Literature in the Language Classroom

A resource book of ideas and activities

Joanne Collie and Stephen Slater

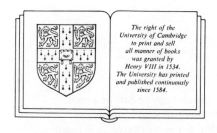

The right of the
University of Cambridge
to print and sell
all manner of books
was granted by
Henry VIII in 1534.
The University has printed
and published continuously
since 1584.

Cambridge University Press
Cambridge
New York   New Rochelle
Melbourne   Sydney

Published by the Press Syndicate of the University of Cambridge
The Pitt Building, Trumpington Street, Cambridge CB2 1RP
32 East 57th Street, New York, NY 10022, USA
10 Stamford Road, Oakleigh, Melbourne 3166, Australia

© Cambridge University Press 1987

First published 1987

Printed in Great Britain
at The Bath Press, Avon

Library of Congress catalogue card number: 87–9377

British Library cataloguing in publication data

Collie, Joanne

Literature in the language classroom: a resource
book of ideas and activities. –
(Cambridge handbooks for language teachers).
1. Language and languages – Study and teaching
2. Literature – Study and teaching
I. Title   II. Slater, Stephen
407'.1   P5B

ISBN 0 521 30996 4   hard covers
ISBN 0 521 31224 8   paperback

WD

Contents

PART A   AIMS AND OBJECTIVES

Reasons for including literature in the language classroom; an outline of our approach; and some answers to general queries that teachers might have.

PART B   PRACTICAL ACTIVITIES IN OUTLINE

A resource bank of activities from which a teacher can choose and which can be applied at different stages when using literary works. In most cases, an illustration is given with the outline, from a range of novels, short stories, plays or poems. (Readers can find descriptions of these works in Appendix 2.) Alternatively, readers are given a reference to the example in Part C.

Contents

PART C WORKING WITH A COMPLETE TEXT

Particular works from four genres are examined in greater detail to show
how the activities outlined in Part B can be adapted. The novel chapter, on
Lord of the Flies, contains the most thorough array of activities, and
readers might prefer to start with this section.

A few hints and a simulation to help teachers prepare their students for
examinations.

Fuller details of works mentioned in the main body of the book and
suggestions for further reading.

Page references to worksheets and figures

Acknowledgements

We should like to thank Michael Swan for his continued advice and guidance, Barbara Thomas and Annemarie Young for their editorial help, and Peter Ducker who designed the book.

We acknowledge with gratitude the students who have helped us explore these ideas and techniques and who have allowed us to reproduce their work in this book.

The authors and publishers are grateful to the following for permission to reproduce material:

Hamish Hamilton for the cover of *When The Wind Blows* on p. 17; William Heinemann Ltd and Viking Penguin Inc., New York for the extracts from *The Talented Mr Ripley* by Patricia Highsmith on pp. 20 and 60; Michael Joseph Ltd, Penguin Books Ltd and Alfred A. Knopf Inc. for the extracts from 'The sound machine' in *Someone Like You* by Roald Dahl on p. 28; Methuen, London for the extracts from *The Applicant* by Harold Pinter on pp. 29 and 30; Jonathan Cape Ltd for the extract from *The Magus* by John Fowles © John Fowles 1966 on p. 31, and Little, Brown and Co., Boston, USA; The Bodley Head Ltd, London and Simon and Schuster Inc. of New York for the extract from *The Human Factor* by Graham Greene on p. 32; Mrs Spark and Harold Ober Associates Inc., New York for the extract from *The Mandelbaum Gate* by Muriel Spark on p. 32; *Radio Times* for the extract on p. 63; The Society of Authors on behalf of the Bernard Shaw Estate for the extract from *Pygmalion* on p. 69; John Harvey and Sons Ltd for the illustrations on pp. 221 and 222; David Higham Associates Ltd for the text of 'The King of China's daughter' by Edith Sitwell on pp. 230–1; 'My Papa's Waltz' by Theodore Roethke on pp. 232–3 is reprinted by permission of Faber and Faber Ltd from *The Collected Poems of Theodore Roethke* and by permission of Doubleday and Co. Inc., New York © 1942 Hearst Magazines Inc.; 'Telephone conversation' by Wole Soyinka on pp. 235–6 first appeared in *Reflections* published by African Universities Press; Oxford University Press for the text of 'The couple upstairs' on p. 240, © OUP 1970, reprinted from *Sugar Daddy* by Hugo Williams (1970); Laurence Pollinger Ltd, the estate of Mrs Frieda Lawrence Ravagli and Viking Penguin Inc., New York for the text of 'To women, as far as I'm concerned' by D. H. Lawrence on p. 244; Jonathan Cape Ltd and A. D. Peters and Co. Ltd for the text of 'You and I' by Roger McGough on p. 246.

The photograph on p. 65 and photograph 1 on p. 198 were taken by Nigel Luckhurst and photographs 2, 3 and 4 on p. 198 are reproduced by permission of Barnaby's Picture Library.

The photographs of Saki on p. 25 were taken from *Saki: A Life of Hector Hugo Munro* by A. J. Langguth, published by Hamish Hamilton and Penguin Books Ltd. We have been unable to trace the copyright owners of the photographs and would welcome information.

Introduction

A corridor outside a classroom. A language teacher spots an intermediate student propped up against a wall, his head in a book.

'What are you reading, Alfredo? Oh, *Animal Farm*. What do you think of it?'

'It's good. I'm enjoying it, though it's difficult for me. But you know, I just need to read something more interesting than the textbook and I heard of this book in my country. Would you have a moment to help me with these parts I've underlined?'

Another corridor, another time. A language teacher, just leaving the classroom, is stopped by a student:

'Could you recommend a novel that I might read to improve my English? I need more vocabulary and reading helps a lot.'

'Mm, well, what sort of books do you like, Martine?'

Inside a classroom, another time again. A language teacher is asking the students' opinion:

'Several students have suggested that we read a novel together. I'm happy to devote one of our hours each week to doing that, if the majority of you want it. What do you say?'

A chorus of replies:

'Yes, that would be interesting. What about *Lord of the Flies*? I've always wanted to try it in English.'

'Oh no, novels are much too difficult. I always have to look up so many words!'

'But then at least you can feel you've really done something.'

'Novels are so long. Just imagine, the same book, week after week, all term. Boring. How about some short stories?'

'I don't like novels. I want to learn to speak English, not just read it.'

The germ for this book sprang from many conversations like these over the years with speakers of other languages who were studying English. Thinking about them, we came to the conclusion that our classroom was something of a microcosm of the English language teaching world generally, reflecting a time when there is much questioning of the relationship between the study of language and literature.

Should we be teaching literature in the foreign language classroom at a pre-university level, or not? This is a question which is certainly in the

1

forefront of debate today, yet it remains controversial and the attitude of many teachers ambivalent. Not so many years ago, there seemed to be a decisive swing against literature in English as a foreign language. The emphasis in modern linguistics on the primacy of the spoken language made many distrust what was seen as essentially a written, crystallised form. Literature was thought of as embodying a static, convoluted kind of language, far removed from the utterances of daily communication. Because of this it was sometimes tarred with an 'elitist' brush and reserved for the most advanced level of study. Even at that level, the need for an arsenal of critical terms, the 'metalanguage' of literary studies, convinced many teachers that it could not be studied satisfactorily in the foreign language. There was dissatisfaction at the amount of time devoted in the native language to appreciation of finer literary points. Moreover, in some cases literature was also seen as carrying an undesirable freight of cultural connotations. What was needed was a more neutral, more functional kind of English, shorn of any implication of cultural imperialism and relevant, in a way that much of literature is not, to the demands of particular uses in business, trade, travel or tourism, advertising, and so on.

Keeping literature off the syllabus, however, has produced a certain amount of unease as well. There is the awkward fact that many learners want and love literary texts, as we have found time and time again. Similarly, they often wish to become more familiar with patterns of social interaction in the country which uses the target language. The created world of fiction portrays these in contextualised situations, and this gradually reveals the codes or assumptions which shape such interaction. Moreover, from the teacher's point of view, literature, which speaks to the heart as much as to the mind, provides material with some emotional colour, that can make fuller contact with the learner's own life, and can thus counterbalance the more fragmented effect of many collections of texts used in the classroom.

We have tried to devise ways of making literature a more significant part of a language teaching programme and of using it in such a way as to further the learner's mastery in the four basic areas of listening, speaking, reading and writing. We believe our approach is most suited to adult or young adult learners, from the intermediate level onwards, including the upper years at secondary school. Many of the activities and the ideas behind them can be successfully adapted across different levels of language proficiency. We wholeheartedly encourage teachers to try them out at lower levels. In our view, the sooner learners can start to enjoy literature in their new language, the better.

1   Teaching literature: why, what and how

Our aim is to provide both new and experienced teachers with very practical help – ideas, approaches and techniques that have worked in our classrooms. To show how we came to be using these, however, we should first like to look briefly at some of the issues which underlie our own attitudes to language learning and its relation to the study of literature. Why is literature beneficial in the language learning process? What works are appropriate in the foreign-language classroom? How can we rethink the way we present and use literature in order to develop a broader range of activities which are more involving for our students?

Why

Firstly, why should a language teacher use literary texts with classes, especially if there is no specific examination requirement to do so and little extra time available?

VALUABLE AUTHENTIC MATERIAL

One of the main reasons might be that literature offers a bountiful and extremely varied body of written material which is 'important' in the sense that it says something about fundamental human issues, and which is enduring rather than ephemeral. Its relevance moves with the passing of time, but seldom disappears completely: the Shakespearean plays whose endings were rewritten to conform to late seventeenth-century taste, and which were later staged to give maximum prominence to their Romantic hero figures, are now explored for their psychoanalytic or dialectical import. In this way, though its meaning does not remain static, a literary work can transcend both time and culture to speak directly to a reader in another country or a different period of history.

Literature is 'authentic' material. By that we simply mean that most works of literature are not fashioned for the specific purpose of teaching a language. Recent course materials have quite rightly incorporated many 'authentic' samples of language – for example, travel timetables, city plans, forms, pamphlets, cartoons, advertisements, newspaper or magazine articles. Learners are thus exposed to language that is as genuine and undistorted as can be managed in the classroom context.

Literature is a valuable complement to such materials, especially once the initial 'survival' level has been passed. In reading literary texts, students have also to cope with language intended for native speakers and thus they gain additional familiarity with many different linguistic uses, forms and conventions of the written mode: with irony, exposition, argument, narration, and so on. And, although it may not be confined within a specific social network in the same way that a bus ticket or an advertisement might be, literature can none the less incorporate a great deal of cultural information.

CULTURAL ENRICHMENT

For many language learners, the ideal way to deepen their understanding of life in the country where that language is spoken – a visit or an extended stay – is just not possible. Some may start learning a language knowing that they are unlikely ever to set foot in an area where it is spoken by the majority of inhabitants. For all such learners, more indirect routes to this form of understanding must be adopted so that they gain an understanding of the way of life of the country: radio programmes, films or videos, newspapers, and, last but not least, literary works. It is true of course that the 'world' of a novel, play, or short story is a created one, yet it offers a full and vivid context in which characters from many social backgrounds can be depicted. A reader can discover their thoughts, feelings, customs, possessions; what they buy, believe in, fear, enjoy; how they speak and behave behind closed doors. This vivid imagined world can quickly give the foreign reader a feel for the codes and preoccupations that structure a real society. Reading the literature of a historical period is, after all, one of the ways we have to help us imagine what life was like in that other foreign territory: our own country's past. Literature is perhaps best seen as a complement to other materials used to increase the foreign learner's insight into the country whose language is being learnt.

LANGUAGE ENRICHMENT

We have said that reading literary works exposes the student to many functions of the written language, but what about other linguistic advantages? Language enrichment is one benefit often sought through literature. While there is little doubt that extensive reading increases a learner's receptive vocabulary and facilitates transfer to a more active form of knowledge, it is sometimes objected that literature does not give learners the kind of vocabulary they really need. It may be 'authentic' in the sense already mentioned, but the language of literary works is, on the whole, not typical of the language of daily life, nor is it like the language used in learners' textbooks. We would not wish students to think that Elizabeth Barrett Browning's 'How do I love thee?' is the kind of utterance normally whispered into a lover's ear nowadays! The objection to literature on the grounds of lexical appropriacy thus has some validity, but it need not be an overriding one if teachers make a judicious choice of the text to be read, considering it as a counterpoise and supplement to other materials.

On the positive side, literature provides a rich context in which individual lexical or syntactical items are made more memorable. Reading a substantial and contextualised body of text, students gain familiarity with many features of the written language – the formation and function of sentences, the variety of possible structures, the different ways of connecting ideas – which broaden and enrich their own writing skills. The extensive reading required in tackling a novel or long play develops the students' ability to make inferences from linguistic clues, and to deduce meaning from context, both useful tools in reading other sorts of material as well. As we shall suggest through many activities in this book, a literary text can serve as an excellent prompt for oral work. In all these ways, a student working with literature is helped with the basic skills of language learning. Moreover, literature helps extend the intermediate or advanced learner's awareness of the range of language itself. Literary language is not always that of daily communication, as we have mentioned, but it is special in its way. It is heightened: sometimes elaborate, sometimes marvellously simple yet, somehow, absolutely 'right'. The compressed quality of much literary language produces unexpected density of meaning. Figurative language yokes levels of experience that were previously distinct, casting new light on familiar sensations and opening up new dimensions of perception in a way that can be exhilarating but also startling and even unsettling.

For these features of literary language to be appreciated, a considerable effort is required on the part of the reader who is tackling the text in a foreign language. But with well-chosen works, the investment of effort can be immensely rewarding, the resulting sense of achievement highly satisfying. At a productive level, students of literature will, we hope, become more creative and adventurous as they begin to appreciate the richness and variety of the language they are trying to master and begin to use some of that potential themselves.

PERSONAL INVOLVEMENT

Above all, literature can be helpful in the language learning process because of the personal involvement it fosters in readers. Core language teaching materials must concentrate on how a language operates both as a rule-based system and as a socio-semantic system. Very often, the process of learning is essentially analytic, piecemeal, and, at the level of the personality, fairly superficial. Engaging imaginatively with literature enables learners to shift the focus of their attention beyond the more mechanical aspects of the foreign language system. When a novel, play or short story is explored over a period of time, the result is that the reader begins to 'inhabit' the text. He or she is drawn into the book. Pinpointing what individual words or phrases may mean becomes less important than pursuing the development of the story. The reader is eager to find out what happens as events unfold; he or she feels close to certain characters and shares their emotional responses. The language becomes 'transparent' – the fiction summons the whole person into its own world.

We believe that this can happen, and can have beneficial effects upon the whole language learning process, as long as the reader is well-motivated, and as long as the experience of engaging with literature is kept sufficiently interesting, varied and non-directive to let the reader feel that he or she is taking possession of a previously unknown territory. Obviously, the choice of a particular literary work will be important in facilitating this creative relationship which the reader establishes with the text. It is this question we should like to consider next.

What

What sort of literature is suitable for use with language learners? The criteria of suitability clearly depend ultimately on each particular group of students, their needs, interests, cultural background and language level. However, one primary factor to consider is, we suggest, whether a particular work is able to stimulate the kind of personal involvement we have just described, by arousing the learners' interest and provoking strong, positive reactions from them. If it is meaningful and enjoyable, reading is more likely to have a lasting and beneficial effect upon the learners' linguistic and cultural knowledge. It is important to choose books, therefore, which are relevant to the life experiences, emotions, or dreams of the learner. Language difficulty has, of course, to be considered as well. Because they have both a linguistic and a cultural gap to bridge, foreign students may not be able to identify with or enjoy a text which they perceive as being fraught with difficulty every step of the way. In the absence of curriculum or exam constraints, it is much better to choose a work that is not too much above the students' normal reading proficiency.

If the language of the literary work is quite straightforward and simple, this may be helpful but is not in itself the most crucial yardstick. Interest, appeal and relevance are all more important. In order for us to justify the additional time and effort which will undoubtedly be needed for learners to come to grips with a work of literature in a language not their own, there must be some special incentive involved. Enjoyment; suspense; a fresh insight into issues which are felt to be close to the heart of people's concerns; the delight of encountering one's own thoughts or situations encapsulated vividly in a work of art; the other, equal delight of finding those same thoughts or situations illuminated by a totally new, unexpected light or perspective: all these are incentives which can lead learners to overcome enthusiastically the linguistic obstacles that might be considered too great in less involving material.

It is therefore well worth the time spent in trying to achieve a good match between a particular group of learners and the literary work they will be asked to read. Questionnaires on tastes and interests can be useful. Another way of proceeding is to give the class a brief summary of three or four possibilities, perhaps with short extracts from the text, and let them choose the one they find the most appealing. A close runner-up can always become the text the class works with next.

How

Once a novel or play has been chosen, how best can the teacher and students work with it? Particular answers to this question will emerge later as our activities are described. In this section we should like to examine more general principles. First we shall describe some of the approaches that are often used when literature is taught. Then we shall outline some of the aims that have guided our quest for ways of supplementing or even, in some cases, replacing these approaches.

Some commonly used approaches to teaching literature

The perennial problem of how to teach languages has in recent years become increasingly guided by the dominant aim of promoting the learner's communicative competence. When, however, the teacher introduces students to the literature of the foreign language, this communicative ideal too often vanishes. The way literature is presented often has a number of typical features.

Sometimes the teacher falls back upon a more traditional classroom role in which he or she sees him or herself as imparting information – about the author, the background to the work, the particular literary conventions that inform the text and so on. Learners are somehow expected to have the ability to take all this in and make it their own.

Often the sheer difficulties of detailed comprehension posed by the intricacy or linguistic subtlety of the language turn the teaching of literature into a massive process of explanation by the teacher or even of translation, with the greater proportion of available classroom time devoted to a step by step exegetical exercise led by the teacher.

At more advanced levels of work with literature, the teacher may resort to the metalanguage of criticism and this may both distance learners from their own response and cause them to undervalue it, whatever the gain in analytical terms.

Even if the teacher hopes to do more to sharpen students' own response to the literary work, there is often little guidance on how to do so. The time-honoured technique of question-and-answer can provide some help. But, unless questions are genuinely open-ended, there is often a feeling on the part of the students that the teacher is slowly but surely edging them to particular answers that he or she has in mind. There is little room for either their own responses or their involvement during such sessions. In short, personal investment is minimal.

All these teacher-centred approaches may foster detailed comprehension but students will probably not have made the text their own. Nor will the classroom process have encouraged them to share their own views with each other, and they may not have used the target language very much.

Aims that underlie our approach

In general terms, our aim is to complement more conventional approaches and so diversify the repertoire of classroom procedures. We hope in this way to put fresh momentum into the teaching of literature, to stimulate students' desire to read, and to encourage their response. More particularly, the following aims have provided a rationale for the kind of activities we outline in later chapters.

MAINTAINING INTEREST AND INVOLVEMENT BY USING A
VARIETY OF STUDENT-CENTRED ACTIVITIES

In establishing a number of ways in which a text could be explored, we have tried to bear in mind that any approach used exclusively can turn to tedium in the classroom. We have found that role play, improvisation, creative writing, discussions, questionnaires, visuals and many other activities which we use successfully to vary our language classes can serve a similar purpose when we teach literature. An array of enjoyable student-centred activities is particularly important when working with students who are not literature specialists and who may not as yet have developed a wish to read literature in the target language on their own initiative. Moreover, the availability of a variety of activities enables the teacher to concentrate on meeting students' weaknesses in particular skill areas – in speaking or listening, for example.

SUPPLEMENTING THE PRINTED PAGE

In devising activities for integrating language and literature we have borne in mind the notion that learning is promoted by involving as many of the students' faculties as possible. By itself, the printed page can be a fairly cold, distancing medium appealing to a restricted part of the reader's visual sense and to the intellect. And yet, of course, the words that make up that printed page can create a whole new world inside the reader's imagination, a world full of warmth and colour. As teachers we try to exploit as fully as possible the emotional dimension that is a very integral part of literature, though it is so often lacking in more neutral language learning texts.

TAPPING THE RESOURCES OF KNOWLEDGE AND EXPERIENCE WITHIN THE GROUP

Pair and group work are now well established as a means both of increasing learners' confidence within the foreign language and also of personalising their contact with it. Although it may seem paradoxical we have found that shared activity can be especially fruitful in helping the learner find a way into what is usually an intensely personal and private experience, that of coming to terms with and inhabiting an author's universe. In the creative endeavour of interpreting this new universe, a group with its various sets of life experiences can act as a rich marshalling device to enhance the individual's awareness both of his or her own responses and of the world created by the literary work.

On a more practical level, working with a group can lessen the difficulties presented by the number of unknowns on a page of literary text. Very often someone else in a group will be able to supply the missing link or fill in an appropriate meaning of a crucial word, or if not, the task of doing so will become a shared one. Shifting attention away from the text itself to such shared activity is often conducive to the creation of a risk-taking atmosphere. With the group's support and control, the individual has greater freedom to explore his or her own reactions and interpretations. Above all, we hope that the group will stimulate learners to reread and ponder the text on their own.

HELPING STUDENTS EXPLORE THEIR OWN RESPONSES TO LITERATURE

This aim has been strongly hinted at within those already discussed. Our activities try to help students to acquire the confidence to develop, express and value their own response. Through this process, we hope that they will become less dependent on received opinion and therefore more interested in and more able to assess other perspectives.

Students who have had to accomplish a range of tasks and activities centred on a literary text, often as a shared activity in groups, may come to be more personally familiar with that text. The effort they have brought to it and the personal investment they have made in it will sharpen their own response, making it more likely that they will want to extend their understanding of it by personal reading at home.

Part A Aims and objectives

USING THE TARGET LANGUAGE

One of the principles which fashions our classroom approach to literature is that of using the target language with the range of activities chosen. We want to give learners the maximum chance of entering the universe of any selected book. This will be facilitated if, instead of trying to transpose it into their own language and cultural experience, they try to put themselves imaginatively into the target situation. The main difficulty with this approach is, of course, that some learners may not yet possess the richness and subtlety of vocabulary and structure in which to couch their response in the target language. We feel that there are a number of ways in which students can be helped to express this response either non-verbally or by making a limited linguistic repertoire go a long way.

If, however, in the discussion following a shared activity there is a reversion to the native language, in groups which have a common first language, then we feel that this is not a disaster. First of all, it usually indicates that the learners are enjoying the task and are engrossed in it; then, too, it shows that learners are bringing their knowledge and experience to bear on the new language, thus identifying with it and personalising it.

Finally, in order to achieve this aim of using the target language as much as possible and framing our approach to the literary text consistently within its own language, we have tried hard to avoid the metalanguage of critical discussion. We feel that concentration on this kind of language can undermine students' confidence in their own response, especially when they are working in the target language.

INTEGRATING LANGUAGE AND LITERATURE

The overall aim, then, of our approach to the teaching of literature is to let the student derive the benefits of communicative and other activities for language improvement within the context of suitable works of literature. Sharing literature with students is a spur to their acquiring these benefits, providing the teacher makes a balanced selection of activities and presents them with confidence. However, before we turn to a description of some activities and techniques that may be helpful, we would like to answer a few of the more detailed practical queries and doubts that practising teachers might still have.

2 In the classroom

In Chapter 1, we argued that shared classroom activities can help learners overcome the difficulties of approaching a work of literature in a foreign language, by giving them new insights and sufficient confidence to stimulate their own rereading at home. However, many teachers who are convinced of the value of literature for their students nevertheless encounter considerable problems when they try to present a particular work to their classes. In our discussions with language teachers, some of these problems surfaced time and again as recurring questions, which we would now like to consider in some detail.

'I'd like to use literature in my non-specialist language classes, but a whole novel seems too much to tackle, and extracts don't spark much interest in my students. What should I do?'

There is no doubt that the sheer length of some works is daunting. Reading or translating a work in class, hour after hour, week after week, can be such a dreary experience that many students never want to open a foreign-language book again.

Extracts provide one type of solution. The advantages are obvious: reading a series of passages from different works produces more variety in the classroom, so that the teacher has a greater chance of avoiding monotony, while still giving learners a taste at least of an author's special flavour.

On the other hand, a student who is only exposed to 'bite-sized chunks' will never have the satisfaction of knowing the overall pattern of a book, which is after all the satisfaction most of us seek when we read something in our own language. Moreover, there are some literary features that cannot be adequately illustrated by a short excerpt: the development of plot or character, for instance, with the gradual involvement of the reader that this implies; or the unfolding of a complex theme through the juxtaposition of contrasting views.

In later chapters, we illustrate an alternative solution, which consists of selecting from a long work a series of extracts which provide the basis for classroom activities. Reading a novel or play thus becomes a combination of classwork and substantial private reading. The entire text need not be read by the teacher and students together; working on carefully chosen

11

selections will maintain momentum and a sense of the whole in class, while the learners' complementary reading at home allows them to form a personal relationship with the text and to feel, at the end, that they have coped satisfactorily with the challenge of a complete book.

'How can I select the right passages to work with in class?'

The criteria we have found most useful in choosing excerpts for classwork are the following: extracts should be interesting in themselves, and if possible close to the students' own interests; they should be an important part of the book's overall pattern; and they should provide good potential for a variety of classroom activities.

Obviously, there is no single solution which will fit all books and all classroom situations. A teacher's selection of passages must vary as he or she attempts to draw upon the different resources within each text, and it will have to take into account the nature and length of the course as well as factors to do with the learners themselves, the level of their linguistic proficiency, for instance, and their own needs and desires.

We hope that the novels and plays we use as illustrations in later chapters will provide examples of how passages can be selected to good effect, so that similar ideas and techniques can be applied to a variety of other works of literature.

'What about the sections not read in class?'

One of our aims in teaching literature is to encourage learners to feel that they *can* read and enjoy books on their own. We therefore ask them to read specified sections at home, often with the support of worksheets which provide either particular help with points of difficulty, or more general help in formulating a response to the passage they are reading. Examples are given in Chapter 4. It is time-consuming to prepare such supportive worksheets when a teacher first works with a book, but well worth the effort, since they can provide a real stimulus to extensive reading. They are also a long-term investment: works of literature do not date very rapidly and can be taught year after year.

It is most important that the parts of a book which are to be read by students on their own should be related to the ongoing pattern of activities in the classroom. Follow-up tasks can be used that depend upon prior home reading, or some aspect of the passage read can be incorporated into the next classroom activity designed to present an unread section. What is essential is to link class and home work, to help maintain an overview of the whole book as we go through it. If this is done, it is no longer necessary to proceed in a strictly linear, chronological fashion. In some cases, for example, parts of a novel might be extracted to provide material for a role-play exercise in the classroom. Students would later be asked to read, as homework, the sections which led up to this situation in the novel. The creative counterpoint which we establish between private reading and group tasks gives us as teachers a much greater freedom in our approach to the long text; in particular, it enables us to break the often tedious linearity of the traditional lock-step process by which a whole class is taken from beginning to end of any work.

'But if we don't read the whole book together, how can I be sure my students really know it well?'

It is true that concentrating on some selected highlights constitutes a form of sampling that does not guarantee an overall grasp of the whole work. But then does any method ever do that? Even if teachers read through and explain every single word of a shorter text in class, can they be sure that what has undoubtedly been taught has also been learnt?

We feel that if we choose extracts carefully and present them through enjoyable group activities, our students have more chance of gaining true familiarity with any work as a whole. After all, such an approach replicates the experience of reading a long text in our own language. We may well read it from beginning to end, but it will not exist as a chronological entity in our minds. Our memory will impose its own overview, lingering upon some aspects rather than others, telescoping events, organising new configurations. It is natural to think and talk about a complex book in terms of its highlights for us as readers, and this is in effect what we are asking our students to do. Nevertheless, we hope that the kind of tasks we have suggested, and especially perhaps in Chapter 6 ('Endings'), will help learners draw together the many strands that constitute their awareness of what an author has achieved in any particular book.

'What can I do about students who are so keen that they race ahead and finish the book out of step with the general pace of the class?'

From our experience, this is inevitable if books are distributed in sets. It should not be discouraged, given that one of our aims is to stimulate reading habits.

What it does mean, however, is that the teacher will have to select classroom activities, and worksheets for home reading, that offer some challenge to this student, perhaps dispensing with activities of prediction or those that would be marred by knowledge of the whole story.

Depending on the type of book read, it is not always a bad thing if students know the ending before the book has been completed. This sometimes frees them to look more closely at each individual part that is being highlighted in class. Group activities or task sheets also make the 'rapid' student reread, sometimes with a new focus of attention, and this is usually very beneficial from both a linguistic and a literary point of view.

'What about other types of literature which do not present a problem of length: short stories, for example, one-act plays, or poems?'

In the foreign-language classroom, poems offer a special kind of reward as well as a challenge all of their own. For this reason, we have discussed possible ways of presenting them in a separate chapter, even though many of the activities outlined for other genres can be adapted to poetry. Short prose works also benefit from the various activities described in Part B. We hope that teachers will be able to use some of these ideas to exploit the particular qualities which make a short text so suitable for less advanced learners. The fact that an entire work of literature can be presented within one or two classroom lessons is extremely rewarding and motivating for such students.

'I don't know whether the methods proposed really deal with my problem, which is that my students find the actual language of literature so difficult that they do not get much out of it.'

Here the answer must lie in selection of an appropriate book. At earlier levels of proficiency, simplified texts may help initiate learners into extensive reading. Activities intended for unabridged texts could be applied to simplified texts and used by students working in groups. This may stimulate interest in literature as well as contributing to language improvement. But although 'graded readers' retain the story line of the original text, much else is lost. At the more advanced level, therefore, it seems to us preferable to choose, whenever possible, books which do not present formidable linguistic difficulties. There are many excellent short works where the style remains fairly simple or uncluttered. We hope that the list of possible titles included in Appendix 2 will prove useful in this respect.

In some cases, choice may be restricted by the availability of books, or by the constraints of a set curriculum. For teachers faced with an imposed book, detecting particular linguistic problems and devising ways of overcoming them will become part of the normal screening activities, the preliminary spade work which is always necessary before we begin to teach a text. It may be that a greater number of linguistically-based activities have to be used for that kind of book; or perhaps more background work will be needed to fill in cultural gaps.

For these books as for others, however, we must try to find some balance between 'pure' language work and other, more creative approaches designed to foster a student's involvement in the text. Quite often, group activities serve to shift a reader's attention away from the minute, intensive attack on a single corner of the text, to a more extensive concern for gist and overall theme. This will prove liberating in the long run for the student previously unable to see the wood for the trees. It is surely motivating to realise that a text can be meaningful and that working with it can be enjoyable, even when there are still quite a few unknowns within it.

PART B   PRACTICAL ACTIVITIES IN OUTLINE

3   First encounters

For students about to explore the unknown territory of a new literary work, the first encounter with it may well be crucial. First impressions can colour their feelings about the whole enterprise they find themselves engaged in. They are likely to be approaching the experience with a mixture of curiosity, excitement and apprehension. The teacher's role must be to play up the sense of adventure while providing a supportive atmosphere that will be reassuring to the students.

The first imperative is usually to try and draw the learners quickly 'into' the text, so that they find it interesting and want to continue reading it on their own. This is much easier to do if the teacher genuinely enjoys the book and can communicate his or her enthusiasm for it: it is worthwhile, therefore, choosing congenial texts if at all possible.

Next, students need to be convinced that the task ahead is not an impossible one; that, even if there are difficult passages to negotiate, it can be done with success and tangible rewards. Many learners fail to persevere with a book because they find the initial encounter simply too daunting. It may be that the first page is bristling with difficult words; or perhaps the territory they have wandered into seems so totally different from their own surroundings that they never quite succeed in identifying with it.

That is why it seems to us well worth spending extra time on orientation and warm-up sessions, either before the book is begun or along with the first reading period. In these sessions, possible lexical difficulties can be incorporated and pre-taught. When the student gets to the text itself, much of the vocabulary will thus be familiar, so that the first reading experience can be easier and more rewarding. It is also useful to explore main themes with students, independently of the way they are articulated in the particular work about to be approached. One of the purposes here is to elicit students' own thoughts and feelings on the issues. When they later turn to the text itself, the preceding discussion or activity will act as a familiar landmark in their new surroundings. It is important for learners to feel that their knowledge and life experience can still provide valuable guidance.

Finally, a warm-up can be designed to set the mood, create interest, or spark curiosity. Sometimes it leads students not to the beginning of the book, but to the first significant or dramatic passage, to whet the appetite.

In some cases, we have devoted the entire class period to activities which, we hope, will make learners *want* to read the text – and we have then left them to get on with the short story or first section of a novel or play, on their own. Even if students do not understand everything perfectly, the fact of reading a foreign work in this way approximates more closely to their experience of reading in their own language. Literature is in a sense taken out of the classroom context and replaced into what we feel is its more 'natural' setting.

The beginning activities suggested in this chapter tend therefore to be rather time-consuming. We hope that teachers will find, as we have, that they are nevertheless worthwhile because they build motivation and foster a love of reading.

Using the title and cover design

The teacher sets the scene and kindles students' curiosity by showing them an intriguing cover design and asking them to speculate about the book, its story and mood.

An example is Raymond Briggs' book *When the Wind Blows*, which portrays the effects upon an elderly English couple of a nuclear attack near their home. The teacher shows the class the cartoon cover design of the book (Figure 1). For easier viewing by the whole class, the drawing

Figure 1

can be transferred to an overhead projector transparency. The title is withheld or covered up in this first stage.

Working with the whole class, the teacher asks them to describe the couple. What kind of people do they seem to be? Urban or country folk? Simple or sophisticated? Rich? Working class? Honest? Patriotic? Law-abiding? Affectionate? Loving? Alike or different from each other? All suggestions are accepted and written up on the board. Students are then asked to speculate on the light behind the couple. What could it be? What feeling do students get about it? Is it something good? Happy? Ominous? Dangerous? What is its relation to the couple?

In a second stage, the teacher explains that the title of the book is taken from a very well-known English lullaby or nursery rhyme (a song to rock small children to sleep). He or she recites, or if possible sings, the lullaby to the class:

> Hush-a-bye baby, on the tree top
> When the wind blows, the cradle will rock
> When the bough breaks, the cradle will fall
> Down will come baby, cradle and all.

The students are asked to guess which *four* words constitute the play's title. What do they feel about this lullaby? Is its mood peaceful? Happy? Ominous? How could it relate to the elderly couple on the cover?

The book is now handed out and reading can begin. It is useful to keep a record of the speculations made about the title as these later help to exemplify the irony of the play.

Getting in the mood

This is a guided fantasy. The teacher asks students to build up a picture of the beginning of the literary work by first setting the scene, and then inviting the class to inhabit this scene in their minds. Once they have done this, they make a note of what they feel, see, say, and so on.

At the end of this 'painting in the mind', students are put into small groups and each group member describes his or her scene to the others. After a brief discussion, the teacher calls the class together. One or two students retell their versions for the benefit of the whole class.

This activity provides an excellent way into Golding's novel *Lord of the Flies*: it is illustrated in detail on p. 94.

Visual prompts

Photos or magazine pictures are often useful in eliciting the response of students to the central situation or theme they are going to meet in a literary work.

Before reading 'The hitchhiker' (in *More Tales of the Unexpected*, by Roald Dahl), for example, students are shown photos of quite different people and asked to say which ones they would be prepared to give a lift to. This makes them more aware of their own attitudes to hitchhikers, and to a person's appearance (see Figure 19 and Worksheet 55).

As a warm-up to 'The war in the bathroom' (in *Dancing Girls and Other Stories*, by Margaret Atwood), magazine pictures are used to get students talking about one of the main themes in this short story: the experience of moving and adjusting to new surroundings (see Figures 21A and 21B).

Using the theme

The teacher takes a major theme from the text and explores it with the class.

For example, in Somerset Maugham's novel *The Moon and Sixpence*, the main character suddenly walks out on his wife, children, home and job. Students are asked to imagine that they have suddenly decided to abandon their own current life situation. How would they do it? Would they plan it in advance? What preparations would they make? Would they tell anyone? What would they take? Where would they go? What kind of new life would they try to build?

The teacher asks students to write the note that they would leave. They are to imagine that they have time to write a short note only – not more than 50 words – and to remember that they may never see the receiver of the note again.

When this is done, the teacher collects the notes and puts them straight into the rubbish bin – and then, of course, invites each student to take one (not their own) out. He or she suggests that the note students are about to read is from the most important person in their lives. They are to try to identify how they feel about what they are reading and jot down their thoughts immediately. The teacher should participate fully by also writing a note and choosing one to read.

This is followed by general discussion about how people felt when they were writing, and reading, the notes.

Students are then given the book to start reading the first section at home.

Key words/sentences

The teacher selects a small number of key words from the first part of the text. In groups, students brainstorm for possible narrative links between the words. When each group has decided on a preferred pattern of connection, a story is built up orally or in written form.

As a variation, key sentences are extracted from the text by the teacher – these produce a somewhat more contextualised framework for the imagination to work on.

'Key words' is illustrated on p. 218 using Saki's 'Sredni Vashtar', and 'key sentences' in Worksheet 63 using Saki's 'The open window' (both stories from *The Penguin Complete Saki*).

Instead of being used to create a story, the key extracts can provide the basis upon which students attempt to build up a first image of a central character, his or her personality, habits, etc. The sentences in Worksheet 1 were drawn from Patricia Highsmith's *The Talented Mr Ripley* and were used in this way, to spark students' interest in Ripley, before beginning to read the novel in class.

Study the following extracts from *The Talented Mr Ripley*. What do they reveal about Tom Ripley, the central character in the book?

His boredom had slipped into another gear. Tom knew the sensations . . . Now he could be maniacally polite for perhaps another whole hour, if he had to be, before something in him exploded and sent him running out of the door.

And now Mr Greenleaf had turned up. Something always turned up. That was Tom's philosophy.

He wouldn't let Mr Greenleaf down. He'd do his very best with Dickie.

Slowly he took off his jacket and untied his tie, watching every move he made as if it were somebody else's movements he was watching.

That had been the only time tonight when he had felt uncomfortable, unreal, the way he might have felt if he had been lying, yet it had been practically the only thing he had said that was true: my parents died when I was very small. I was raised by my aunt in Boston.

Mr Greenleaf came into the room. His figure seemed to pulsate and grow larger and larger. Tom blinked his eyes, feeling a sudden terror of him, an impulse to attack him before he was attacked.

Tom wanted to get out of the apartment. And yet he still wanted to go to Europe, and wanted Mr Greenleaf to approve of him.

Worksheet 1

Questionnaires

Learners are given a questionnaire to fill in, to determine their attitude to the issues raised by the book's central theme. An example is given for 'The war in the bathroom' (see Worksheet 65).

A 'pyramiding' technique is often useful with questionnaires. That is to say: each student fills in their own, then compares results with one other partner. Through discussion, they are to try to arrive at the same set of answers. The two then compare their new set of answers with that of another pair, and so on.

Listening-in

This is a listening activity for teachers who have easy access to recording facilities. With a friend or other native speaker, the teacher makes a recording of two people discussing their reaction to a particular literary work. Many different contexts can be imagined: friends discussing a novel they have both read or a television adaptation, two people coming out of the theatre, an interview for the class or school journal, etc. For advanced classes, recording a fairly spontaneous, unscripted conversation would be ideal – but this is not often possible, and, in any case, using truly unscripted material often presents quite a lot of difficulty when it comes to devising the accompanying tasks.

The example given is a compromise, using scripted material in the semi-formal situation of an interview for a school newspaper, with non-native but fluent speakers of English. It was used to present *Animal Farm* by George Orwell to a 'lower advanced' multilingual class (just post Cambridge First Certificate).

Students listen to the recording once, without taking notes. They are then paired, one given Worksheet 2A, the other Worksheet 2B. They are given a few minutes to fill in any details they remember, then they hear the recording again in sections, with a few minutes to fill in more details at each pause. After they have heard the recording once again, the pair together completes both worksheets, then compares their answers with a neighbouring pair. General feedback completes the activity.

SCRIPT FOR 'LISTENING-IN'

Sven, a Swedish doctor, is on a study visit to London. During his stay, he visits a friend's son who is studying English at a language school. Another student at the school interviews Sven about his trip to the theatre to see a stage adaptation of George Orwell's *Animal Farm*.

Karin: What did you think of the play?
Sven: It was really good . . . er . . . the actors were very good and looked just like animals. The hens jerked their heads very real . . . realistically and the horses clip-clopped all over the stage. The cat was good too, slinking by so quietly.
Karin: It sounds rather unusual. Just how many more animals were there?
Sven: Well . . . er . . . there was Muriel, the goat who could read . . . and some dancing sheep who interrupted meetings singing 'Four legs good, two

Listen to Karin interviewing Sven about the animal characters in *Animal Farm*. Then try to fill in as many details as you can in the boxes below.

Kind of animal	Name	What do we know about this animal?
1.		
2.		
3.		
4.		
5.		
6.		
7.		
8.		

Worksheet 2A

Listen to Karin interviewing Sven. Then try to complete the following sentences so that they tell the story of what happens in *Animal Farm*.

Once upon a time there were some animals that decided to revolt against their human masters. They were led by the cleverest animals .... They succeeded in taking over the farm and running it. Their first leader was .... He wanted ....

But although he was clever and kind, he was not strong enough. A more powerful animal called .... managed to take his place as leader. He did this by .... The animals were convinced by this new leader and followed him faithfully even though he behaved .... Boxer, the horse, worked especially hard. His motto was .... But when he got old and tired, ... The donkey, on the other hand, was not at all impressed by what the animals had achieved because he said that ....

Worksheet 2B

legs bad' and blindly repeated anything they were told. Oh yes, and the pigs ... they took over the farm and led the revolt ...

Karin: What exactly is the story about? It all sounds rather confusing.

Sven: Erm ... well ... the animals take over the farm. Snowball, their first leader, wants the animals to be equal and happy but he doesn't last long ... a more powerful pig, Napoleon, takes over using dogs ... trained dogs. He's not very nice but very clever ... he ... er ... tricks the other animals and uses them. The poor horse called Boxer ... he kept repeating that Napoleon was always right, but he suffered for it.

Karin: Do the animals turn against Napoleon?

Sven: Ah ... that would be telling ... you must go to see it with your colleagues.

Karin: OK. Just one more question. Is there a moral to the story? It sounds like a sort of ... fa ... fable to me.

Sven: A moral? ... Yes, I suppose there are many if you think deeply about it ... er ... the old donkey in the story is probably right when he says that things never change, never really change, I mean.

Karin: I'm afraid I must stop the interview now ... Thank you very much for talking to me.

Sven: It was a pleasure. I look forward to reading about the interview in your school magazine.

Biographical montage

Some teachers prefer to talk about the author before starting the text, using this background knowledge as a way in to the work. There are various activities which can be used if this approach is retained. They are also useful after the book has been read, as follow-up material.

Biography montage is one such activity and others follow. The teacher collects some photos, objects, place names: anything which is relevant to the author's life (see Figure 2). These are mounted on to a large piece of poster card (or pinned to a wall or notice-board). The class is invited to speculate about the meaning of the items in the montage, either in groups or as a whole class.

Follow-up writing activities could include: reconstructing missing entries from the author's diaries, using the visual prompts on the montage; writing (or completing) sub-titles or a short text about each of the items, so that the montage becomes an illustrated biography; or, for less advanced classes, matching short texts of this kind (perhaps gapped) with the items on the montage.

Creating a sketch of the author

The teacher shows a photograph of the author (or several taken at different periods of his or her life) and asks the class to build up an intuitive character portrayal (see Figure 3 which shows photographs of Saki). This could be done in groups, allowing time at the end for the resulting sketches to be compared.

Figure 2

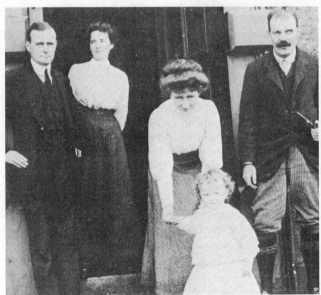

Figure 3

Guessing at missing information

The teacher gives some biographical information but omits certain important facts or aspects of the author's life. The class speculates about the missing parts (for example, education, married life, political beliefs). In groups, learners can fill in missing details, then compare their guesses with those of other groups.

It is hoped that this activity will spur students' curiosity about the author and make them want to know more.

Worksheet 3 is an example for this activity. It is based on the life of Hector Hugh Munro. A similar activity can also usefully *follow* the reading of a particular work.

Make guesses to fill in the details about H. H. Munro.

H. H. Munro was born on 18 December, 1870 in Burma, where his father was an officer in the British military police. In 1872, the family went back to England where a tragedy occurred: ....

The father returned to Burma, and Hector and his brother and sister were brought up by their grandmother and two maiden aunts. Hector was a frail but rather mischievous child. When he was nine, something happened which disrupted his schooling: ....

He was sent to Bedford Grammar School but remained there only four terms. His education continued to be interrupted by ill health.

His first job was with .... in Burma. But he fell ill and had to return to England.

He worked as a .... from 1902 until 1909. During this time he was sent to the Balkan States, then to St Petersburg. He then abandoned a regular salaried job to devote himself to ....
in London. He was an extremely patriotic man and when war was declared in 1914 immediately enlisted as a trooper in the army.

There was one thing he never did in his life: ....
The way he died in 1916 was: ....

Answers: His mother was charged by a runaway cow in a field, and died. / He had severe brain fever. / the military police / foreign correspondent for a newspaper / writing fiction / get married / in battle.

Worksheet 3

Biographical lie-detecting

The teacher gives a brief and truthful introduction to an author's life (oral or written text, slides, video, etc.). Then one written sentence is given to each member of a group of four students. Each sentence adds a new detail about the author's life, but one of the four is not true. Each group compares their four sentences and nominates the false one. The teacher asks each group for its choice and the reasons for it. He or she then reveals the lie, offering additional biographical details as a text for homework reading.

For example, students are given some biographical details about George Bernard Shaw:

Born 1856 / father a corn miller who was a heavy drinker / his parents' marriage was an unhappy one / mother left the family home in Dublin and moved to London with Shaw's two sisters / Shaw joined them in 1876 / Shaw had various jobs – assistant to a land agent, book reviewer, music critic / married a rich Irishwoman at the age of 42 / Nobel Prize for Literature 1925 / wrote more plays than Shakespeare / died in Hertfordshire in 1950.

Next students are asked to consider the following additional facts and try to spot the false one*:

1. Shaw made provision in his will for over £350,000 to be given to the campaign for spelling reform.
2. Shaw was a supporter of the fascist ideology.
3. Shaw never had any children.
4. Shaw was a lifelong teetotaller.

If preferred, the teacher can compile more sets of biographical facts and play a version of 'Call my bluff'. Students are divided into groups of four and given sets of four facts about Shaw's life. In each set, one fact is incorrect. Each member of the group reads out his or her one 'fact' and another group guesses which fact is the false one. It is essential for the students to have some biographical information about the author before this game is played, otherwise guesses are completely blind.

Star diagrams

This activity and the ones that follow are to be used when students begin to read the work.

Assuming key words have not been listed and used as a warm-up activity prior to reading, the teacher asks learners to extract important words from the first section of the text used. In groups, students skim

---

* The second statement is false.

through the first passage and extract words or expressions to be listed under a number of headings: colour words, words that indicate mood or movement, words that express feelings, etc. The object of the exercise is partly linguistic (to expand vocabulary) and partly literary (to sensitise students to the way an author presents a description or a theme, to make them aware of the lexical patterning that structures a work of literature).

An example of this activity, using a five-point star diagram, is given for *Lord of the Flies* (see Figures 9A and 9B).

Sentence whispers

This activity is especially suitable for large classes. The class is put into four or five lines of students (each line having a minimum of four students). The teacher cuts up into four sections the first passage to be read and gives the first section to line A, the second to line B, the third to line C and the fourth to line D. The student at the front of each line reads his or her section. He or she then whispers it (once or twice only) from memory into the ear of the student next in the line, who passes it on similarly until the student at the end receives the whispered message. Then the students at the end of the line retell the sequence, starting with line A. Immediately afterwards, the teacher asks the front students to read their sentences consecutively. Differences between versions are discussed and then the class is asked to predict what will happen next, or to discuss the title, from the information gathered up to this point.

Learners usually find the activity amusing; the aim is simply to get them 'into' the story quickly and painlessly. Roald Dahl's short story 'The sound machine' (in *Someone Like You*) works well with this technique. The opening passage could be cut up in the following way:

Section given to line A:

It was a warm summer evening and Klausner walked quickly through the front gate and around the side of the house and into the garden at the back.

Section given to line B:

He went on down the garden until he came to a wooden shed and he unlocked the door, went inside and closed the door behind him.

Section given to line C:

The interior of the shed was an unpainted room. Against one wall on the left there was a long wooden workbench.

Section given to line D:

(and) on it, among a littering of wires and batteries and small sharp tools there stood a black box about three feet long.

28

Point of order

This 'jigsaw' ordering activity is especially suitable for beginning plays. It usually whets the curiosity of the students, as well as providing valuable phonological practice in stress and intonation patterns.

The teacher places six chairs at the front of the class, and asks for six volunteers to come and sit on them. Each one is given a card on which has been typed one exchange from the beginning of the play. These are not given in order. Each student in turn reads his or her card out loud to the class. The class must then place the six readers in the right order, so that starting from one end, they read the speeches in an order which makes sense and corresponds to the beginning of the play. When this has been done to their satisfaction, the teacher asks the class to situate what is happening, and make predictions about the play's development. The procedure can then be repeated with the next six lines of the play, with six new volunteers.

We have used this technique very successfully to present Harold Pinter's short sketch *Applicant* (in Redamond and Tennyson's *Contemporary One-Act Plays*). The six students are given a slip of paper each, on which is typed:

1. I am, actually, yes.
2. Ah, good morning.
3. Yes. You're applying for this vacant post, aren't you?
4. Are you Mr Lamb?
5. Oh, good morning, miss.
6. That's right.

The teacher asks the class to find the right order. It is usually necessary to help students with the language they will need to give orders to reshuffle the seated students: for example, 'Move up two places, Kari', 'Juan, change places with Maria', 'Stand up and wait a minute, Annette', 'Sit on the third chair, Tsung', 'Read your part again, Vasiliki'. When the class is satisfied that they have got the right order, the teacher asks all six to read their parts again, consecutively. (The right order in this case is 2, 5, 4, 6, 3, 1.) He or she then asks the class: How many characters are there in this play? Who are they? Man? Woman? What are they doing? Where are they?

Most classes will have guessed that the scene is set at a job interview. The teacher then asks them to suggest how each one of the two characters feels. Have any of the students ever been to an interview of any kind? How did they feel? Nervous? Happy? Expectant? etc.

Having thus set the scene, the teacher asks for five more volunteers to come forward and do the next bit of the play in the same way. The correct order in this case is:

1. Are you a physicist?
2. Oh yes, indeed, it's my whole life.
3. Good. Now our procedure is, that before we discuss the applicant's qualifi-
    cations, we like to subject him to a little test to determine his psychological
    suitability. You've no objection?
4. Oh, good heavens, no.
5. Jolly good.

When a satisfactory order has been achieved, the teacher asks students
what new information they have learned about the characters. What kind
of test is about to be given, do they think? How will the applicant react?
Do they think this is a good idea during a job interview?

The class can then proceed to the role play described in the next
activity, or to a reading of the play. If the class has enjoyed the ordering
activity, it can even be repeated a third time, because the next part of the
play begins to seem distinctly bizarre:

1. Please sit down. Can I fit these to your palms?
2. What are they?
3. Electrodes.
4. Oh yes, of course, funny little things.
5. Now the earphones.
6. I say how amusing.
7. Now I plug in.

Students are once again invited to speculate on what kind of test is going
to be administered. Students are usually intrigued enough to be willing to
act out a role play of the interview as they predict it from this point. They
are then amazed and amused when they read the remaining section of this
short sketch, which does not conform to their expectations!

Choose the prediction

Having read the first section of a text, students are asked to study a range
of possible continuations of the story line. Then they choose the one they
consider the author would have used. The list of predictions can, alternatively, be arranged in order of suitability. In groups, choices are compared
and justified.

Bernard Malamud's story 'The model' (in *Selected Stories*) makes an
excellent text for this activity. It is about an elderly man who is an
amateur painter. He hires a model who duly arrives at his house and poses
while he paints her. Suddenly she gets up and comes towards him . . .

Students are offered the following predictions of what is to come:

1. The model weeps on the man's shoulder and tells him that she needs
    money to pay for her mother's operation. He finds out that he knows the
    girl's mother . . .

30

2. The model is actually an artist. She is convinced that the man is not a genuine artist, merely a voyeur. She punishes him by making him pose while she paints him . . .

3. She confesses that she is wanted by the police for murdering an elderly man because he resembled an uncle of hers who had brutally tortured her as a child. She tells the man that his face looks familiar . . .

4. The model seizes his painting and rips it up. She accuses him of exploiting women and demands to be compensated. When he refuses to co-operate, she telephones some feminist friends and invites them to come to the man's house . . .

Sealing the time capsule

Assuming that all students have read the opening section of the work together, this is another activity to follow that reading. Each learner is given a small piece of card on which to record his or her predictions about likely events that will occur as the story unfolds. The teacher can prompt with questions if necessary, or individual writing can follow a general brainstorming session when as many possibilities as can be imagined are quickly reviewed. The cards are then collected, to be sealed in a 'time capsule' envelope where they will remain until the class reaches the end of the book. Follow-up at that point is described in Chapter 6 ('Endings').

Comparing beginnings

The teacher takes three or four opening paragraphs from novels or short stories with fairly similar beginnings, and asks the class to respond to the contrasts. This is especially fruitful with novels in which the main character is described in the first paragraph. Lists or grids can be completed showing physical and psychological attributes, to act as a basis for prediction of future development. The exercise makes students more aware of the particular features of an author's prose style, and may be used to foster students' own powers of description in English.

The first example shows extremely brief but vivid first paragraphs taken from twentieth-century novels; the second example is of lengthier nineteenth-century descriptions opening a novel.

Here are the beginning paragraphs of three modern novels, in which a main character is presented:

1. I was born in 1927, the only child of middle-class parents, both English, and themselves born in the grotesquely elongated shadow, which they never rose sufficiently above history to leave, of that monstrous dwarf Queen Victoria. I was sent to a public school, I wasted two years doing my national service, I went to Oxford; and there I began to discover I was not the person I wanted to be.

(from *The Magus* by John Fowles)

31

2. Castle, ever since he had joined the firm as a young recruit more than thirty
    years ago, had taken his lunch in a public house behind St James's Street,
    not far from the office. If he had been asked why he lunched there, he would
    have referred to the excellent quality of the sausages; he might have
    preferred a different bitter from Watney's, but the quality of the sausages
    outweighed that. He was always prepared to account for his actions, even
    the most innocent, and he was always strictly on time.

    (from *The Human Factor* by Graham Greene)

3. Sometimes, instead of a letter to thank his hostess, Freddy Hamilton would
    compose a set of formal verses – rondeaux redoubles, villanelles, rondels
    or Sicilian octaves – to express his thanks neatly. It was part of his modest
    nature to do this. He always felt he had perhaps been boring during his
    stay, and it was one's duty in life to be agreeable. Not so much at the time
    as afterwards, he felt it keenly on his conscience that he had said no word
    between the soup and the fish when the bright talk began; he felt at fault in
    retrospect of the cocktail hours when he had contributed nothing but the
    smile for which he had been renowned in his pram and, in the following
    fifty years, elsewhere.

    (from *The Mandelbaum Gate* by Muriel Spark)

Here are three similar opening passages from nineteenth-century novels:

1. It was admitted by all her friends, and also by her enemies – who were in
    truth the more numerous and active body of the two – that Lizzie Greystock
    had done very well with herself. We will tell the story of Lizzie Greystock
    from the beginning, but we will not dwell over it at great length, as we
    might do if we loved her. She was the only child of old Admiral Greystock
    who in the latter years of his life was much perplexed by the possession of
    a daughter. The admiral was a man who liked whist, wine – and wickedness
    in general we may perhaps say, and whose ambition it was to live every day
    of his life up to the end of it. People say that he succeeded, and that the
    whist, wine and wickedness were there, at the side even of his dying bed.
    He had no particular fortune, and yet his daughter, when she was little
    more than a child, went about everywhere with jewels on her fingers, and
    red gems hanging round her neck, and yellow gems pendent from her ears,
    and white gems shining in her black hair. She was hardly nineteen when
    her father died and she was taken home by that dreadful old termagant, her
    aunt Lady Linlithgow. Lizzie would have sooner gone to any other friend or
    relative, had there been any other friend or relative to take her possessed of
    a house in town.

    (from *The Eustace Diamonds* by Anthony Trollope)

2. 'Edith!' said Margaret, gently, 'Edith!'
        But as Margaret half suspected, Edith had fallen asleep. She lay curled up
    on the sofa in the back drawing-room in Harley Street, looking very lovely
    in her white muslin and blue ribbons. If Titania had ever been dressed in

white muslin and blue ribbons, and had fallen asleep on a crimson damask sofa in a back drawing-room, Edith might have been taken for her. Margaret was struck afresh by her cousin's beauty. They had grown up together from childhood, and all along Edith had been remarked upon by every one, except Margaret, for her prettiness; but Margaret had never thought about it until the last few days, when the prospect of soon losing her companion seemed to give force to every sweet quality and charm which Edith possessed. They had been talking about wedding dresses, and wedding ceremonies; and Captain Lennox, and what he had told Edith about her future life at Corfu, where his regiment was stationed; and the difficulty of keeping a piano in good tune (a difficulty which Edith seemed to consider as one of the most formidable that could befall her in her married life), and what gowns she should want in the visits to Scotland, which would immediately succeed her marriage; but the whispered tone had latterly become more drowsy; and Margaret, after a pause of a few minutes, found, as she fancied, that in spite of the buzz in the next room, Edith had rolled herself up into a soft ball of muslin and ribbon, and silken curls, and gone off into a peaceful little after-dinner nap.

(from *North and South* by Elizabeth Gaskell)

3. My godmother lived in a handsome house in the clean and ancient town of Bretton. Her husband's family had been residents there for generations, and bore, indeed, the name of their birthplace – Bretton of Bretton: whether by coincidence, or because some remote ancestor had been a personage of sufficient importance to leave his name to his neighbourhood, I know not.

   When I was a girl I went to Bretton twice a year, and well I liked the visit. The house and its inmates specially suited me. The large peaceful rooms, the well-arranged furniture, the clear wide windows, the balcony outside, looking down on a fine antique street, where Sundays and holidays seemed always to abide – so quiet was its atmosphere, so clean its pavement – these things pleased me well.

(from *Villette* by Charlotte Brontë)

What happens next?

This activity can take the form of a role play. Students, in groups, discuss possible continuations, then either improvise them and act them, or prepare, script and act them out. This is an ideal follow-up for the 'ordering' activity described earlier and is suitable for the same sketch 'Applicant'.

An alternative activity is predictive writing. After the students have read (or listened to) the first section of text, the teacher asks them to write the story/dialogue/letter/note/telegram that follows from the situation in the first passage. For less proficient learners, writing activities should involve something simpler such as form-filling or completion of one of the above forms of writing.

V. S. Pritchett's short story 'A family man' (in *Collected Stories*) can serve here as an illustration of the technique. The first section of the story informs the reader that Berenice is a college lecturer who is having an affair with a married man, William Cork. A knock at the door announces the unexpected arrival of a large woman. It is Mrs Cork.

Students are asked to write the ensuing dialogue, either as homework or in pairs, each taking the role of one of the ladies. Before dialogues are created, the teacher speculates with the class about the likely form of the conversation, level of politeness, whether Mrs Cork knows of the affair, etc.

The aim is obviously to make learners want to read the continuation on their own. The form the piece of writing takes depends entirely on the particular text. In H. G. Wells' short story 'The man who could work miracles' (in *Selected Short Stories*), for example, a man who did not previously believe in miracles suddenly finds himself performing them to his own amazement and everyone else's in the local inn. An appropriate writing task to follow the first section of this story would be the report the constable writes on the curious happenings down at the pub.

Writing Chapter 0

Students are asked to write the paragraphs that come immediately *before* the first section of the work which they have just encountered. This is described in more detail for *Lord of the Flies* on p. 95.

Signpost questions

The teacher examines the first significant passage in the text in order to devise comprehension questions which signpost aspects important to the work as a whole: setting, character, or particular themes. The aim is to encourage students to attend to these aspects as the reading progresses.

Editorial suggestions

This is a simulation in which the class is divided into groups. Each group is to be the editorial panel of a publishing house. The first passage of the book, which students have now read, is the draft sent in by the author. The panel's task is to draw up suggestions (concerning style, the unfolding of the plot, characterisation, etc.) for the author. More advanced learners can be asked to write the letter which the editors send; intermediate students could be asked to tick appropriate responses from a computerised list of suggestions normally sent to all authors by this publishing house. A possible second stage would be for students to form new groups. The groups now represent the board which considers the various editorial suggestions made, or letters sent, and chooses the best one.

For plays, students are the panel of selection for a national repertory theatre company, responsible for choosing the next play to be put on.

4 Maintaining momentum

The activities described in this chapter and the next can be used at almost any point in a literary work, and can be applied to the various genres. If the work chosen is not a very long one (a short story, single-act play, or short poem) the teacher can usually present it with one activity, carefully selected amongst those outlined, to help learners understand, enjoy, and appreciate the work.

For lengthier plays, novels, or even longer short stories, however, the teacher will have to section the text and work through it in some way. It is in this situation that a mixture of class activities and home reading can best be used. This will introduce variety into the classroom, maintain momentum and personalise the student's response. It is also most likely to encourage extensive reading habits. Although long works are sometimes read from beginning to end in class, we feel that this is not such a satisfactory procedure. It leaves little time for anything but the reading itself, accompanied perhaps by rapid comments or exegesis by the teacher. Moreover, a lock-step pace is imposed on each member of the class, thereby undermining the creation of a productive tension between group and individual response.

If we assume, then, that a combination of home and class work is to be adopted, a whole range of possibilities opens up for the teacher once a literary work has been started. Teachers must ask themselves the following questions:

What scope does a particular literary work offer for furthering one or several language skills?
Each novel, short story or play can spark off a wealth of different activities. Tasks and exercises based on a literary text can provide valuable practice in listening, speaking or writing, as well as improving reading skills. Literary works of all kinds are now becoming increasingly available in spoken form on cassettes. These can be especially useful in providing extensive listening practice. The chunks heard at one time can be longer than would be possible with many other types of recorded passage, because once a book has been started, students are within a familiar context and have a whole set of expectations about what they are hearing. These are two conditions which are recognised as being helpful to comprehension in a foreign language. Similarly, a shared book provides a network of familiar vocabulary, which means that it can be used for

oral or written work with a minimum of pre-teaching of new words or expressions.

Which parts of the work are to be dealt with in class and which at home?
Here, of course, the teacher will be guided by the level of proficiency, interest and motivation in the class. Some activities need more support in the way of vocabulary pre-teaching, some require a higher level of creativity and imagination from the students. The difficulty of the book, or of any particular passage in it, will also influence the length of the section that can comfortably be read at home. The same approach cannot be used or recommended for all classes. As a general rule, however, it is best to plan lesson activities around the book's highlights: a turning point in the plot, for example, or a scene that furthers the development of characterisation.

How can the best use be made of limited classroom time?
In timetabling lessons, a teacher will want to take into account the following four aspects, any or all of which may occur within class time.

1. Follow-up from home reading: Some of the worksheets which learners are using to help them with their individual work will lead to checking or feedback in class. The first few minutes of a lesson may thus be taken up with a quick review of the task set, to ensure that the section read at home has indeed been understood, to correct or compare answers, to encourage discussion on issues raised, etc. This is a way of allowing learners to pool their resources to overcome difficulties, or simply to find out how others have responded to the text.

2. Ongoing snowball activities: A point to bear in mind is that the method we are proposing can make for a piecemeal set of experiences from the learner's point of view. It is therefore most important for the teacher to plan some way of helping students to retain an overview of all the parts read to date. A few minutes can usefully be set aside in each lesson for one of the snowball activities described later in this chapter.

3. Presenting the new section: The main part of the lesson will often focus on a new passage in the book, which need not follow immediately from the point the students have reached in their own reading. A section just a bit further on can be chosen for class treatment, leaving students quite often curious enough to want to read the intervening part. At other times, class time is used to introduce a new aspect or theme, using a passage students have read at home, with the aim of deepening their insight into the book's literary features.

4. Looking forward: At the end of the class, a few minutes will usually be needed so that the teacher can set the section to be read at home, distribute worksheets to accompany this home reading, and add whatever instructions or explanations are needed.

Home reading with worksheets

Our way of dealing with long texts means that learners will be expected to read quite substantial sections of the book on their own. We would now like to look at how a teacher can make that task easier for the students.

Basically, we suggest that, as often as possible, students be given worksheets to accompany home reading. These can and should be varied in their format, and are usually designed to help with comprehension of the passage set, on the level of language, ideas, or characterisation. When time is at a premium, the worksheet can be planned to generate little or no class follow-up. Self-access answer sheets can be provided. In other cases, a worksheet might raise questions of response or interpretation, and a shared feedback or discussion time in class becomes a necessary follow-up.

The following suggestions indicate the range of possibilities open to the teacher.

Question-and-answer worksheets

In many ways these are the most familiar of all, and the easiest to prepare. Care must be used, however, to avoid the kind of situation where the student merely gives what is obviously the desired 'right' answer; or questions that simply lead students to a particular point in the text, where the answer is clearly to be found.

The following examples show two slightly different approaches, for a class reading Tennessee Williams' *The Glass Menagerie* (in *Penguin Plays*). In this play, set in the south of the United States, a family of three struggle on the edge of poverty. The crippled daughter is shy and withdrawn; the son, a frustrated writer, is forced to work in a shoe factory to support all three; while the mother, living on memories of her own pampered youth, pins all her hopes on somehow finding a husband for her daughter. The first two scenes have been presented in class. Students must now read Scene III on their own. This scene consists of three parts: first, Tom, the son, tells the audience about his mother's growing obsession with finding a husband for Laura; next, we see Amanda, the mother, trying to sell magazine subscriptions over the phone to raise money to buy what she imagines Laura will need for her courtship and marriage; finally, a violent quarrel breaks out between Amanda and Tom. The questions on both worksheets focus mainly on the first and third sections of the scene as these carry plot and theme; the middle part recurs as a kind of pattern which will be picked up later on in the play.

Worksheet 4A consists of questions only, and is thus quite open-ended. Worksheet 4B uses the same questions but gives students more guidance by asking them to choose from various possibilities. In both worksheets, however, the first four questions require factual, right-or-wrong answers, while the next four ask for interpretation and are therefore open to different answers.

It is always useful to allow some time for students to compare the way they have answered the type of questions set in the second half of these questionnaires. This can act as a spark to discussion concerning characterisation in this scene. Asking students to justify their choices can also make them more aware of the process of inference by which readers or spectators arrive at conclusions about the characters or the dramatic situation. A slightly different example of open-ended questions used to encourage students to speculate, interpret, and probe beneath the surface text, is given for the short story 'The edge' (in *Malgudi Days* by R. K. Narayan) (see Worksheet 60).

Question worksheets leading to pair work in class

Half the class is given one set of questions relating to the passage set as home reading, the other half another set. (For example, a teacher working with Worksheets 4A or 4B for *The Glass Menagerie*, could give half

---

Read Scene III of *The Glass Menagerie*. Do not worry too much about words you do not know. Try to get the general meaning if you possibly can without using a dictionary. Then answer the following questions.

1. Amanda is very disappointed that Laura will not take lessons to become a typist. What plan for Laura replaces this one in her mother's mind?
2. Amanda thinks she will need money to carry out her plans for Laura. What does she do to earn that money?
3. Tom and Amanda have a violent quarrel. What did Amanda do that has made Tom so angry?
4. What has Tom been doing when Amanda interrupts him?
5. How would you describe the way Amanda treats Tom?
6. Why does Amanda not believe Tom when he says he is going to the movies?
7. Why does Amanda object to Tom's going out?
8. What is Tom's view of his relationship with his family?

Worksheet 4A

Read Scene III of *The Glass Menagerie*. Do not worry too much about words you do not know. Try to get the general meaning if you possibly can without using a dictionary. Then tick the right answer to the questions below. For questions 5–8, there may be more than one appropriate answer. In that case, tick all possible answers, then number them according to how important they seem: 1, 2, 3, etc. For these questions, a line has been left for you to add other possibilities.

1. Amanda is very disappointed that Laura will not take lessons to become a typist. What plan for Laura replaces this one in her mother's mind?
   ☐ Tom must work harder to support Laura.
   ☐ She herself will find work to support Laura.
   ☐ A husband must be found for Laura.

2. Amanda thinks she will need money to carry out her plans for Laura. What does she do to earn that money?
   ☐ She works in a rope factory.
   ☐ She sells magazine subscriptions over the phone.
   ☐ She begins to write stories for a woman's magazine.

3. Tom and Amanda have a violent quarrel. What did Amanda do that has made Tom so angry?
   ☐ Amanda would not let Tom read the novels of D. H. Lawrence.
   ☐ Amanda scolded Tom for swearing in front of Laura.
   ☐ Amanda scolded Tom for tracking mud and filth all over her clean floors.

4. What has Tom been doing when Amanda interrupts him?
   ☐ Sleeping.
   ☐ Getting dressed to go out.
   ☐ Writing.

5. How would you describe the way Amanda treats Tom?
   ☐ She treats him as though he were still a child.
   ☐ She is harsh and unfeeling.
   ☐ She scolds him because she is worried about the family's future, and especially about Laura.
   ☐ She never stops nagging him.
   ☐ She is a caring mother, really, but she doesn't realise the effect she is having on her son.
   ☐ She is totally selfish and does not see him as a person.
   ☐ ....

6. Why does Amanda not believe Tom when he says he is going to the movies?
   ☐ She thinks this is impossible because she does not know anyone else who goes to the cinema every night.
   ☐ She is trying to find any excuse to quarrel with Tom.
   ☐ She wants to believe the worst of him.
   ☐ She wants to make him feel guilty.
   ☐ She is trying to make him stay at home.
   ☐ ....

7. Why does Amanda object to Tom's going out?
   ☐ Because it makes him tired next day and she is afraid this may make him lose his job.
   ☐ Because she is lonely and would like him to stay with her in the evenings.
   ☐ Because she does not want him to do anything on his own, away from the family – she fears he will go away like his father.
   ☐ Because she is concerned for his health.
   ☐ Because she thinks he is 'up to no good' – she is concerned for his moral health.
   ☐ ....

8. What is Tom's view of his relationship with his family?
   ☐ He feels he is a slave to his family.
   ☐ He resents working so hard for them, and having nothing of his own in return.
   ☐ He resents sacrificing his own writing career for them.
   ☐ He feels he is not free in his own home.
   ☐ He hates his mother for treating him like a child.
   ☐ He dearly loves his sister.
   ☐ He pities his sister.
   ☐ ....

Worksheet 4B

the class the four even-numbered questions, and the other half the odd numbers.) Students are told to prepare answers to their questions as they read through the set section, but they do not have to write them out.

At the beginning of the next lesson, each student is paired with someone who received a different worksheet. In turn, they ask their questions and monitor the answers given orally by the other student.

Part B   Practical activities in outline

'Do it yourself' questionnaires

When students have worked once or twice with worksheets given to them by the teacher, they often enjoy the challenge of devising such a questionnaire themselves. The class is set a passage to read, with the task of thinking up and writing two or three questions on it. In the next lesson, students are paired and ask each other their questions; or all the questions are put into a container and drawn out to be answered by the class working as a whole.

Another successful procedure is to set each half of the class a different passage to read. Each student prepares a worksheet to accompany his or her section – it is best to indicate the number of questions to be included, in the interests of overall fairness. At the next lesson, students exchange worksheets with someone from the other half of the class. They now read their partner's section from the book and answer the questions on it. The next lesson must obviously include some feedback time for the pairs, and this often generates useful discussion on what each student considers important in the passage, and 'worthy of a question'.

The same procedure can be used with the different types of worksheet outlined next.

Complete the sentences

For variety, and for linguistic practice, a teacher can use the format of incomplete sentences, instead of questions and answers. Worksheet 5 is

---

Read the beginning of Scene V from *The Glass Menagerie*. Then complete the following sentences.

1. Amanda would like Tom to comb his hair because if he did so ....
2. Amanda says that if Tom stopped smoking, he ....
3. Tom feels he is living a dull life. When he goes out on the fire escape, though, he sees other people leading more exciting lives. He thinks if only he ....
4. Amanda makes a wish on the moon. If she could have her wish, she ....
5. Amanda says to Tom, as she has done many times before, that it would be very nice for Laura if Tom ....

Worksheet 5

an example of an extremely simple worksheet to accompany home reading, again of Tennessee Williams' *The Glass Menagerie*, but this time from the beginning of Scene V. Students are asked to provide fairly straightforward answers to complete the sentences, but in so doing they practise the second conditional forms: 'If he did . . . he could . . . or he would . . . '. Further examples are given for *Lord of the Flies* in Worksheet 25 and on p. 116.

True or false

Once again, this is an easily devised type of worksheet. It provides help for students by paraphrasing difficult sentences. Worksheet 6 is an example from the beginning of chapter 3 in *The Great Gatsby* by F. Scott Fitzgerald, which describes the prodigious parties given by Gatsby in his New York mansion.

Summaries with gaps

Summaries can give rise to useful group work in class, as we shall see later. For the moment, we would like to consider their use simply as a means of facilitating home reading, either with self-access answer sheets, or with time allowed for students to compare and discuss their answers in class.

The most straightforward type of summary exercise is the gapped summary. This helps readers by providing them with an almost complete, and simply phrased, description of the main points of the section they are tackling. The gaps are usually key words or expressions, which only a reading of the appropriate passage can reveal. Self-access answer sheets are useful here.

The example is taken from *Pygmalion*, the popular play by George Bernard Shaw, about a professor of phonetics who takes a poor flower girl from the slums of London and transforms her by changing her clothes, her manners, and her speech. The gaps are to be filled with factual statements, except for the very last one, which asks for interpretation (see Worksheet 7).

Summaries with incomplete sentences

A slightly more challenging variant consists of a summary with incomplete sentences. The learner has a bit more writing to do to complete the sentences and thus ensure a fluent and accurate summary. The teacher takes in the worksheets and marks them for content and language proficiency. An example is given for *Romeo and Juliet* (see Worksheet 44).

Read the first half of chapter 3 of *The Great Gatsby* and decide whether the following statements are true or false.

T	F	
		1. Gatsby's parties always started at dusk.
		2. Gatsby stood at the door to greet guests as they arrived.
		3. It took six servants to squeeze the hundreds of oranges and lemons used to make drinks for the parties.
		4. It took eight servants to clean up afterwards.
		5. The food was all made by Gatsby's own cook in his kitchens.
		6. A huge variety of food was spread out on tables outdoors, under a canvas top.
		7. In a bar in the hall, guests could help themselves to all kinds of drinks, some familiar and some very strange.
		8. All Gatsby's guests knew each other before the party.
		9. There was a very large orchestra to play music at the parties.
		10. The guests all arrived by train.
		11. All Gatsby's guests had to show invitation cards at the door before they were allowed in to the party.
		12. The guests wore bright colours and the most fashionable clothes and hair-dos.
		13. The guests tended to stay in their own little groups all evening.
		14. Everyone knew the party had really started when girls started dancing on the platform.
		15. The parties became very noisy as the evenings wore on.

Worksheet 6

Read the scene in Act II of *Pygmalion* where Liza's father comes to see Professor Higgins. Then fill in the following summary, using an appropriate word or expression.

In this scene, Alfred Doolittle, a .... by trade, comes to see Henry Higgins. His manner is that of a man who is .... He seems quite used to saying what he thinks and feels. Having heard that his daughter Liza has come to live with Higgins, he has decided to try to use the situation to .... At first, he tries to .... the Professor, saying he wants his daughter back. Higgins replies by insisting that Doolittle must .... immediately. Higgins threatens to tell .... about Doolittle's attempt to blackmail him. Doolittle explains that he was not responsible for Liza's coming and only heard about it from .... The Professor rings for his house-keeper and tells her to let Doolittle take Liza away. But just as he is about to leave, defeated, Doolittle makes an appeal to Higgins as a '................................'. It is clear he thinks Higgins wants Liza for pur-poses that have little to do with language training! Doolittle says Higgins can keep Liza if he .... When Higgins is shocked, Doolittle says he is not a moral person because .... All he wants is .... to compensate him for the loss of his daughter. When Higgins offers him twice the sum requested, however, Doolittle refuses, saying too much money is .... In the end, Higgins gives in and .... because he is impressed by Doolittle's ....

Worksheet 7

Summary comparison

The teacher writes two summaries of a section to be read at home. Students must choose the best one, justifying their choice. Differences between the summaries can be 'fine-tuned' according to the level of the group. At the simplest level, one of the summaries omits certain key points; at a more difficult level, both summaries are fairly accurate but one may contain incorrect inference or interpretation. At a still more advanced level, the best summary may be chosen for style, perhaps using such criteria as:

– Which summary do you think the author himself would prefer?
– Which would be preferable for: a literary magazine?
　　　　　　　　　　　　　　　a popular newspaper?
　　　　　　　　　　　　　　　a class of language learners at an elementary level?
　　　　　　　　　　　　　　　etc.

Two different types of summary comparisons are illustrated for *Lord of the Flies* (see Worksheets 22 and 29).

Key points for summaries

From a section read at home, students are asked to list the five key points which would form the basis for a continuously written summary. Key points can be related to events or to character development. Since the latter type, especially, calls for interpretation, it is useful to compare choice of key points in class, perhaps asking each group to produce a common list, by negotiation. The teacher supplies his or her own list for comparison and discussion.

Alternatively, the teacher provides the class with a list of key points for a section they are about to read at home, and asks them to tick each one off as they read. Then they have to supply one missing point, or delete one irrelevant point. The latter can be checked by self-access answer sheets.

Jumbled events

'Ordering' worksheets offer a great deal of support to students as they read, because they give most of the facts needed to make sense of the passage. All they have to do is find the right order or sequence. There is a puzzle element to them which appeals, and extra elements of challenge can be added.

In its simplest form, the student is given a jumbled list of a certain number of events that occur in the home-reading passage, and asked to place them in their correct sequence. A few incorrect events can be included which must be spotted and discarded; or one or two key events may be left out, to be supplied by the reader. An example of a jumbled list including some false choices is given for *Lord of the Flies* (see Worksheet 33). Another example, where the facts are all accurate but, once ordered, must be fitted into a flow diagram, is given for 'The edge' (see Worksheets 61A and 61B).

Continuous summaries may be used instead of a list of happenings. There are examples in both the novel and play chapters.

Choosing an interpretation

Here, instead of events, students are given a series of different interpretations of events in the passage they are reading. They can be asked to sort these into order of importance, choose the one nearest to their own ideas, or write their own interpretation, selecting if they wish elements from those given. An example is given for *Lord of the Flies* (see Worksheet 32).

Value judgment worksheets

Most of the worksheets we have been discussing focus on helping learners understand the literary work. There are times, however, when a teacher will want the students to go beyond basic comprehension and consider some of the moral or aesthetic issues raised by a particular text. A worksheet to accompany home reading can do much to pave the way for fruitful class discussion – it is a means of drawing attention to the special areas the teacher might wish to highlight. Comparing answers that require interpretation and value judgments can also provide a stimulus to analysis and extend a reader's range of literary response.

Worksheet 8 is based upon the scene in *Pygmalion* for which we have already provided a gapped summary (Worksheet 7). Except in advanced classes where it would not be needed, Worksheet 7 can be used as a preparatory exercise, so that the teacher can ensure that everyone has understood the basics of what happens in this part of the play. But the bare summary of events does not begin to pin down everything that is actually happening on stage. The scene is a crucial one for plot and characterisation. Dramatically, it presents an amusing but very powerful conflict in wit and will between two men who, despite the contrast in their social position, are equally clever, confident, ruthless, and determined to get their own way. Morally, the scene is profoundly ambivalent, full of contradictions about what constitutes honesty, sincerity, and 'decent' feelings about one's family and one's fellow human beings. These are some of the areas Worksheet 8 encourages students to explore. They are asked to respond to a set of statements by grouping them in order of importance or preference, as they read the scene at home. In class, choices are compared, discussed, justified. This is best done in groups, with each group being asked to establish an overall profile of the attitudes expressed by the priorities most of them have chosen. The general class discussion which follows can be quite wide-ranging and illuminating.

》》》→

Read the scene in Act II of *Pygmalion* where Liza's father comes to see Professor Higgins. Then study the following sets of statements. From each set, choose the *three* statements which seem to you most appropriate, and put them in order of importance: first, second and third. Be prepared to justify your choice by reference to the scene.

Henry Higgins
a) Higgins is an example of upper-class morality: totally self-centred, caring for no one else but himself.
b) Higgins is a realist: he accepts things as they are.
c) Higgins is a ruthless manipulator who lets nothing stand in his way.
d) Higgins is really quite a kindly man beneath his crusty exterior.
e) Higgins is a bully because he is unsure of himself and wants to hide his insecurity.
f) Higgins is a gentleman with a gentleman's code of honour.

Alfred Doolittle
a) Doolittle is an extraordinarily callous man, willing to sell his own daughter for £5.
b) Doolittle's behaviour can be excused: society has never given him anything, and so he owes it nothing.
c) Doolittle is completely selfish: he thinks only of himself, and does not care what is happening to his daughter.
d) Doolittle is refreshingly free from ordinary morality and social conventions.
e) Doolittle is sincere: he is remarkably open about his own shortcomings.
f) Doolittle is not only 'an old liar', but he is a clever and persuasive liar at that.

The morality that emerges from this scene
a) If you are clever enough you can get away with anything.
b) Morality is a luxury only the rich can afford.
c) Appearance is all.
d) Be true to your own self, nothing else matters.
e) Civilisation and its conventions constitute a strait-jacket that any thinking person will want to avoid.
f) Any code of honour is a thin veneer disguising dishonesty.
g) It is better not to have too much money: it makes a man too prudent.
h) Cleanliness is next to godliness.
i) .... (Write your own.)

Worksheet 8

Chessboard

Another way of getting students to consider the implications of given elements in a literary work is to ask them to place statements from it on either the white squares (for positive, 'good' elements) or black squares (for negative or 'bad' elements) of a chessboard-shaped grid. This often serves to underline the ambiguity of the work of art. An example is given for *Lord of the Flies* (see Figure 12).

Choosing a moral

Giving a 'moral' for a short story, novel or poem is a traditional way of drawing out the ideas or values that are implicit within it. Sometimes, however, simply asking a class: 'What would you say is the moral to this story?' produces rather disappointing results. Students usually come up with better ideas if they have time to mull over the question, and if they are given something to spark their interest and get them started. A worksheet to be done at home while they read the last section of the text, with results compared in the next lesson, often generates better discussion.

Worksheet 9 lists several alternative morals for the short story 'The man who could work miracles', by H. G. Wells in *Selected Short Stories*. (A simplified version is available for intermediate-level students in *Outstanding Short Stories* by G. C. Thornley.) This is a story about an ordinary man who suddenly and unaccountably finds himself able to do any-

---

Read to the end of 'The man who could work miracles'. Then choose the moral which you think most appropriate. If none seems suitable to you, write one of your own. Be prepared to justify your choice.

The moral of this short story is:
1. 'Don't give the ordinary man power – he can't use it sensibly.'
2. 'Do-gooders only succeed in doing evil.'
3. 'If you have a power or talent, trust your own ability to use it.'
4. 'People who are supposed to have superior wisdom often lack ordinary common sense.'
5. 'Position and personality are entirely different things.'
6. 'Power corrupts.'
7. 'Thank goodness human beings are not all-powerful.'
8. 'Leave miracles to God.'
9. Your own: '.................................'

Worksheet 9

thing at all, just by wishing it. The village clergyman, consulted about it, attempts to channel this new power for the good of humanity, but his efforts are misguided and the world is only saved from total catastrophe by the miracle worker's wish that he be relieved of his power and returned to the moment before he suddenly acquired it. Another example requiring more interpretation is given in Worksheet 57 for the story 'The spread of Ian Nichol' (in *Unlikely Stories, Mostly*, by Alasdair Gray).

Language worksheets

The section to be read at home sometimes presents vocabulary or other language difficulties, and an accompanying worksheet is designed to make reading easier for the learner. In other cases, the teacher might wish to highlight a writer's rich or metaphorical language, or ensure that particular terms or structures encountered in a literary text are internalised and become part of a student's active vocabulary. In all cases, this kind of worksheet depends very much on the actual text, its level of difficulty, its particular stylistic qualities, and so on. It is quite difficult to give any general rules, or to illustrate out of context. We therefore give a brief list of various types, with page references to indicate illustrations given within the context of the discussion of complete works of literature in later chapters.

MATCHING

The simplest way to help students with texts that have difficult words, expressions, or structures is to give them simple definitions for problem words, or simplified rephrased sentences, which they are asked to match with the more complex original.

Examples of two kinds of worksheet of this type are to be found in the chapter on *Romeo and Juliet*: one gives modern colloquial sentences, in jumbled order, which the student must match to the speeches in one scene of the play (see Worksheet 51); the other gives a series of rephrased, simplified sentences, some of which are accurate, others not: the student's task is to distinguish between them (see Worksheet 43).

EXTRACTING AND CLASSIFYING VOCABULARY FROM THE TEXT

When a teacher wants to highlight words either for comprehension or for stylistic analysis, students are asked to extract specific kinds of words or expressions from a part of the work studied. A visual means of indicating different categories of words is the star diagram given for *Lord of the Flies*, which can be used as a class or home reading activity (see Figures 9A and 9B).

WORDS OR EXPRESSIONS TO CHARACTERISE A TEXT

To enrich learners' vocabulary, the teacher can give them a whole series of terms or expressions that must be assigned to specific features or characters in their book. Examples are given for *Lord of the Flies* (see Worksheets 14 and 36), grids for characterisation work (see Worksheet 15) and for the short story 'The star' (see Worksheet 56).

LITERAL AND METAPHORICAL MEANING

Worksheets can be used to sensitise students to the metaphorical dimension of words in the book they are reading. Examples can be found in Chapter 8 (see Figure 16 and Worksheets 47 and 48).

SIMPLE GRAMMAR OR STRUCTURE WORK

The text of a book often offers excellent opportunities to practise specific areas of language. The advantage of the literary text is that it provides a context for language work. Exercises can be quite open-ended, so that in addition to language improvement, they incorporate student response. Some examples are: 'preposition practice' (see p. 115) and 'structural exercise' (see p. 116).

WORD PUZZLES WITH FOLLOW-UP WRITING EXERCISES

Word puzzles are simple to create, with follow-up writing tasks designed to help learners use their new vocabulary. Examples can be found in Worksheets 31A and 31B.

WORKSHEETS FOCUSSING ON THE PERFORMATIVE FUNCTION OF LANGUAGE

Such a worksheet, illustrated in *Lord of the Flies* (see Worksheet 34) can be given to accompany home reading, followed by class discussion.

Snowball activities

These are activities which continue, and are added to progressively, as students read through a long work. They help to maintain an overview of the entire book, provide a valuable aid to memory, and reduce a lengthy text to manageable proportions.

Retelling the story

Valuable oral practice for classes can be provided by retelling the story so far as a chain activity. This also helps to keep the whole narrative in the mind of the reader. Large classes can be divided into story-telling groups so that each student gets a turn. The activity can be combined with vocabulary work, as in the example in *Lord of the Flies* or with work on character portrayal (see p. 120).

Wall charts and other visual displays

Visual prompts are extremely helpful to learners working their way through a long, and sometimes complex, work. They function as a constant reminder of the book's various elements. Wall charts can be of several kinds:

SNOWBALL SUMMARIES

A traditional way of retaining an idea of chronology is to ask students to write a summary of what happens as each part of the book unfolds. We have found that this is indeed a useful tool for both comprehension and revision; but keeping it going can easily become a repetitive chore, so that early chapters tend to be dealt with more fully than middle or end sections.

One way of minimising tedium is to make the activity into a shared one for the whole class. The representation of events is done on a large wall chart (or, if circumstances make this difficult, in one notebook which is available for all members of the class to consult, and copy into their own books if they wish). The class is divided into teams, each assigned responsibility for the creation of one or more sections of the chart.

An example involving a three-fold summary of events, themes, and the reactions of characters, is given for *Lord of the Flies* (see Figure 10).

MONTAGE

In the same way that an author's life can be used for a montage (see Figure 2) the various aspects of a work – plot, character, setting – can form the basis for a growing visual display. Magazine pictures, drawings, photographs, suitable pieces of creative writing or extracts from critical works, quotations, character sketches that have been drawn or written by the students can all be added gradually.

GRAPHIC REPRESENTATIONS

These could be sequentially arranged diagrams or other forms of visual representation focussing on different elements of a particular work. Here are some examples:

– Representations of the development of the plot. If the teacher plans to section the reading of a long text into ten parts, for instance, the chart would consist of ten divisions, each one exemplifying in some concrete way what happens in that part of the book. Memorable quotes can be added. Each part can be encapsulated in a symbolic shape which reminds the reader of some particular feature of that section of the work. An example is shown for *Romeo and Juliet* (see Figure 17).

- Representations of characters, their introduction into the story, their growing or changing relationship with each other. These could be in the form of a large class grid, on which new information is jotted down as reading progresses. For added visual interest and memorability, a different colour can be used for each character, or non-linear forms adopted: for example, information about various characters is added gradually to large outlines of each one that have been drawn on a wall chart: the 'flow' of character development is represented along a wavy line, showing the 'ups' and the 'downs' in a particular character's fortunes, or morale; finally, the relationship between characters is portrayed graphically on a type of 'snakes and ladders' board ('ladders' for a closer or more amicable time, 'snakes' for conflict or discord).
- Representations of the setting in which the action occurs. Once again, an imaginative variation on a standard linear form can often prove more interesting for learners to create, and easier for them to remember. The star diagram used to describe the setting in *Lord of the Flies*, for example (see Figures 9A and 9B) could be repeated at various points in books where there is a change of setting, thus providing a snowball variant.

Wall charts or diagrams can be class-based, with groups given responsibility for one planned sequence in the overall diagram. Alternatively, different groups can have their own displays, leading to discussion about *why* each particular item or symbol was chosen. Apart from being useful in stimulating oral work, the latter option helps break down the idea of a 'definitive' version of literary criticism. Different responses are seen to be possible and fruitful.

Reassessing

An overview can be maintained by simply redoing a particular exercise at various points in a book. For example, a grid used to crystallise a first insight into motivation and personality (see Worksheet 15) can be collected and kept by the teacher. Several chapters later, learners are given a second copy of the same grid to fill out again, drawing now on their expanded knowledge of the character. Comparison of earlier and later views is often instructive!

Continuing predictions

In situations where it is possible, that is, where students are all reading at about the same pace, they can be asked to predict the likely course of events near the beginning, then again at later stages of their reading. This fosters momentum, and it can take the form of oral work, with the teacher or, better still, one of the learners asking appropriate questions: What is going to happen? What is likely to be the fate of X . . . ? Choices could be offered: Here are three possibilities . . . Which do you think is the most likely? Why?

A variation which our students have found interesting is the following: after reading the first section of the book, students are asked to complete a series of statements in writing. Here is an example for *Lord of the Flies*:

I think Piggy will ....
I think the children will/will not be rescued because ....
I think the greatest danger they face is ....
I think they will succeed in ....
I think they will fail in ....
I think they will find it easiest to ....
I think they will find it hardest to ....

These are pinned up and reviewed after a few lessons. Are early predictions still valid? Why/why not? How would they need to be changed in the light of our new knowledge?

A variation of the preceding exercise also provides training in making inferences from given data, a skill which is an important element in reading comprehension.

From a set of facts, learners are asked to deduce likely consequences. For example, from early chapters of *Lord of the Flies*:

In this chapter, we see the beginnings of conflict between Jack and Ralph. From this we can foresee that ....
Jack taunts Piggy and won't let him speak. This may lead to ....

The stress laid on facts in this version trains learners to be attentive to the possible consequences of events in the story they are reading. Having done this once, students could initiate the process themselves for the next section of a long text. That is, working in groups, they extract from a passage which they have just read, the *facts* upon which inferences can be made. Each group's facts are then passed on to another group, whose task it is to work out possible conclusions.

Decision points

At certain points in reading a book, learners are asked to write a sentence or paragraph in answer to a question of the type: Why did X make this decision? take this step? change her mind?

Here are some examples:

Why did Ripley decide to kill Dickie Greenleaf? (*The Talented Mr Ripley* by
  Patricia Highsmith)
Why does Daisy stay with Tom? (*The Great Gatsby* by F. Scott Fitzgerald)
Why does Liza decide to stay with Higgins when he is so rude to her?
  (*Pygmalion* by George Bernard Shaw)
Why do people keep going to Doctor Fischer's parties? (*Doctor Fischer of
  Geneva* by Graham Greene)

The teacher collects the answers. He or she then writes or types out a
selection of the answers, chosen to illustrate the widest range of reasons
(the rather tedious recopying is to ensure anonymity and allow some
unobtrusive language correction by the teacher, if need be). Later on,
when students have read further, the selection is either pinned up for all
to see or, if it is possible to duplicate it, distributed to the students.

It is now easier for learners to assess whether additional information
gained since writing their answers can affect their ideas about the question asked, what new answers would now have to be given, why certain
answers were fuller, closer to the mark than others, and so on.

With more advanced groups, this activity can be used for quite useful
language work: the sentences or paragraphs, instead of being corrected,
are rewritten or typed with either all errors left in, or with one specific
type left in (for example, omission of articles, verb tenses, etc.). Students,
working in groups, see how many of the errors they can spot and correct.
This kind of work is usually enjoyable for them – but it is probably best
to use it sparingly: after such intense scrutiny of the *way* ideas have been
expressed, it is quite often difficult to go on to a discussion of *what* the
sentences formulate. In this as in so many other activities, it is important
to try to vary and balance the kind of work learners are doing.

Writing ongoing diaries

As the long text unfolds, students are asked to keep a diary recording
events and feelings. Different students can imagine that they are different
characters and keep the diary which 'their' person would have written as
each new circumstance in the book develops. This ensures a range of
diaries written from different perspectives. It is important to provide
some opportunity for students to compare diaries, and discuss them, at
the end of the book. An exhibition of diaries could be organised.

Fly on the wall

Instead of taking on a character's role, students, alternatively, can act as
'flies on the wall' and imagine that they are present in the book as themselves, though invisible. Their diaries therefore contain their own obser-

vations and comments. The responsibility of building up an accumulated range of 'fly-on-the-wall' views can be a shared one. The teacher divides the long text into a number of sections equal to the number of students in the class. Each learner draws a number and is then responsible for writing a commentary on the part of the book corresponding to the number. These could be put on a wall chart, or in a decorated book kept especially for this purpose and containing one section per student. The binders now available, into which sheets of paper can be slotted betwen protective plastic, seem ideal for this activity. According to the level of the class and his or her own teaching priorities, a teacher could decide to correct the written comments before incorporating them into the book, or leave them as each student produced, 'warts and all'.

Other writing tasks can be similarly added to snowball wall charts or notebooks as reading progresses.

Language projects

An activity to be done in groups, each group being assigned one specific language aspect to study as the class reads through a text. See Worksheet 42 for an example using *Romeo and Juliet*.

5 Exploiting highlights

Once progress through the literary work is being sustained by supported home reading, and with snowball activities developing and maintaining a growing sense of narrative and characterisation, the teacher can select from an additional range of imaginative activities in order to exploit the highlights of the work. These activities will further encourage the students to explore and express their own response to the literary work. Moreover, if the teacher's selection is judicious, this will enable him or her to attend to particular deficiencies in one or more of the students' language skills at the same time as they are absorbed in the drama of a novel or play.

The activities described in this chapter are ideas or templates which can be modified or adapted according to the particular literary work being read and the type and level of students involved. Once again, we emphasise that they can be used at different points in the text.

Although the majority of the activities are grouped under skill headings, many of them integrate several language skills and reflect our wish to use literature as a stimulus to oral work, especially in groups. The result we believe will be not only a general improvement in the students' all-round ability in the target language, but also an enjoyable relationship with the literature of that tongue.

Writing activities

Literary works provide a wealth of contexts for interesting writing activities in the classroom. We group here a variety of activities that have a writing component, though many lead naturally into game, discussion or drama follow-ups and thus develop into multi-skill exercises. The progression in this section is from more controlled writing activities to more creative ones.

Connectors and summary writing

The teacher gives the class a list of connectors, for example:

furthermore	however	to sum up
nevertheless	meanwhile	to make matters worse
even so	on the other hand	

Students are set a passage to read at home. In the next class lesson, they are asked, in pairs, to write a summary of this section, using each of the connectors in the list appropriately. The teacher gives them a maximum number of words. There is comparison and discussion of the results.

As a follow-up in the next lesson, the same connectors are written on slips of paper and put into a box. Students have been set a further home-reading passage. Each student now chooses a slip of paper with a connector. In groups, they relate the events of the new passage read, in turn, using the connector chosen. If it is not possible for them to use it, they are allowed to substitute a totally different connector, which they write on a slip of paper to add to the stock. Repetition of connectors is not allowed!

Similar work can be done with markers that help clarify the logical progression of an essay, for example: 'one reason for this is . . . ' and 'take, for example . . . '

As these activities help students develop awareness of ways of connecting ideas, they are useful preparation for writing essays.

Summarising the summary

One novel way of carrying out summary work is to make it progressive. Students are divided into three groups. Each writes a summary of the section read, with a maximum number of words, for example, 70. They then pass on their summary to the next group, which must reduce it to half its length, that is, to 35 words. This is now passed on to the third group, which halves the length again, to 17 words. Each group is thus involved in reducing all three summaries. Final versions are read out and changes discussed.

Creative conversation writing

Writing dialogues is a good way for students to explore their view of a character or fictional situation. The exchanges are kept simple so that they remain effective even if learners have not yet achieved perfect control of the target language.

The most obvious and successful way of creating conversation based on literary works is to take scenes in which there is no speech available and ask the class to imagine the conversation that took place, then write it, in groups or pairs. For example, a character arrives on the scene, having just been with someone else: students are asked to write the previous conversation, which is not in the literary work itself. Characters who are not placed alone together in the work can be given that opportunity in the reader's imagination. Poems also provide excellent contexts for conversation writing, and several examples are given in Chapter 10. The exact format of the task will of course vary according to the particular situation in each literary work. In *Lord of the Flies*, for example, students are asked to write a monologue (see p. 150), while after reading the short play *The Sandbox*, they are asked to create a sketch (see p. 194). In all these cases, the dialogues written can be the basis for excellent role play or dramatisation. Students usually enjoy performing their own works!

Another popular way of creating dialogues is to have them written 'in the round' as follows.

The teacher having set the scene, each student writes the first utterance, imagining that they are character A. They then pass their slip of paper to their right-hand neighbour. Everyone now reads the utterance they have received, and, imagining they are now character B, write a reply to it on the paper before them. They then pass the paper back to their left-hand neighbour, that is, the learner who originally wrote the first exchange. Each student is now character A once again, and replies to character B's part of the dialogue. At the end of the activity, each learner will have helped build up two dialogues, one in which they have consistently been character A, the other in which they have been character B. This technique often makes dialogue writing more enjoyable because it contains an element of surprise: each learner must react to the part of the conversation written by another student. It also has the advantage of being suitable for any size of class. An illustration can be found in the imagined dialogue between Romeo and Old Capulet in *Romeo and Juliet* (see p. 178).

Thought bubbles

As learners become familiar with a work of the imagination, the teacher will wish them to become aware of the creative interplay that exists within it, between the 'outer' world of action and appearance, and the 'inner' world of thought and feeling. He or she will want them to notice, too, that readers can be given a varying set of clues about these worlds: sometimes the readers are told only what a character does or says, at other times they are also told what the character thinks; sometimes there is comment from a narrator, at other times not. There are assumptions which every reader has to make to interpret the clues given and to create, in a sense, a new world that is merely pointed to, in the text. The following task helps students make these assumptions explicit. In so doing they will, it is hoped, gain a fuller understanding both of the imaginary world itself, and also of the narrative or dramatic codes by which an author creates, and a reader re-creates, this complex world of the imagination.

The task is simple: students are asked to write the 'inner' dialogue that parallels the 'outer' dialogue given in the literary work. A way of making this more visual, concrete, and interesting, is illustrated for the poem 'Telephone conversation' (see Worksheet 67). Here, a cartoon has been drawn showing what each character says; learners have to fill in the

Part B   *Practical activities in outline*

Read the passage on pp. 69–70 of *The Talented Mr Ripley*, where Dickie comes into his room, to find Tom trying on his clothes. The dialogue on the left is what they say to each other. On the right is what each of them is thinking. With your partner, write what each character really thinks. The first two parts have been done, but you can change these if they do not represent what you consider each character to be thinking. Remember the novelist has given some clues in the passage!

	What each character says	*What he is thinking*
Dickie:	What're you *doing*?	How dare you come into my room secretly and sneak into my clothes! It's disgusting!
Tom:	Oh – just amusing myself.	What shall I do? Where can I hide? Oh, my God, he knows! I hate him!
Tom:	Sorry, Dickie. Dickie, I'm sorry if . . .	
Dickie:	I wish you'd get out of my clothes. Shoes too? Are you crazy?	
Tom:	No. Did you make it up with Marge?	
Dickie:	Marge and I are fine. Another thing I want to say, but clearly. I'm not queer. I don't know if you have the idea that I am or not.	
Tom:	Queer? I never thought you were queer.	
Dickie:	Well, Marge thinks *you* are.	
Tom:	Why? Why should she? What've I ever done?	
Dickie:	It's just the way you act.	

Worksheet 10

'thought bubbles' to indicate each person's simultaneous, though unuttered, thoughts and feelings.

The cartoon is not, however, an essential feature. In Worksheet 10, designed for a highlight scene in *The Talented Mr Ripley* by Patricia Highsmith, the spoken dialogue is given on the left, and students are asked to write the accompanying thought dialogue on the right. In this case, the attention of students is drawn to the fact that some clues are given in the narrative (for example, the author says that Tom is embarrassed at the beginning of the scene) and that these must be taken into account in establishing the parallel inner script.

Cries for help

It is often the case that a highlight scene in a literary work presents one of the characters, or several, in some dire predicament. Students are asked to write the note or short letter that such a character dashes off as a plea for help. In a state of peril or anguish, obviously, communication is paramount: no one is going to worry unduly about the odd spelling or syntax mistake as long as it does not impede possible comprehension of the message. The context can therefore be a liberating one for learners who are not too confident of their mastery of the written mode. An example is given for *Lord of the Flies* ('Letter in a bottle', p. 116 and Figure 11) but the situation can be varied for a great number of different texts: students can be asked to write the note which the girl tries to smuggle out in John Fowles' *The Collector* (before the class has reached that point in the novel); or which Mrs Wilson tries to get out to Tom when she has been locked up by her husband in *The Great Gatsby* by F. Scott Fitzgerald; or which Friar Lawrence sends to Romeo in *Romeo and Juliet*; or which John writes to the Reservation asking to be rescued, in Aldous Huxley's *Brave New World*, etc.

Poems

Writing poems in the foreign language can be surprisingly enjoyable for learners, as long as the whole activity is done within a very relaxed and non-directive framework. The aim is to crystallise a personal, felt response to a literary situation. It is usually better, therefore, not to impose constraints of rhythm or rhyme. Formal limitations, on the other hand, can be quite rewarding. Students usually enjoy writing poems whose shape, for example, reproduces the main theme, as in George Herbert's famous examples. Poems with a set number of syllables, as in the various Japanese models, or whose first letters in each line spell a name, are also popular. Examples are given in the poetry chapter, and in *Lord of the Flies* (see p. 123).

.9 February **MONDAY RADIO**

art of the Summer Term.
sive Mr Beeston, and a
ed teacher: a pre-occupied
rown, and – 'where have
children gone? . . .'
rchant ....ROY SPENCER
ʼson ....ROSEMARY MILLER
.....PRUDENCE OLIVER
....ROBERT LYNAM
ʼ?K DENHAM

ᵉcause ᵃ...   ʼᵗⁱᵒ ⁿᵃⁱ
know that *how* you give birth
can matter a great deal.
Corinne Julius visits one of the
Caesarian Support Groups
which have been growing up
round the country.
Serial:
The Diary of a Good Neighbour
by DORIS LESSING
abridged in 12 episodes
by MEG CLARKE
Read by **Janet Suzman** (1)
Jane Somers, a successful
magazine journalist, feels that
she failed both her husband and
her mother when they were
dying of cancer. But then life
presents her with a second
chance in an unlikely encounter
with an old woman – Maudie
Fowler.
(Music: Claude Bolling's Suite for
cello and jazz piano)
Editor SANDRA CHALMERS

1.55-3.0 *VHF/FM*

6.ᴏ   ᴏ. O'Clock News
with Pᴇᴛᴇʀ DONALDSON
Half an hour of reports
from the BBC correspondents
around the world
including **Financial Report**

6.30 The News Quiz
The last seven days from a
peculiar viewpoint, the chair of
Barry Took. Trying to make
sense of it, *Private Eye*'s
Richard Ingrams, his gifted
satirist **John Wells**, *Observer*
Editor **Donald Trelford** and
Punch supremo **Alan Coren**
Written and compiled by
JOHN LANGDON with the
Producer HARRY THOMPSON. *Stereo*
(Broadcast on Saturday at 12.27 pm)

7.0 News

ᵉⁿⁱⁿᵍ ...ˢᶜⁱ
A weekly review of discoverᵢₑₛ
and developments from the
world's leading laboratories.
Producer GEOFF DEEHAN
(Re-broadcast next Saturday)

8.15 The Monday Play
The Diary by BRIAN GLANVILLE
with **Mary Ellis** as Alice
Jane Asher as Helen
and **Robert Harris** as Vanbrugh
In her villa outside Florence,
Alice lives the life of a great
lady, waited and doted on.
However, her mother was a
particular friend of Edward VII
and her daughter is a raffish
bohemian. There are skeletons
in her cupboard – and in her
diary!
Clovis ....HENRY STAMPER
The Rev Deeley ....PETER MARINKER
Holmes ....KERRY SHALE
Giuseppe ....TIM REYNOLDS
Directed by GRAHAM GAULD
Stereo (Re-broadcast next Saturday)

ᵃ Kaleᵢᵈ...
Presented by Michaᵉ
Producer JOHN BOUNDY
Editor ANNE WINDER
(Re-broadcast tomorroᵣ

10.15 A Book at Iᵉ
Missing Persons bʸ
abridged in ten paᵣ
DONALD BANCROFT
Read by **Patricia R**
6: *The Prodigal. Sₜ*

10.30 The World
Presented by **Davi**
Editor BLAIR THOMSC

11.15
The Financial W

11.30 *LW*
Tᵒday ⁱⁿ Pᵃ ʼ

ᵒᵍrammes w.
ᵒn Wednesdays froᵤ ₄ ₘₐᵣₓᵣ on
BBC2. Other material –
software, print support, slides
available from BBC Enterprises.
The following programmes are a
selection of short self-help units.
The CSA programme should be
used in conjunction with the
CSA software pack.
12.30 1: *Control*
12.40 2: *Making Things Move*
12.50 3: *Materials and
Components*
1.0 4: *Structures* (CSA)
Producer JULIAN COLEMAN. *Stereo (e)*

Note
*Approximate time
*Programmes can only be received in
stereo by switching to VHF/FM*
(R) denotes repeat
*(e) This programme may be recorded
by educational institutions for non-
commercial use. For details write to:*
*BBC Education, Villiers House,
London W5 2PA*

ᴇLY *(R) (e)*

ᵃrnoon Play
ᵗ**Lesson**
CAMPBELL. *Stereo*
ᵣ *Saturday at 7.0 pm)*

ʼoscope

ᵉⁿ explores the past
ᵉⁿt of Russian art
which currently
ᵒndon's Barbican

ᵤₛt Friday)

by **Gordon Clough**
ᵢe **Singleton**
ᴇK LEWIS
ᵐ *VHF/FM* 5.50-5.55 pm

Figure 4

Using authentic formats

There are many non-literary formats which can be imported into the context of the literary work and used to spur writing about it. In each of the following examples, students are first shown an 'authentic' model, so that they have some awareness of the usual layout, style, length and register.

GUIDE TO A TV OR RADIO SERIAL

Students imagine that the work they are studying is being serialised on radio or TV. They are shown an example of the 'Guide to TV and radio' section in a newspaper or magazine (see Figure 4). They must then write a very brief account of one particular scene of their work, as though for that publication. (This could also be used as an ongoing snowball activity.)

NEWSPAPER ARTICLES

A newspaper article or feature is to be written about the highlight scene chosen. Students are shown examples of genuine newspaper articles, if possible from more than one type of publication. They are asked to write about the events in the literary work as though for one of these newspapers. They can be given a headline as a prompt, and a maximum number of words. This is exemplified for the short story 'The hitchhiker' (see p. 200) and *Lord of the Flies* (see p. 155).

REPORTS

These practise a more official register, an impersonal kind of writing. In each case, it may be necessary to familiarise students with the conventions of report writing by studying examples with them beforehand. Different types of report might be 'minutes of the meeting' exemplified in *Lord of the Flies* (see p. 129), an insurance or police report, or a school report as in *Lord of the Flies* (see Figure 13 and Worksheet 35).

AN 'AGONY AUNT' COLUMN

Examples of a group writing activity based upon the idea of seeking the advice of an 'agony aunt' column in a newspaper are given for *The Sandbox* (see Worksheets 53A and 53B).

EPITAPHS

A lapidary comment on a deceased character! Once again, it is best if examples can be provided (see Figure 5). This is an excellent pretext for a very brief appreciation of a character, and one that seems to be always very popular with students (see Worksheet 39).

⋙→

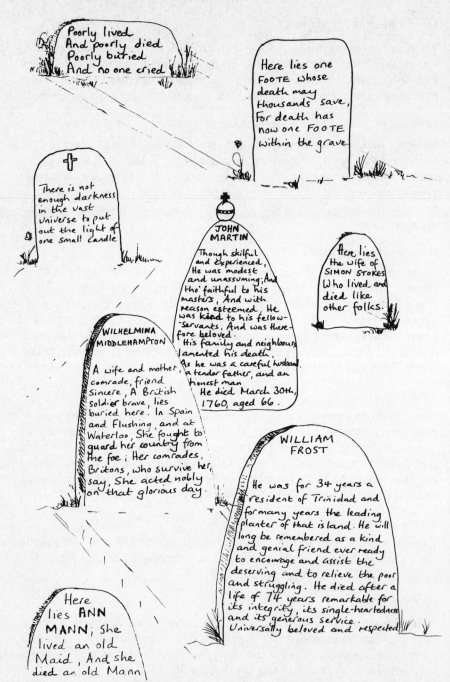

Poorly lived
And poorly died
Poorly buried
And no one cried

Here lies one
FOOTE whose
death may
thousands save,
For death has
now one FOOTE
within the grave.

There is not
enough darkness
in the vast
universe to put
out the light of
one small candle

JOHN MARTIN

Though skilful
and experienced,
He was modest
and unassuming; And
tho' faithful to his
masters, And with
reason esteemed, He
was kind to his fellow-
-servants, And was there-
fore beloved.
His family and neighbours
lamented his death,
As he was a careful husband,
a tender father, and an
honest man
He died March 30th,
1760, aged 66.

Here lies
the wife of
SIMON STOKES
Who lived and
died like
other folks.

WILHELMINA MIDDLEHAMPTON

A wife and mother,
comrade, friend
Sincere, A British
soldier brave, lies
buried here. In Spain
and Flushing, and at
Waterloo, She fought to
guard her country from
the foe; Her comrades,
Britons, who survive her,
say, She acted nobly
on that glorious day.

WILLIAM FROST

He was for 34 years a
resident of Trinidad and
for many years the leading
planter of that island. He will
long be remembered as a kind
and genial friend ever ready
to encourage and assist the
deserving and to relieve the poor
and struggling. He died after a
life of 74 years remarkable for
its integrity, its single-heartedness
and its generous service.
Universally beloved and respected

Here
lies ANN
MANN; She
lived an old
Maid, And she
died an old Mann

Figure 5

MISSING POSTER

This is a format which is applicable to many literary works. Students are shown an example of such a poster (see Figure 6), then asked to write one for a character who has gone missing, for example:

- Simon, in *Lord of the Flies* (see p. 121).
- Liza, before her father catches up with her at Professor Higgins' home, in *Pygmalion*.
- The victim in *The Collector*.
- The young boy in Alasdair Gray's *The Star* (in *Unlikely Stories, Mostly*).

etc.

MISSING

Have you seen this girl?
MARCIA, aged 14, was
last seen on 12 January in
Tooting, South London.
She is 5ft 1in tall, has
grey–blue eyes and short,
blond hair.
At the time she went
missing she was wearing
dark blue corduroy
trousers, a beige jumper
and a black woolly jacket.

Anyone knowing the whereabouts of this girl should
get in touch with the Tooting Police:
TELEPHONE (01) 630 1121

Figure 6

Listening and reading activities

Reading sections of a literary text in class, especially dramatic scenes, or those involving dialogue, where another dimension can be added through the voice, leads to useful listening practice for foreign learners. If cassettes or records of the work are available, these can be helpful, as can video recordings. However, the teacher's reading of a section is also valuable, as well as being often enjoyable and relaxing for students. He or she can get the meaning across by miming, gestures, facial expression, or by mimetic emphasis, for example 'sl . . . o . . . o . . . wly' drawn out, or 'in a twinkle' said very briskly, or 'tearfully' with tears in the voice. Non-native teachers sometimes feel unduly reticent about reading aloud to their students: they can be extremely effective if they do so, because the creation of atmosphere, and the communication of meaning and drama are both much more important than perfect pronunciation or stress patterns.

The students can sometimes be told just to listen for the pleasure of it, if this is appropriate to the classroom situation and to the particular group: many learners enjoy this. It does help them create their fantasy response to the text and become involved in it. Occasionally, learners like listening with their eyes shut; at other times, this makes them feel too self-conscious. Obviously, it is important to adapt activities to particular groups, and to vary them. Straightforward listening can be followed in the next lesson by listening with worksheets for specific purposes.

Listening

After a suitable warm-up, students listen to an entire short work, or a section of a longer one, before reading the printed version. This works well with both poems and short stories, and examples are given in the chapters on these genres. (See especially 'The hitchhiker', and 'The war in the bathroom'.)

Listening to a section can be enriching and interesting, even if some of the class have already read the text. The experience of hearing the section always brings some new detail to the fore. Some personal response can be encouraged in the form of jottings or doodlings, as in *Lord of the Flies* (see pp. 151 and 160).

Activities to accompany reading or listening

These are grouped together because many of the worksheets devised to help with reading can also be used profitably when students listen to a text. Some examples of tasks used in class to further either reading or listening skills are:

GRIDS

These can focus on different aspects of a particular work: development of character or plot, descriptive language, attitudes to issues raised, etc. Several examples are given in *Lord of the Flies*; the use of grids to accompany listening is exemplified in 'The war in the bathroom' (see p. 225).

SELECTING AND ORDERING TASKS

The examples given in the section on home reading can be adapted to accompany listening. An example is shown for 'The edge' (see Worksheet 59).

JIGSAW READING OR LISTENING

In the tradition of jigsaw activities, this kind of reading or listening creates a gap in the narrative. Different groups are given either different texts or different recordings, and by consultation with each other, must reconstitute a complete narrative. The example given for the short story 'Destiny and the bullet' is worked out for reading, but could be adapted to listening (see p. 217). In either case, it also provides valuable oral practice.

I KNOW WHAT YOU SAID, BUT WHAT DO YOU MEAN?

Studying what a particular utterance can actually mean in different circumstances is an activity that can accompany either reading or listening. Worksheet 34 in the chapter on *Lord of the Flies* could be used with the printed page, or with a cassette recording of this particular section.

Finally, some of the listening tasks outlined in the next chapter can also be adapted to be used with highlights of a book, as well as with the entire work once it has been read by the class.

Parallel reading

Many literary works make statements or pose questions about larger issues or themes which the teacher would like the students to think about and discuss. Occasionally, a book's themes can be examined more revealingly or more thoroughly through the medium of other sources: through similar or contrasting short stories, poems, essays, newspaper articles, or critical works. These can be set as reading assignments (either whole or in extract form) and comparisons, contrasts or parallels drawn out in class discussion. For example, one central theme in *Lord of the Flies* concerns the experience of being cut off from the controls and the support of one's own society. The same theme appears in other works, like the well-known novels *The Coral Island* by R. M. Ballantyne or *Treasure Island* by R. L. Stevenson, the play *The Admirable Crichton* by J. M. Barrie, and the recent non-fiction work *Castaway* by Lucy Irvine. Examples of extracts from *The Coral Island* used to complement discussion of certain aspects of *Lord of the Flies* are given in that chapter (see pp. 103–6). Examples of other parallel texts are discussed in the chapters on short stories or plays.

To further habits of extensive reading, different groups in a class could be given different parallel texts to read. When this has been done, new groups are constituted, each member of which has read a different text. Each learner tells their story and describes their conclusions about it to others in their group. The group's task is to establish as many parallels as they can between each work read and the main book studied. Results are pinned up for the class to compare and discuss.

Oral activities

Of all the categories in the present chapter, that of 'oral activities' is the least complete and self-contained. This is because so many of our activities incorporate an oral component, whatever other skills they also aim to foster. The great majority of our classroom activities, for example, are based on group work, which stimulates oral practice. The warm-up sessions which lead into more detailed examination of literary works are similarly designed to elicit spoken response; many of the worksheets used to accompany home reading give rise to oral feedback and discussion in the next class lesson.

What follows is, therefore, an outlining of *some* of the activities which can be more especially beneficial in promoting oral skills. Most of these are amply illustrated later in the book, within the context of whole works, and especially in the chapter on *Lord of the Flies*. The entire range cannot of course be used with any one work: they are offered as ideas from which to choose, in order to link reading a text with improving mastery of the spoken language.

This section progresses from two activities with a phonological emphasis, through structured discussion to more creative activities.

Mini-reading aloud

This activity aims to develop student awareness of intonation, rhythm, stress and other features of spoken language. Its starting point is the selection of a dramatic piece of dialogue from a known part of the literary work. Thereafter the activity can take various forms. One approach is to put students into groups of three and ask each group to study a different section of the extract. They read it silently together and then try to mark the main stresses and discuss the attitudes and feelings of the speakers, identifying any particular words that would bring out those feelings. Pauses after sense units or for special emphasis are also discussed. The teacher is available to give help where required but does not actually model the extract.

After this preparatory phase, the groups decide on the speakers for their extracts, and a 'conductor' to maintain rhythm and lend encouragement and feedback. After rehearsals, there is a public performance by each group in the correct sequence.

With classes that have worked through a range of literary works, including poems, during their course, an end of course 'concert' can be produced with several prepared extracts forming the programme.

The following extract from Shaw's *Pygmalion* is an excellent example of a piece eminently suited to mini-reading aloud. For more detailed examples with poems, see pp. 229 and 233.

HIGGINS [*in despairing wrath outside*] What the devil have I done with my slippers? [*He appears at the door*].

LIZA [*snatching up the slippers, and hurling them at him one after the other with all her force*] There are your slippers. And there. Take your slippers; and may you never have a day's luck with them!

HIGGINS [*astounded*] What on earth–! [*He comes to her*]. Whats the matter? Get up. [*He pulls her up*]. Anything wrong?

LIZA [*breathless*] Nothing wrong – with you. Ive won your bet for you, havnt I? Thats enough for you. *I* dont matter, I suppose.

HIGGINS. You won my bet! You! Presumptuous insect! *I* won it. What did you throw those slippers at me for?

LIZA. Because I wanted to smash your face. I'd like to kill you, you selfish brute. Why didnt you leave me where you picked me out of – in the gutter? You thank God it's all over, and that now you can throw me back again there, do you? [*She crisps her fingers frantically*].

HIGGINS [*looking at her in cool wonder*] The creature is nervous, after all.

LIZA [*gives a suffocated scream of fury, and instinctively darts her nails at his face*]!!

HIGGINS [*catching her wrists*] Ah! would you? Claws in, you cat. How dare you shew your temper to me? Sit down and be quiet. [*He throws her roughly into the easy-chair*].

LIZA [*crushed by superior strength and weight*] Whats to become of me? Whats to become of me?

HIGGINS. How the devil do I know whats to become of you? What does it matter what becomes of you?

> LIZA. You dont care. I know you dont care. You wouldnt care
> if I was dead. I'm nothing to you – not so much as them slippers.
> HIGGINS [*thundering*] Those slippers.
> LIZA [*with bitter submission*] Those slippers. I didnt think it
> made any difference now.

(from *Pygmalion* Act IV)

Oral summaries

Delivering an oral summary of a section read at home gives the student good practice while affording the teacher a check that the reading has indeed been done. In a simple variation, two or three individuals are asked to record on cassette a summary of the section read at home. A time limit is set for each summary. The class listens to all three, jotting down any points of divergence between them, or omissions.

Choose the statement

This is the first of a series of activities based on the idea of sparking discussion by means of a concrete task. The technique is particularly fruitful when applied to discussion of literary texts. While avoiding excessive abstraction or teacher domination, it builds students' confidence in the value of their own response.

'Choose the statement' is an easy activity to organise. It is, in essence, discussion based upon an open-ended multiple choice. Students are provided with a list of statements about a character, an event, a theme, etc. They are then asked, individually or in groups, to choose the *one* which is closest to their own view.

For example, in John Fowles' novel *The Collector*, a girl is kidnapped and held captive in a quiet country house, by a strange, lonely young man. The class is given the following statements:

1. The man captures the girl because he is sexually attracted to her.
2. The man captures the girl because he has very little self-confidence.
3. The man captures the girl because he is mentally disturbed.
4. The man captures the girl because he wants to possess her totally.
5. The man captures the girl because he wants to kill her.

When they have chosen, individuals or groups are invited to explain the reasons behind their choice. A way of eliciting livelier discussion at this point is to ask learners to give one reason for rejecting each of the discarded statements, rather than one reason for choosing as they did. This often provokes more talk about alternative possible choices.

Another example, using short paragraphs, is given for *Lord of the Flies* (see Worksheet 32).

Discussions based on questionnaires

Questionnaires are usually very helpful in sparking discussion. A simple kind lists statements with answer boxes to be ticked, such as: agree / disagree / not sure. These can be prepared to be filled in at home, with follow-up in the next lesson; alternatively, they can be completed during class time. Students are then asked to discuss their choices with fellow students, either in pairs or in groups. Worksheet 11 is based on *Brave New World* by Aldous Huxley.

Other examples are given in later chapters: for example, Worksheet 27 in *Lord of the Flies* and Worksheets 46 and 52 in *Romeo and Juliet*.

Tick the appropriate box.

	Agree	Disagree	Not sure
1. The Bokanovsky process is an acceptable alternative to natural childbirth because you grow up knowing where you are.	☐	☐	☐
2. Staying younger for longer is an attractive aspect of life in the Brave New World.	☐	☐	☐
3. The control of individual emotions is an effective way of preventing time-wasting and loss of productive energy.	☐	☐	☐
4. Frequent, brief relationships are a realistic alternative to the pressures of married life.	☐	☐	☐
5. Sexual relationships are better in the Brave New World because they are simple and direct, and don't arouse anxiety or guilt.	☐	☐	☐

Worksheet 11

Discussions based on grids and worksheets

The variety of grids or worksheets leading to discussion is almost endless. Some elicit a personal response, as in 'The power of the group' (*Lord of the Flies*, Worksheet 38), where students are asked for their own experiences and feelings. Others involve matching, as in 'Solutions' (*Lord of the Flies*, Worksheet 37) where possible alternative solutions have to be matched with the most appropriate character. Some give a list to be put in order of importance, as in 'A good leader' (*Lord of the Flies*, p. 157) or 'The tragedy would not have happened if . . . ' (*Romeo and Juliet*, p. 189). Many of the worksheets or grids used to build up familiarity with various characters and chart the development of their personality as the literary work unfolds, incorporate an element of controversy and can thus be useful in promoting discussion. An example of such a worksheet, designed to elicit students' response to a rather mysterious central character, is given for 'The war in the bathroom' (see Worksheet 66). A worksheet can also be used as a first stimulus, leading to the 'continuum' discussion exercise described next.

Continuum

At a certain point in their reading, students are asked to express their reaction to aspects in the book by choosing a point on a continuous line drawn between two opposing views, or two extreme characteristics. This can be done in the following ways:
- On paper. For example, students place the book's main characters on a point along the following lines.

callous _____	kind
serious _____	frivolous
forceful _____	weak

There is oral follow-up: comparison of completed forms, justification of choices, discussion of implications. Another example is given in *Lord of the Flies* (see Worksheet 17).
- Along a wall of the room. One corner represents one extreme, the other its opposite. Students go and stand at the point against the wall which represents their judgment of the opinion expressed. As differences of opinion are thus vividly revealed, this activity often produces spontaneous discussion of the element of the book that is being highlighted. Examples are given for a poem (see p. 243) and for *Lord of the Flies* (see pp. 129–30).

Codes

Most literary works have a social and political dimension in the sense that they portray relationships which involve codes of behaviour and hierarchies of power. Sometimes these codes have the overt quality of laws or rules, in other cases they are expectations to be inferred from a set of given data. The following activities are variations, designed to help learners articulate explicitly and discuss the often implicit set of constraints which give a book its internal tension.

RULE MAKING

Students, in groups, are asked to formulate a set of rules which apply to a particular situation in the literary work they are reading. They either imagine that they are in that setting and decide on *their* own rules, or they can try to decide what rules seem to be implied within the context of the book itself. An example from *Lord of the Flies* is given in Worksheet 24.

HOW TO . . .

Instead of rules, students are asked to formulate advice on coping with the social situation they find in the literary work. This allows for considerable variation.

Illustrations might include:
1. *The Great Gatsby*: 'How to be a social success'
   Some classes benefit from being given a set format, for example:

   'To be a social success you must: ....
   ....
   ....

2. *Brave New World*: 'How to be happy'
3. *The Collector*: 'How to persuade your captor to release you'
   'How to . . . ' can be extended by asking students to draw up a similar list for their own contemporary situation.

HOW SHOULD THEY . . . ? HOW SHOULD YOU . . . ?

In this activity, students put themselves, imaginatively, into a particular situation in the literary work. They have a list of 'How should you . . . ?' questions to answer, upon which they must try to achieve a group consensus.

For example, in Muriel Spark's short story 'The twins' (in *The Go-Away Bird and Other Stories*), the narrator has a series of uncomfortable experiences when she goes to visit an old school friend, Jennie, and her husband Simon. The couple's children, angelic-looking twins, seem to have an uncanny divisive effect upon the world of grown-ups. Students are given Worksheet 12 and asked to give answers, in pairs or small groups.

Read to the end of 'The twins'.

You are going to stay at Jennie and Simon's house.
1. How long should you stay?
2. How should you react if one of the twins asks you for money?
3. Should you discuss the twins' behaviour with Jennie? If so, what should you say?
4. Should you interfere between parents and children?
5. If Simon says something about Jennie, should you mention it to her?
6. What should you do if you receive a letter from Simon after your visit?

Worksheet 12

Filling in the gaps

Novels, stories, plays or poems give only partial portrayals of situations and characters, leaving plenty of room for inference. A straightforward activity is to ask groups of students to make inferences about missing aspects and then to discuss these. Discussion is sparked by requesting students to provide justifications for their guesses: in other words, what known facts have they used to build up their inferred picture?

For example, in Graham Greene's *Doctor Fischer of Geneva*, we know very little of the doctor's background or early life. The teacher gives each group a set of questions:

What was Doctor Fischer like at school?
Did he have many friends?
What was his favourite subject?
Did he often get into trouble?
Was he close to his parents?
Did he cry a lot?
Did he play practical jokes?

In a general class feedback session, groups compare their answers and explain the particular part of the text which led them to their conclusions.

Debates

Many books suggest controversial issues that can give rise to interesting debates in the classroom. The formal structure, especially if fairly short time limits are set, is often helpful for learners expressing themselves in the foreign language. One example is described in detail in *Lord of the Flies* (see p. 159); another subject for a debate motion is given for the short story 'Destiny and the bullet' (see p. 217).

Friendly persuasion

In this activity, pairs of students take on prescribed roles: one tries to persuade the other of the merits or drawbacks of a course of action, or of a certain character in a literary work. For example, one learner is given the role of a friend of the 'collector', in John Fowles' novel of that title. His or her task is to persuade the manager of a fashion model agency (the other student) that the 'collector' would be the ideal photographer they are seeking.

In George Orwell's *Nineteen Eighty-Four*, one student could be a friend of O'Brien's, trying to get him employed as a psychiatric nurse by persuading the nursing officer. The 'friend' tries hard to be convincing, while the other role player attempts to resist by asking pointed questions, in this case, for example: Is your friend fond of people? Is he compassionate? Are you sure he isn't too aggressive?, etc.

For groups which need help to be inventive, guidelines can be offered on role cards.

It may be useful to practise the language of persuasion, and of resistance to it, before the first role play. If necessary, students can be given some examples of the kind of expressions they will need.

Helpful expressions for persuaders

She's / He's ever so (+ adj.).
She's / He's the most . . .
I've never met anyone who is as (+ adj.) as she / he is.
Go on, give her / him a chance.
Why don't you give her / him a chance? You won't regret it.
She / He will not disappoint you / let you down.
Can't you see your way to letting him / her have a go?
She's / He's just the sort of person who . . .
If anyone can do it, she / he can.

Helpful expressions for those resisting persuasion

That's all very well, but . . .
She / He isn't really what I'm after / looking for.
She / He sounds a bit (+ adj.).
She / He isn't quite what I / we have in mind.
I see your point, but . . .
I'm not convinced that she / he is the right person for the job / situation.
She / He must have one or two weak points.
I'm sorry but I only have your word to go on.

A similar activity, but cast in the form of 'Accuse and deny' is described in *Lord of the Flies* (see p. 157).

Improvisations

At a certain point in the reading of a literary text, students are asked to devise alternative outcomes to the events they are encountering in the story. They are then asked to plan an improvised dramatisation of one such outcome, and perform it for the class. If necessary, they can be given one or two possibilities to start them off.

Here and there

These two activities are designed to extend students' understanding and appreciation of characterisation within the literary work.

HERE

Students are asked to speculate about how particular characters would behave and what they would feel or say, in an imagined situation which is not part of the work itself.

Ideas for situations are most successful when they are linked to learners' own lives. For example, a character is imagined in the town where the students live. Where would that character go? stay? What would he/she eat? want to do? talk about? buy? Then, the character is invited into each student's home or room. Where would he/she sit, what would he/she notice in the room, what would the conversation be about? In a third stage, the character is placed in an urgent, interesting new situation which calls for some reaction: predictions are made about the character's likely response. For instance, a woman rushes up to the character and demands money because she has lost hers and must pay the rent or be evicted. What is the character's reaction?

In small classes, this can be done by students simply 'fantasising out loud'. In larger classes, the activity works best when based on a worksheet outlining the new situations and asking students to fill in the character's imagined response. When this has been done, either at home or in class, answers are discussed in groups. In a general feedback session, the teacher can then ask the students to draw out the implications of the choices they made, as far as their views of the character's personality are concerned.

THERE

The preceding situation is reversed. Someone who is not a character in the literary work is imported into it and his or her likely actions, reactions, and impact are discussed. For instance, in a book with a male hero, the class is asked to imagine what differences, if any, a female equivalent would make to events and relationships.

Alternatively, a member of the class is chosen and 'dropped in' to a particular situation in the work, either to replace a character, or to be involved. The fantasy involves working out differences in behaviour and outlook between the character and the student substitute or, in the second case, imagining what the student would do to try to influence people and events once introduced into the plot. This usually provides lively discussion, and can also be adapted for role play or improvisation. An example, 'You have the conch', is outlined in Chapter 7 (see p. 120).

Role plays

The context provided by works of literature facilitates the creation of role-play situations. Sometimes, however, learners feel rather awed at the prospect of depicting characters or events already vividly drawn in the book. In this case, 'extra-textual' situations, such as those imagined in the preceding exercise, can be particularly helpful. An example is given for *Lord of the Flies*, in which the boys who are stranded on a desert island are imagined back in an ordinary school setting (see 'Interview with a school counsellor', p. 146).

Another successful technique for implementing role play with longer novels or stories is to take themes from the text and create parallel settings, but with totally different characters. Afterwards, the work itself is compared with the created role play. For example, John, the savage in *Brave New World*, illustrates the fate of the outsider who is brought into a social pattern that he finds alien and that eventually destroys him. A parallel role play takes the plight of the first extra-terrestrial beings (thankfully humanoid and able to speak English) who want to make a life on Earth but suffer the pressures of media attention. The role play involves a press conference in which questions are prepared by teams of journalists, while the extra-terrestrials prepare a description of their society, which has minimised technology in favour of a return to more natural living.

Parallel role plays work well with younger learners, especially if the text is a difficult one, or set in the past, as in a Shakespearean play. *West Side Story* could perhaps be cited as a popular 'parallel' presentation of *Romeo and Juliet*!

Trailers

This is another way of making the business of dramatising a novel or other work into a more manageable task for learners. Anyone who goes to films or watches television is familiar with the notion of a 'trailer', that is, a short advertising clip designed to promote a film or television programme. It usually consists of a narrative 'voice-over' extolling the film, interspersed with extremely brief, intriguing shots taken from the tensest or most spectacular moments of the film's action.

In groups, students are given the task of concocting a two-minute 'trailer' to advertise the work being read, using the particular highlights of a chapter. This will be presented to the class in the following way: one learner, the presenter, reads the 'voice-over' narrative, while other students, at the appropriate point, act out the dramatic highlights of the plot, or simply adopt frozen postures to depict them.

We have found that even less imaginative or shyer learners can manage the very limited acting involved in these brief scenes. The activity is usually extremely amusing, and also generates interesting discussion springing from the fact that different groups produce such varying interpretations of the literary work's most dramatic moments. An illustration is given for the short story 'Sredni Vashtar' (see p. 219), and another for *Lord of the Flies* (see p. 121).

Moviemaker

This is a more complex activity, which involves adapting a highlight to make one scene of a 'film' or 'television programme'. Students can be given fairly detailed instructions to help them visualise their task. Each group in a class can be set a slightly different scene, so that there is variety when the 'films' are acted out in front of the class, and so that the contrast can lead to discussion about differences in interpretation. An illustration, including three different sets of instructions for three 'production units', can be found in the chapter on *Lord of the Flies* (see p. 127).

6 Endings

Coming to the end of a literary work is really only a staging point, a temporary distancing from a continuing process of appreciation and understanding. The activities described in this chapter reflect a wish to keep each student's own sense of the literary work alive, and aim to involve students in sharing views and reviews.

We have compiled a range of activities but it is worth remembering that several of the activities outlined in Chapters 4 and 5 are also entirely appropriate at this stage in the literary work. This has been indicated earlier, where applicable.

As many of the activities in this chapter involve an integration of language skills, we have decided not to arrange them under single skill sub-headings. However, there is a broad progression. First we outline activities which produce a strong visual impact. Next those with an emphasis on discussion are described, and so on through listening-based activities, writing tasks and finally, role play and drama work.

Cover designs

Asking students to provide a design for the book's paperback cover is a way of eliciting and crystallising their overall response to the work they have just been reading. This can be done individually, or as a group activity; but, as students are asked to depict their own response, it may be better to keep groups small, possibly even to get students working in pairs. Their brief is the following: they are working for the publisher's graphics department and are responsible for planning a cover that will both represent the spirit of the book and be likely to appeal to potential readers.

It is important in any activity of this kind to provide some support for students who are not too confident about their artistic ability. It is often more fruitful to suggest ways in which students can express their response without being asked to draw. Collage is an effective technique, for which suitable materials are:
- Magazine pictures, to be cut out and glued on to large sheets of coloured poster card.
- A kit of adhesive geometrical shapes in different sizes and colours, to be combined to form abstract or symbolic designs. This often produces

Figure 7

striking and imaginative representations of a book. Figure 7 is an example of such a cover design.

When the designs are complete, an exhibition is held in the classroom. Each 'designer' or design team presents its cover to the class and talks about the effect they were trying to communicate. Students are free to question the designers, or to comment on similarities or contrasts. If there is insufficient time for everyone to discuss their cover, they are asked to write what they would have included in their presentation, and these written comments can later be pinned up alongside the designs.

Writing a 'blurb' for the back cover

As preparation for this activity, the teacher reads out the cover blurb for two or three novels or plays which the students are unlikely to know. These are then displayed, and students are asked to rank them in order of appeal. They discuss the format and any special features which affected their response.

In groups or pairs, students are then to write the blurb for the book they have been studying, including at least one quote from the work, which they feel is bound to draw in someone browsing in a bookshop.

Sculpting

This activity concentrates attention on the principal characters in a book or play. One student volunteers or is chosen to be the sculptor. The names of the main characters are placed individually on slips of paper and put into a bag. Students take one slip each until they are all gone. The sculptor chooses a 'character' and asks him or her to stand, sit, or take up any position or expression which seems appropriate to that character's essential personality traits.

A cleared area of the classroom is the sculpting arena. Another 'character' is now asked to come forward and the sculptor places him or her in an appropriate position relative to the first character, that is, near if the sculptor sees them as close, or far apart if they have little connection with each other. The characters can be facing each other, back to back, holding hands, huddled together, in fact, whatever the sculptor chooses. Once positioned, characters remain in their positions until the sculpting is complete. When this is done, the sculptor discusses his or her thoughts with others in the class, who comment on their view of the characters. If there is time, several more sculptings can be carried out.

The activity is surprisingly powerful and memorable, and works particularly well with books that have a good number of interrelated characters. It leads to a lot of discussion and reveals differences in individual perceptions. Although perhaps best with adults or mature adolescents,

Figure 8

sculpting does appeal to a wide range of students. When it is first introduced, or with more unadventurous classes, the teacher should be the first sculptor. Figure 8 is an example for *Lord of the Flies*.

Unsealing the time capsule

When predictions about the development of the plot or characters have been put into a sealed 'time capsule' at the beginning (see Chapter 3), now is the time to open it. Discussion centres on *why* students made their original predictions, and what happened later in the book to confirm or disprove them.

Point of no return

In groups, learners decide upon the 'point of no return' in the unfolding of the novel, play or short story just read. This can perhaps be done most easily by duplicating an instruction card and distributing it to each group (see Worksheet 13).

A pyramiding technique is used: students decide upon their point in pairs, then in groups of four, and so on. This usually generates lively discussion and a thorough revision of the book.

We have now read (title) and we know its outcome.
    Looking back, can you say what, precisely, was the 'point of no
return' – that is, the point at which the outcome became *inevitable*.
(This can be a point in the events or the development of a character.)
    Write down the point that you have agreed upon in your group.
    If you do not think there *was* such a point, give reasons for thinking
that the outcome was *not* inevitable.

Worksheet 13

What if . . . ?

This is a discussion activity, which can be a follow-up to 'point of no
return'. Students imagine the moment *before* the 'point of no return'.
What if circumstances had been different? What alternative choices could
the characters have made? What other effects upon the reader could have
been attained by the writer? (By implied contrast, what special effects
derive from the book's special configuration, and what reasons can the
author have had for arranging things the way he or she did?)

This exercise can give rise to much useful language work. The topic
requires past conditionals (If X had happened, Y would have resulted . . .)
and past modals (could have made; could have been attained; might
have . . . ; should have . . .). Pre-teaching or revision of these forms may
therefore be appropriate with some classes. An example is given for *Lord
of the Flies* (see p. 153).

Team competitions

Team competitions are a traditional but still useful and enjoyable way of
reminding students about various strands of the book, so that they have
all the material available to start building up an overall view. It can be
done by straightforward questions, or by using quotes: Who said this?
Where? When?

The questions can be prepared by the teacher or, better still, by students
in groups setting questions for the rival team. The combing of the book to
find suitable questions or quotes is in itself a useful revision exercise.

Just a minute

This classroom game is based on the popular radio programme, in which
contestants try to speak for 60 seconds on a given topic, without hesi-

tation, deviation or repetition. A stopwatch is needed (a large chess clock is ideal). Themes from the book are written on slips of paper (by the teacher or by students working in pairs). For example, themes for *Romeo and Juliet* could include: love, violence, feuds, loyalty to one's friends, compassion, friendship, anger, fate, happiness, civil strife within a city, arranged marriages, usefulness of balconies, the blindness of youth, etc. If it seems necessary, students are allowed to take away topics and consider them in preparation for the game.

The topics are then put into a hat. Four learners play at a time: the teacher or a student 'gamesmaster' chooses a topic from the hat and designates the contestant who must try to speak on that theme for 60 seconds. If he or she hesitates, deviates, or repeats any word except the theme words (articles, prepositions, conjunctions don't count!), he or she can be challenged by one of the three other contestants. A successful challenger can then continue to speak for the rest of the minute. Points are awarded for successful challenges, and for the contestant who is still talking when the 60 seconds are up.

Although the game can be played at any point during the reading of a particular book, it is particularly suited to the end, when students have most material available and the exercise is useful for revision. A slightly easier version is given for *Lord of the Flies* (see p. 124).

Retelling the story

Relating the story seems a fairly unsophisticated way of going over a book just read, yet there is no doubt that it can provide valuable oral practice in the foreign language – much of the vocabulary needed will be known, but using it can help make it part of the learners' active lexis, while the narrative mode will usually allow them to use a variety of tenses, link words, and other discourse markers.

For small classes, each student is given a number, then all the numbers are written on slips of paper and put into a hat. The learner whose number is drawn first starts off, relating the story from the beginning, until interrupted by the teacher's buzzer or gong. Another number is drawn and that student continues the narration. This can sometimes generate animated discussion about points omitted or related out of sequence.

A note on error correction: overt correction by the teacher will prove much too disruptive during such an activity. It is better to jot down recurring errors for discussion afterwards. An excellent error correction technique for small and fairly relaxed groups is recording the entire storytelling, then playing it back and asking learners to note any errors they can spot.

Critical forum

Where this is practicable, recorded discussions or conversations about a book which has been read by the entire class provide ideal material for listening comprehension practice: the familiar context, and the learners' expectations derived from their knowledge of the book, help them to make inferences about what they are hearing, thereby facilitating understanding. There are several ways in which listening tasks can be varied to provide interest.

SPOT THE ERROR

With a friend or a native speaker, the teacher records a conversation (unscripted, or 'lightly' scripted in note form) between two people talking about the book. One or more errors of fact or of sequencing are introduced. Students are asked to note errors as they listen.

As follow-up, students, working in pairs or small groups, write and then record similar conversations or monologues about various aspects of the book: plot, analysis of motivation, character development, discussion of style, etc. Groups then exchange recordings and try to spot the error(s). This activity can also be done in a language laboratory, and is suited to the more advanced levels, when students do not have too much resistance to the idea of recording their own voices.

CRITICAL COMMENT

The teacher records a critical commentary on the book just read (from radio discussions, school broadcasts, etc.) or records his or her own or a native speaker's reading of a printed text. If this is not possible, the exercise can still be done by the teacher simply reading a prepared text to the class. There are several tasks which can be used to accompany such a recorded commentary:
- Summary: Students are asked to list the two or three main points made by the speaker, or to choose (from three possibilities) the best summary of the points made.
- Note-taking: Students are asked to take notes which they later expand into a paragraph.
- Gapped text: If the text is fairly short, the teacher can give students the entire text with some key words or expressions deleted, to be supplied by listeners. For longer texts, only main sentences are given, again with blanks to be filled.

Choosing highlights

The teacher shows the class a sealed envelope in which is listed his or her choice of three 'highlights', that is, points in the book which he or she considers to be crucial to its overall effect, for example because of their importance in the unfolding of the plot, the light they throw on character or motivation, the building-up of a picture of a certain society, and so on. He or she then asks students, individually, to do the same.

Learners then get together in groups of three to compare their lists of highlights, justify their choices, and compile a new list which represents their consensus. Having to explain their own views and argue for or against those of others can make students bring out their own thoughts and range more freely in expressing their reaction to the book than they might do if they were responding to more straightforward questions about it. At the end, a student is asked to open the teacher's envelope and read its contents to the rest of the class. The teacher justifies his or her choices and asks for comments on similarities or differences of opinion.

As written follow-up, students write a paragraph on each one of their group's highlights, justifying their choice and showing its importance for the book as a whole.

A variation of this activity is described in *Lord of the Flies* (see p. 161).

It will be seen that in this activity, while learners retain the support of the group, have access to their companions' ideas and have the opportunity of testing their own views in discussion, they are moving towards practice in answering fairly standard types of essay questions and thus preparing for exams.

Round robin

The class is divided into small groups. Five people per group is just about right. The task set is to summarise the book in five sentences (or six sentences for a group of six, etc.). Each person in the group writes the first sentence, then passes that piece of paper on to his or her right-hand neighbour, who writes the second sentence and then passes the paper on to the person on the right, and so on. At the end, a group will have five summaries, to which each of its members has contributed one sentence. These five are then passed on to another group. Each group reviews the five it has received, chooses the one it likes best and says why. If a group cannot agree on a choice, it is allowed to use parts of different summaries in order to build up what it considers to be a complete, accurate and well-written synopsis.

For less advanced classes, a variation of the above activity can be used for individual rather than group work. A summary of the book is given in ten sentences with three choices for each sentence (30 sentences in total). Learners choose the best of the three in each case and then write out their complete summary. Comparison of the choices made can provoke discussion about the grounds for choosing one sentence rather than another.

Short writing tasks

LETTERS

One character writes to different people. Students are asked to write the letter that X (one of the main characters) sends after the end of the book to explain what happened, and how it came to happen as it did. Different registers are practised by varying the people to whom the letters are to be sent (that is, X will write in a different way to his mother/wife/best friend/headmaster/solicitor/boss/MP, etc.). Students read and compare corrected letters to appreciate differences of content and style.

Alternatively, different characters write to each other about the events they have lived through. In Patricia Highsmith's *The Talented Mr Ripley*, for instance, half the class is Marge writing to Tom, the other half Tom writing to Marge. Letters are exchanged, and, if appropriate, the activity is extended so that each person replies to the letter received.

LAST PAGE PLUS ONE

If the book allows for such progression, students write the next few paragraphs after the end of the book.

THE BOOK ON A POSTCARD

The challenge here is to fit an appreciation of a literary work into a very limited compass. Students are asked to write about the book in exactly 50 words. The compression quite often produces interesting pieces of writing. An example is given for *Lord of the Flies* (see Figure 15).

Writing essays

Some of the grids used during the reading of a work for the purpose of extending students' understanding of plot and character can be used after the end of the book as material on which to base essay writing, if this is seen as desirable or necessary for exam preparation. Examples are given for the short stories 'The edge' (see Worksheet 62) and 'Sredni Vashtar' (see Worksheet 64).

Adapting the literary work for another audience

This activity is suitable for an advanced group. It involves rewriting the literary work for a different audience; for example, for a child, an elementary learner, a horror movie director, etc. Most learners reaching the upper-intermediate or advanced stage will have encountered graded readers or other forms of simplified text, at some point in their language studies. They usually respond with interest to the challenge of creating such a text themselves.

A prompt is often useful to start the activity. For example, a group of students asked to retell *Doctor Fischer of Geneva* as a fairy story for children, can be given the following beginning:

Once upon a time there was a wicked baron who lived in a large and gloomy palace. He was so rich that people were . . .

The activity can be an oral or a writing task. A similar beginning produced the following adaptation for younger readers of Saki's short story 'Tobermory' (in *The Penguin Complete Saki*):

Once upon a time there was a magician who cast a spell on a cat called Tobermory. The cat was suddenly able to talk to humans. At first, everybody was excited and delighted and asked the cat lots of questions just to hear his voice. But then they became alarmed when they realised that the cat could also talk about things it saw and heard while wandering quietly around the house at all hours of the day or night. Can you imagine what the people decided to do to protect their secret? Well, they tried to poison his food but Tobermory wasn't hungry for food. He had gone off to find a friend. Panic broke out in the household! Tobermory was going to tell everything to the whole world! What a relief when they found that Tobermory was killed in a fight with another cat. The poor magician was very sad as he needed a special animal for his spell. He went away high and low and found a much bigger animal – an elephant. But he got the spell all wrong and made the elephant very angry. Instead of talking, the elephant jumped up and down – on the magician!

From telegrams to newspaper reports

This is a four-part writing/role-play activity especially suitable for books that contain a lot of action and a dramatic ending. Parts may be used independently if time constraints prevent a fuller treatment. The class is divided into four or eight groups.

Part 1: The task for each group is to write a telegram (an appropriate word limit is set) giving the gist of what has happened in the book read, as though from a foreign correspondent to his newspaper. This is more interesting if the special conventions of telegram writing have been examined beforehand. One amusing way of doing so is to look with students at the totally inept telegrams sent by William, the central character of Evelyn Waugh's *Scoop*.

Part 2: Each group hands its telegram to the next group. Telegrams are read and discussed. Then, *on the basis of the telegram in hand*, the groups write a newspaper report of the events. Students might be encouraged to decide the kind of newspaper for which they are going to write their article; for example, a scandal sheet, or a more sober 'quality' newspaper, etc. It is usually best for the teacher to specify the length of the article, and also the time available for the writing task. We have found that group writing tasks of this kind can provide valuable help and support for students whose oral facility outstrips their ability to express themselves in writing. To allow these students to contribute fully, however, it is often best to keep groups relatively small.

Part 3: Groups pass on to the next group their report, together with the originating telegram and the title or description of the newspaper for which it was written. Groups now become an editorial panel: they read the articles submitted to them, suggest corrections, note omissions or overstatements, discuss the 'newsworthiness' of the presentation.

Part 4: When groups are satisfied that the corrected article is in a reasonable state (or at the end of the specified time) they once again hand it on to the next group. One thing remains to be done: supply a striking headline for the article. Groups read the article submitted, then try to encapsulate its essential facts in an eye-catching – or even sensational! – formula.

An important follow-up to this activity is the posting-up of all four articles, complete with original telegrams and headlines, so that students can see the entire process.

Press conference

This activity constitutes a logical follow-on from the writing/role-play activity just outlined, but it can also stand on its own as a way of getting students to put themselves back into the literary work they have just finished, and to discuss it.

The roles taken are the following:
1. A Press Conference Officer who conducts the press conference, calls on reporters to speak, keeps order and brings the proceedings to a close.
2. One, two or three characters from the book (as appropriate) are questioned by reporters and give their version of the events they have just been involved in.
3. The rest of the class can be reporters. According to the number of students involved and their level of proficiency, they can be given general, or fairly detailed, instructions. This is most easily done by using role cards. An example follows, taken from Graham Greene's *Doctor Fischer of Geneva.*

The use of individual role cards means that each reporter can be given different 'angles' of the story to investigate, and this tends to ensure a more lively press conference. More advanced students will need to be given fewer guidance questions than intermediate learners. When appropriate, they can be asked to conform to the kind of questions which typify different types of publication: a scandal sheet, a Sunday newspaper, a television news team, etc.

Here is an example role card for *Doctor Fischer of Geneva*:

Role card
You are a reporter for *The Sunday Globe*. Your editor wants you to write a story about the death of the wealthy Doctor Fischer. The inquest is now over, and Mr Jones and Mr Steiner have agreed to give a press conference about the mysterious affair.

Your editor would especially like you to find out:
- How often Doctor Fischer entertained his circle of friends.
- What they did at these gatherings (the rumours the paper published last week have not really been substantiated).
- The amount of money involved in the last party.

Dramatic adaptations

Having finished reading their novel, short story, or poem, students are asked to turn a scene they consider crucial into a short theatre or television play. The class is divided into groups, each one choosing a scene and producing a dramatised version to be put on for the class. It is sometimes best to let this be a voluntary activity organised, with more or less elaborate staging effects, props, music, etc., by the drama enthusiasts of the class, perhaps as an end-of-term activity. This allows quieter students to contribute to the creating of setting, costumes, etc. We have found that the class performance, however short, or however far from perfect, is usually enjoyed immensely by most students, and that it does make the scene memorable for them – it is usually this very scene which is later chosen to illustrate points made in essays or exams!

A television 'reportage' used as a follow-up activity to the reading of a short story, 'The edge', is described on p. 214.

Balloon debates

This traditional form of debate can be adapted with great success as a way of allowing learners to explore the complexities of the characters in a novel or play.

PREPARATION

The teacher chooses five or six of the main characters in the book read. The class is divided into that number of groups, each of which is assigned one of the characters. The groups now have the task of choosing two of their members to take on the role of their character: one for each round of the debate. The members of the group help prepare their representatives, by finding suitable arguments for their character's survival, and good ways of expressing them.

THE DEBATE

The class imagines that the five characters are sailing high in a hot-air balloon, when they start to lose altitude disastrously. To prevent a crash, all but two of the characters must be thrown overboard.

Each character (first representative of each group) has an opportunity to make a speech outlining the reasons why he or she should be allowed to remain in the balloon and survive. The teacher, or a student, presides. After this first speech, the class votes for the two most convincing characters. The two survivors (second representatives) make a speech, summing up the crucial reasons, and trying to add new ones, for their continued survival. Finally, the class votes for the last remaining survivor.

We have found this to be a popular activity. Since everyone has read the book, they have a common base of vocabulary and a shared knowledge which facilitates the exercise. Students often comment with surprise on the insight they have suddenly gained into their character's psychology, because they have been forced to put themselves into his or her place, imaginatively. One student, for example, claimed to have suddenly felt an unexpected compassion for Mrs Wilson, the victim in F. Scott Fitzgerald's *The Great Gatsby*, when she had to plead her case in the balloon.

Improvisations

Classes where role play is popular can be given a slightly freer task after the entire book has been read: to produce a dramatised version of the chapter *after* the end of the book. The following activity is one way of doing this.

INQUEST

Many books lend themselves to a recapitulative role play based upon an inquiry of some sort into the events that have occurred. Some examples would be:
— An inquest on board the ship which has rescued the survivors of *Lord of the Flies*, conducted by the ship's captain (see p. 161).
— A coroner's inquest into the death of Gatsby, or Doctor Fischer of Geneva, or the victim in *The Collector* by John Fowles.

One student is nominated the coroner. He or she calls the inquest, interviews witnesses, and eventually makes a report. The class is divided into groups, each of which prepares one 'witness' — a surviving character in the book – for interrogation. It may be necessary to provide a coroner's team to help him or her question witnesses and make a report.

Variations on this judgement theme might be:
– A divorce court judge's inquiry (awarding custody of 'the twins' in Muriel Spark's short story of that title, for example).
– A court martial.
– A school's disciplinary committee, etc.

Everything depends on the particular book, its setting, characters, and situation.

7   A novel: *Lord of the Flies*
by William Golding

The novel we have selected to demonstrate the range of activities available in presenting a work of literature is the modern classic *Lord of the Flies*, by William Golding. There are many reasons for our choice. Golding is a major twentieth-century English writer, whose works are read and studied throughout the world. *Lord of the Flies* deals with the ever-topical and universal themes of violence, social control, human nature, survival in conditions of adversity – yet in a setting that is neither culture-specific nor restricted to one time. Its schoolboy characters have in fact been removed from their own context to be placed in elemental conditions that reveal their true selves. This gives the book the aspect of a fable, which is at once strong and simple enough to catch the imagination of most readers. The book suits a readership of almost any age, and we have read it successfully with a range of classes, from intermediate to advanced learners. Its rich, associative, metaphorical language provides a challenge, but comprehension is definitely aided by the clear context, as well as by the novel's strong characterisation and plot. Last, but certainly not least, *Lord of the Flies* has a strong pull on the reader's involvement, from the very first page.

For convenience, we have divided the novel into 12 sections corresponding to its 12 chapters. We have labelled these I–XII to distinguish them from the chapters of this book (1–10). For each chapter of *Lord of the Flies*, we shall describe a large and varied number of classroom and homework activities. At various times, these have been used with success in our classes, but obviously they represent a range of choices, not a scheme of work. Teachers must choose and adapt according to their own situation, constraints, particular group of learners, and teaching style. The activities are a set of ideas and resources to stimulate variety in the classroom.

The only words of advice we would like to add are these:
1. Try to select activities which complement each other and form a suitable balance, for example between language-enrichment activities and ones designed to deepen the students' understanding of the book and elicit a response.
2. Do not select too many activities in case this harms the simple involvement through reading that the individual builds. Remember reading is often a quiet, private activity and one we strongly wish to encourage.

3. Do not lose sight of the principal aim of the whole operation, which is to foster enjoyment of reading in the learner. An important gift we can give the student is the realisation that further reading and rereading can be enriching. You can never really 'finish' a book, except on a superficial level. Rereading always produces new insight, new perceptions, a deepened response.

4. It is a good idea to vary the mode of presentation: silent reading, for example, can be followed by listening to the passage on a cassette, so that this 'revisiting' of the text feels like a different experience and challenges other areas of the learner's abilities.

5. Unless you are obliged to use prescribed texts, choose works that you know and like, and which are likely to appeal to the students you teach. Using activities of the kind we describe requires a good deal of imaginative involvement on the part of the teacher – much better that this groundwork should be enjoyable rather than a chore!

Chapter I   The sound of the shell (pages 7–34)*

From the first page, the reader is taken immediately into the atmosphere of the book. The setting is an exotic tropical island where two English boys find themselves wandering about, having been dropped to safety before the crash of their plane, which had been attacked. To the boys, the island seems to promise an enchanted, adult-free life. Gradually, as more boys emerge, they hold a meeting and elect Ralph as chief. Jack, the leader of a group of choirboys and the other candidate for leadership, takes to hunting; but the first time he chases a piglet, he cannot quite bring himself to kill it.

This chapter is quite long and is therefore best divided into class and home reading. Since the island setting is such a strong part of the novel's appeal in the beginning, we have planned a detailed warm-up activity prior to reading, in order to focus upon this aspect and build up a sense of expectation.

In the mood

This warm-up activity is a simple but effective way of building familiarity with the setting of the novel prior to reading, and preferably before the texts are distributed to the students.

The teacher informs the class that he or she is going to ask them to create a picture of the beginning of the book in their minds. The class are

---

* Page references are to the paperback edition of *Lord of the Flies*, Faber and Faber, London, 1958.

asked to relax, close their eyes and try to make a large empty space for their imagination to work on.

Students are then told to imagine that they are 11 years old again, and they are asked: What do you look like? What is your hair like? your clothes? your shoes? How tall are you? What do you like doing? What things are you interested in? (Pause for mind painting.)

Next, the teacher tells students to imagine that they have been dropped on to a tropical island, from a plane just before it crashed. They are alone. It is very hot. What are their first thoughts, and what do they do to start with? After allowing time for pictures to be built, the teacher asks the students to open their eyes and to jot down, quickly, these thoughts and initial actions.

Students close their eyes again and are asked to imagine what things they *see* on the island, what they *hear*, *touch* and *feel*. Again, after a pause, students open their eyes and write down their sensations.

Finally, students are told that suddenly, another child of about the same age appears from the undergrowth. He was on the plane too. What do they talk about with the other child? What do they feel? Sad? Excited? Frightened? Again, students open their eyes and jot down their thoughts.

At this point the teacher asks the class to leave the island of their imagination. He or she puts them into pairs or threes and each person describes their scene to the others. After a few minutes, the teacher calls the learners together again, for one or two 'pictures' to be described to the whole class.

The students are now 'in the picture' as far as the book is concerned and proceed either to read the first two pages or to listen to them and to note down some broad differences between their pictures and that in the book. They are asked not to worry about unknown words at this stage.

Finally, there is general class discussion of differences noted and of points of special interest or difficulty in this initial section.

Retrospective writing

If sufficient time is available, students, in small groups, are asked to reconstruct, from details given in the first two pages, the events which happened just before the opening of the novel. This is a planning session which will lead to students individually writing the last few paragraphs of the imaginary chapter which would *precede* the opening section of *Lord of the Flies*. This writing task can then be completed in class, or set as homework.

Part C Working with a complete text

Two worksheets to support home reading

Students are asked to read the first half of the chapter, with an emphasis on gaining a first insight into the personalities of Piggy and Ralph, the two boys introduced in this section. Worksheets 14 and 15 help this first contact with the characters, by not demanding too much intensive text work. We want to encourage learners, from the beginning, to read confidently for gist.

Each of the worksheets illustrated can give rise to oral feedback in class. Worksheet 15 provides excellent support for a structured speaking task. Students are asked to give short talks based upon the notes they have jotted down in one particular box of the grid. They speak in turn, for a maximum of one minute, as requested by the teacher.

Read pages 7–18 of *Lord of the Flies*, then decide which of the characteristics in the box belongs more readily to which boy. List each one below the appropriate name. Use a dictionary if necessary.

Piggy   *Ralph*

....

....   athletic   friendly   ....
                                         wealthy   realistic
....   courageous   ....

....   fair   ....
                                     wise   short-sighted
....   reserved   asthmatic   ....
                                     pessimistic
....   orphaned   reckless   ....

....   intelligent   confident   tall   ....
                                  fat   prudent
....

Worksheet 14

96

Read pages 7–18 of *Lord of the Flies*. Write brief notes in each box as appropriate.

	Piggy	*Ralph*
Personality		
Appearance		
Attitude towards being on the island		
Attitude towards the other boy		
Information about parents		

Worksheet 15

Memory exercise (pages 7–18)

Worksheet 16 is for a class game or for homework.

Which boy said the following? Tick the right name.

	Piggy	Ralph
1. 'And this is what the tube done.'		
2. 'Sucks to your auntie.'		
3. 'You can't half swim well.'		
4. 'So long as you don't tell the others.'		
5. 'He's a commander in the Navy.'		
6. 'We may stay here till we die.'		
7. 'Get my clothes.'		
8. 'Gosh.'		

Can you remember what they were talking about, and why? Now find page references for each, and check your answer.

Worksheet 16

Class reading (pages 23–4)

The teacher reads out loud (or plays a cassette of) the section about the election of a chief. In a general class discussion, students are then asked to list all the qualities they would seek in a leader, if they were in the boys' position on the island. The teacher keeps the list, to link to an activity designed to develop this theme later on in the book (see p. 157).

Character portrayal

Worksheet 17 is to accompany home reading (to the end of the chapter).

This activity can be repeated half-way through the book, and again when the entire book has been read. The teacher keeps the earlier graphs to demonstrate the evolution of the students' awareness of characterisation, as the book unfolds.

Put a mark for each boy (X for Piggy, O for Ralph, ★ for Jack) on each
of the following lines, according to your judgment of their character,
so far. If you have no idea, leave blank.

self-confidence   LOW _____ HIGH
intelligence   LOW _____ HIGH
athleticism   LOW _____ HIGH
sensitivity   LOW _____ HIGH
cruelty   LOW _____ HIGH
anxiety   LOW _____ HIGH
friendliness   LOW _____ HIGH
loneliness   LOW _____ HIGH

Worksheet 17

'Correcting' Piggy's English

The aim of this activity is to make explicit the kind of English Piggy speaks
and, through feedback and discussion, elicit what this tells the reader
about Piggy's background and education (see Worksheet 18).

You have noticed that Piggy speaks a different kind of English from
that spoken by Ralph or Jack. A strict, traditional schoolmaster might
well frown at some of the things Piggy says. Choose at least three
things that Piggy says. Write down his words, then write down what
a traditional schoolmaster might want him to say.

Example: Piggy says: And this is what the tube done.

The schoolmaster says: And this is what the tube did.

1. Piggy says: ....
   The schoolmaster says: ....
2. Piggy says: ....
   The schoolmaster says: ....
3. Piggy says: ....
   The schoolmaster says: ....

Worksheet 18

What could I kill?

A questionnaire (Worksheet 19) is given to students, either before or after reading the final two pages of the first chapter. Responses are compared first in groups, then in a general class discussion.

An interesting follow-up would be class reading and discussion of the parallel situation in Worksheet 21 which is an extract from *The Coral Island* by R. M. Ballantyne.

Look at the creatures listed below. If you think you could kill any of them, put a tick in the first column. In the second column, explain circumstances in which you would do so, for example 'if starving', 'in self-defence', etc.

Creature	Yes?	Circumstances?
ant frog hen cat snake pig horse human		

Worksheet 19

Star diagram

This activity aims to foster students' understanding and appreciation of words and expressions used to describe the setting.

In class, after the first chapter has been read, students are divided into four groups. Each group is assigned one element of the island setting:

Group 1: words that describe water, the sea, the lagoon.
Group 2: words that describe the sand, the beach, the sea-shore.
Group 3: words that describe the jungle and its vegetation.
Group 4: words that describe mountains, rocks and cliffs.

Together, students skim through the first chapter, extracting words or phrases which refer to their element. Their task is then to arrange these in an order that shows which words are visual, which are tactile, which are metaphorical, and so on. One way of doing this is to use a five-point star diagram. Each group is given an empty star shape on a large card, and then groups its descriptive words into five appropriate categories. Illustrations for two of the elements are given in Figures 9A (words that describe the jungle and the vegetation on the island) and 9B (words that describe water: the sea, the lagoon, the coral reef).

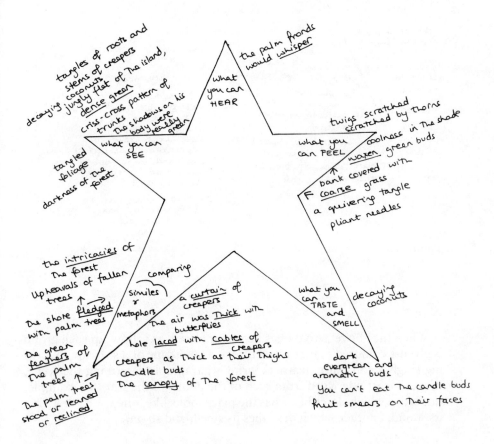

Figure 9A

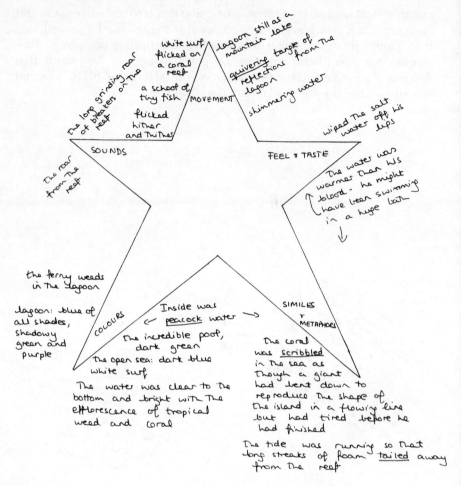

The handwritten notes on the star diagram read:

MOVEMENT (top point):
- white surf flicked on a coral reef
- a school of tiny fish flicked hither and thither
- lagoon still as a mountain lake
- quivering tangle of reflections from the lagoon
- shimmering water

SOUNDS (upper left point):
- The long grinding roar of breakers on the reef
- The roar from the reef

FEEL & TASTE (upper right point):
- wiped the salt water off his lips
- The water was warmer than his blood – he might have been swimming in a huge bath

COLOURS (lower left point):
- the ferny weeds in the lagoon
- lagoon: blue of all shades, shadowy green and purple
- Inside was peacock water
- The incredible pool, dark green
- The open sea: dark blue white surf
- The water was clear to the bottom and bright with the efflorescence of tropical weed and coral

SIMILES & METAPHORS (lower right point):
- The coral was scribbled in the sea as though a giant had bent down to reproduce the shape of the island in a flowing line but had tired before he had finished
- The tide was running so that long streaks of foam tailed away from the reef

Figure 9B

When the above activity has been completed, as follow-up each group is given a coloured magazine picture of a landscape or a seascape. Working singly or in pairs, learners write a paragraph describing the scene, using at least one word from each of the points of the star (for example, one word which describes what the place looks like, one which describes its sound, another which describes its smell, and so on).

Parallel reading

The Coral Island: a Tale of the Pacific Ocean is a famous adventure story written for young readers, by R. M. Ballantyne. Like *Treasure Island* by R. L. Stevenson, it has provided, for generations of English-speaking adolescents, an ever-popular tale of dangerous, exciting exploits carried out by three young men in the glamorous setting of the South Sea islands. Its three boyish heroes are called Ralph, the narrator, Jack, the leader, and Peterkin the hunter of pigs. Beside the obvious parallel of the names, there are many clues which show that Golding's novel constitutes a deliberate and often ironical counterpoint for this classic, which so many of his adult readers would remember from their childhood. Comparison of selected passages from it can throw interesting light, for the advanced foreign student, on the exact nature and quality of what Golding does with a similar setting and what seems at first sight a fairly similar situation.

Two extracts are given here. Worksheet 20, with a grid for comparisons, focusses on the setting; Worksheet 21, for reading and discussion, can be used as a follow-up to Worksheet 19.

Read the following extract from *The Coral Island* in which three young sailors, Jack, 18, Ralph, 15, and Peterkin, 14, find themselves alone on an uninhabited coral island after a shipwreck. Then fill in the boxes with appropriate quotations.

This was now the first time that I had looked well about me since landing, as the spot where I had been laid was covered with thick bushes, which almost hid the country from our view. As we now emerged from among these and walked down the sandy beach together, I cast my eyes about and truly my heart glowed within me and my spirits rose at the beautiful prospect which I beheld on every side. The gale had suddenly died away, just as if it had blown furiously till it dashed our ship upon the rocks, and had nothing more to do after accomplishing that. The island upon which we stood was hilly, and covered almost everywhere with the most beautiful and richly-coloured trees, bushes and shrubs, none of which I knew the names of at that time except, indeed, the cocoa-nut palms, which I recognised at once from the many pictures that I had seen of them before I left home. A sandy beach of dazzling whiteness lined this bright green shore, and upon it there fell a gentle ripple of the sea. This last astonished me much, for I recollected that at home the sea used to fall in huge billows on the shore long after a storm had subsided. But on casting my glance out to sea, the cause became apparent. About a mile distant from the shore, I saw the great billows of the ocean rolling like a green wall, and falling with a long, loud roar upon a low coral reef, where they were dashed into white foam and flung up in clouds of spray. This spray sometimes flew exceedingly high, and every here and there a beautiful rainbow was formed for a moment among the falling drops. We afterwards found that this coral reef extended quite round the island, and formed a natural breakwater to it. Beyond this the sea rose and tossed violently from the effects of the storm; but between the reef and the shore it was as calm and as smooth as a pond.

My heart was filled with more delight than I can express at sight of so many glorious objects, and my thoughts turned suddenly to the contemplation of the Creator of them all. I mention this the more gladly because at that time, I am ashamed to say, I very seldom thought of my Creator, although I was constantly surrounded by the most beautiful and wonderful of His works. I observed, from the expression of my companion's countenance, that he too derived much joy from the splendid scenery, which was all the more agreeable to us after our long voyage on the salt sea. There the breeze was fresh and cold, but here it was delightfully mild; and when a puff blew off the land, it came laden with the most exquisite perfume that can be imagined.

	The Coral Island	Lord of the Flies
1. *Shore/beach* Colour, sound, smell words Similes and metaphors		
2. *The sea/lagoon* Colour, sound, smell words Similes and metaphors		/
3. *Trees/vegetation* Colour, sound, smell words Similes and metaphors		
4. *Reactions of the main characters*		*Ralph Jack Piggy*

Tick which description is:

Simpler?		
More vivid, colourful?		
More concrete?		
More metaphorical?		
More poetic?		
The one you prefer?		

Worksheet 20

Read the following extract from *The Coral Island* in which Jack and Ralph come across a family of slumbering pigs. Jot down the difference in attitude between Jack and Ralph in *The Coral Island* and Jack and Ralph in *Lord of the Flies*.

The ground at the foot of this tree was thickly strewn with the fallen fruit, in the midst of which lay sleeping, in every possible attitude, at least twenty hogs of all ages and sizes, apparently quite surfeited with a recent banquet.

Jack and I could scarce restrain our laughter as we gazed at these coarse, ill-looking animals while they lay groaning and snoring heavily amid the remains of their supper.

'Now, Ralph,' said Jack, in a low whisper, 'put a stone in your sling – a good big one – and let fly at that fat fellow with his back toward you. I'll try to put an arrow into yon little pig.'

'Don't you think we had better put them up first?' I whispered; 'it seems cruel to kill them while asleep.'

'If I wanted *sport*, Ralph, I would certainly set them up; but as we only want *pork*, we'll let them lie. Besides, we're not sure of killing them; so, fire away.'

Thus admonished, I slung my stone with so good aim that it went bang against the hog's flank as if against the head of a drum; but it had no other effect than that of causing the animal to start to its feet, with a frightful yell of surprise, and scamper away. At the same instant Jack's bow twanged, and the arrow pinned the little pig to the ground by the ear.

'I've missed, after all,' cried Jack, darting forward with uplifted axe, while the little pig uttered a loud squeal, tore the arrow from the ground, and ran away with it, along with the whole drove, into the bushes and disappeared, though we heard them screaming long afterwards in the distance.

(*Returning to their encampment, the two boys do not find their companion Peterkin but they soon hear 'a chorus of yells from the hogs, and a loud hurrah'.*)

We turned hastily towards the direction whence the sound came, and soon descried Peterkin walking along the beach towards us with a little pig transfixed on the end of his long spear!

'Well done, my boy!' exclaimed Jack, slapping him on the shoulder when he came up; 'you're the best shot amongst us.'

Worksheet 21

A snowball summary

Figure 10 shows an example of the gradual building of a three-fold summary as the book is read: of events, themes, and the reactions of characters. The class is divided into four teams, A, B, C, and D. Each team has responsibility for preparing three of the book's chapters, as the class reads gradually through the novel.

Chapter/ Team	Events	Themes	The boys' reactions
I/A	Ralph and Piggy meet on the island. They swim in a pool and find a conch. Ralph blows the conch to call the other boys. Others arrive. Piggy takes names. Ralph is elected leader. Ralph, Jack and Simon explore the island. They climb to the top of a mountain. Jack tries but fails to kill a pig.	Glamour of life on the island. Leadership. What it means to kill.	Joy of freedom. Glamour of exploring the island. Friendship, shared endeavours.
II/B	Afternoon meeting. A small boy speaks of a snake beast. They pile up wood for a fire and light it with Piggy's glasses. The forest is on fire.	First ideas on rules for survival.	Fear (littluns). Content (biguns). Friendship, joy of adventures.
III/C	Jack hunts. The others build shelters. Ralph and Jack quarrel. Simon finds a secret place in the forest.	Selfishness of people, indifference to others' desires.	Slight disillusionment. Fear held in. Frustration setting in.
IV/D	The life led by the littluns. Roger teases Henry at the water's edge. Jack paints his face. Ralph sights a ship but their fire is out. Jack and hunters come back with a pig. Jack resents criticism, attacks Piggy, breaks his glasses. They roast and eat the pig.	Civilisation and its inhibitions. Release in anonymity behind mask. Glamour of hunt vs. work and responsibility. Violence.	 Elation of hunt-camaraderie. Ralph changes sides.

(Figure 10)

⠀⠀ »»→

V/A	Ralph holds a meeting to restate the rules of the island.	Qualities for leadership.	New-found under-standing (R.).
	The littluns talk of their fear.	Irrationality and power of fear.	
	Simon suggests the beast is within them.		J. – aggression.
	The meeting breaks up – Piggy and Ralph and Simon long for the lost adult world.	Rules/Chaos and hatred.	Wearisome life with responsi-bilities.
VI/B	There is a battle in the sky above the island during the night.		Fear. R. – tired of responsibilities.
	A parachute comes down and is caught on the mountain top.		J. – aggression, assertion of his leadership.
	Sam and Eric make the fire in the morning and see what they think is a beast.		Simon – inability to communi-cate rational views.
	The twins tell the others about it.		
	The biguns go to search for the beast.	Bravery/ Cowardice.	
	Ralph and Jack search the Castle Rock.		
	The boys roll a huge stone into the sea.	Games the boys play.	
VII/C	The boys set off to look for the beast on the mountain.		
	Ralph daydreams of his home life.		R. – new compre-hension.
	The boys hunt a boar, Ralph hits it with his spear; but it escapes.	Violence within man's heart. Blood-lust.	
	There is a mock hunt, Robert is a pretend pig.		
	The boys follow the pig-run to the base of the mountain.		
	Simon goes back alone to tell Piggy.		

	Ralph and Jack in conflict – decide to go up the mountain in the dark. Only Roger joins them. Jack goes first, sees the beast. The three boys go to look, see it and flee.	Antagonism, hatred.	Roger – adventurous. J. – hatred, desire to dominate, aggression.
VIII/D	Jack calls an assembly to replace Ralph as leader. The others refuse. He goes off on his own. Piggy suggests a fire on the beach. The choir joins Jack. They hunt and kill a pig. Jack leaves the head on a stick for the beast. Simon watches them. He hears the Lord of the Flies talking to him. Jack and his hunters raid the fire, invite the others to their feast.	The reason for things going wrong. The darkness inside our hearts.	P. – relief at J.'s going. J. and hunters – desire fun, loss of inhibitions behind paint, 'fulfilment' of killing. S. – perception about people.
IX/A	Simon climbs the mountain and sees the dead parachutist. Ralph and Piggy go to Jack's feast and eat. A storm breaks. The boys dance in a mock hunt. Simon crawls in among them and is mistaken for the beast. He is killed. The parachute is blown into the sea. Simon's body is washed out to sea.	Power/Authority. Violence. The importance of ritual. Crowd violence, mob psychology.	S. – does rational thing but cannot communicate it. Boys caught up in violent ritual.

⫸→

X/B	The boys cannot admit the events of the previous night – hide it from themselves. Jack organises his band at Castle Rock. The hunters raid the others' camp to steal Piggy's glasses.	Guilt.	R. and P. – guilt, bad conscience. J. – increasing violence.
XI/C	Ralph, Piggy and twins go to Castle Rock to recover Piggy's glasses. Jack orders twins caught and bound. Jack and Ralph fight. Roger dislodges huge rock. Piggy is hit and swept out to sea. Ralph flees pursued by spears.	Concealing paint liberates into savagery. Underlying cruelty outs 'playing the game'.	J. – triumphant aggression, power. R. – hunted, in terror.
XII/D	Ralph is outcast. He smashes skull of the Lord of the Flies. He climbs up to Sam and Eric on watch. They tell him he is to be hunted next day. Ralph hides in a thicket. Jack has rocks hurled down, then sets forest on fire. Ralph is pursued through undergrowth. Ralph runs out to the beach. Ship's officers appear to rescue the boys.	Chaos, cruelty, disorder, violence unleashed in boys. 'Savagery'. The end of innocence. The darkness in man's heart.	R. – terror of the hunted. J. – total power, cruelty.

Figure 10

Chapter II   Fire on the mountain (pages 35–51)

The second chapter marks the appearance of cracks in the boys' capacity to organise themselves for survival and to co-exist amicably amidst underlying fear of their new environment. The safety of their 'old' life is receding fast.

There are numerous activities that work successfully with most groups. At 16 pages, the chapter is short enough for home reading with worksheets. Alternatively, home reading could be combined with highlights read in class by the teacher or prerecorded on cassette. Once again, it would not be useful to be too prescriptive, as language learning groups vary so widely.

Summary comparison

The class is asked to study the summaries of chapter II in Worksheet 22 and decide, individually or in groups, which they prefer, and why. In this exercise, the summaries are not meant to be authoritative; they can be ascribed to previous groups of students if this helps learners feel freer to criticise. The 'why' part can be done as class follow-up discussion or as individual written work to accompany home reading. In both cases, it is helpful for students to have in mind some criteria which would make one

---

Read the following summaries. Decide which is preferable and say why.

Summary A
Basically chapter II deals with the problems the boys have when they try to organise themselves for survival. There are doubts about the possibility of rescue and some of the smaller boys are frightened by snake-like beasts. The decision is made to light a fire to aid rescue but the boys have no survival skills and the fire gets out of control. Disagreements start to break out between Piggy, Jack and Ralph.

Summary B
Basically chapter II concerns the making of rules. The older boys are looking forward to the adventure of life on the island and are confident of rescue. One of the younger boys is frightened of what he calls a 'beastie' but it is merely his fear feeding his imagination. The boys light a fire very haphazardly. Piggy is critical of the boys' lack of organisation and the first signs of discontent become apparent.

Worksheet 22

summary better than another, that is, relevance of points brought out, comprehensiveness, concision, style in which the summary is written. Depending on the level and nature of the class, a teacher could give these to help the learners see why one summary is preferable to another; or he or she could ask them to compare two or more summaries and, in small groups, evolve a set of criteria for good summary writing, based upon their comparison.

Discussion about why one summary is preferable to the other can be followed by the group task of rewriting one to provide a more satisfactory summary, more complete, without irrelevant details, etc.

This activity is useful in helping basic comprehension of the events and themes in the chapter. It also focusses attention on stylistic matters, and it aims to develop the reading and writing skills which are traditionally thought to be fostered by précis work: the ability to identify and extract key concepts in a lengthy prose passage, distinguish between essential points and illustrative or supportive material, and finally, express ideas concisely. The activity may therefore be appropriate to more advanced levels. Examples of summary comparison focussing more particularly on comprehension (and therefore incorporating a 'right' or 'wrong' view) which may be more appropriate for intermediate learners, are given for chapter VI on p. 133.

Grids

Worksheet 23 can accompany home reading or be done in groups in class. The aim is to further develop students' understanding of the three central characters in the novel.

Once again, if it is appropriate, the teacher can create a large grid for display on a class wall, on which all characters are included as they occur and personal traits added as they are revealed. This is useful vocabulary work as well as providing a handy visual checklist of characters for students to refer to as reading progresses.

Rules

A major theme in this and subsequent chapters is that of rules: the imposing of order upon chaos in nature, and in human nature. Here are two ways of helping learners deepen their insight into the issues raised:
- Retrieving rules from the novel. Students in groups are given Worksheet 24. Completed rules are pinned up so that they can be compared and discussed.
- A short simulation. This is best done as a small-group activity in class. It can precede the reading of chapter II, to set the scene and make students aware of the importance of this theme, or it can follow their

In chapter II of *Lord of the Flies*, we find out a lot more about three of the main characters – Piggy, Ralph and Jack. Study the list of words below. Use your dictionary, if necessary. Then, as you read chapter II, pick out short quotes with page references which seem to you to illustrate the types of behaviour listed. Write them into the appropriate boxes. Some boxes have been filled in to give you an example. Add other types of behaviour to the list if you can.

Type of behaviour	Piggy	Ralph	Jack
1. childish			"All the same, you need an army– for hunting." p.35
2. mature, thoughtful	"… acting like a crowd of kids" p.42		
3. frightened			
4. violent, aggressive			
5. caring, reassuring like a parent		"…there aren't any grown-ups. We shall have to look after ourselves." p.36	
6. good leadership			
7.			
8.			

Worksheet 23

As you read pages 35–42 of *Lord of the Flies*, you will find that the boys start to make rules for their 'new' society. How many rules can you find? List them on the scroll below in order of importance.

Rules of our Island

Worksheet 24

first home reading. It invariably leads to a great deal of discussion. Adapt the formula to suit particular groups.

With an older, or specially imaginative group, the activity can be open-ended. The group is told they are suddenly stranded on an island, isolated from the rest of the world: they will probably have to spend the rest of their lives together. This is their first meeting to discuss basic rules, decide about the social organisation they wish to adopt, elect leaders if they wish, etc. (A follow-up discussion on punishments for breaking rules appears later, in the next section on chapter III.)

With a less advanced or less adventurous group, it is probably a good idea to give a list of rules for life in a commune or other self-enclosed system, and ask students either to select the three or four most important rules, or to order the complete list, from the most to the least important. A time limit is set.

In both cases, once groups have decided on basic rules, results are compared and discussed, and parallels drawn with the boys' situation in the novel.

Simple language work

It is entirely in order to use the text of a novel to practise specific areas of language, though in our experience this should be done briefly so as to maintain the 'magic' of the narrative and the reader's immersion in its fantasy. The following examples are taken from chapter II.

Preposition work:

Fill in the blanks with *one* appropriate word.

1. We're .... an uninhabited island.
2. He slammed his knife .... a trunk.
3. He gaped .... them for a moment.
4. Jack snatched the glasses .... his face.
5. There hasn't been the trace .... a ship.

Phrasal verbs:

Fill in the blanks with *one* appropriate word.

1. The shouting died ....
2. He sighed, bent and laced .... his shoes.
3. We shall have to look .... ourselves.
4. He cleared his throat and went ....
5. I'll split .... the choir – my hunters, that is – into groups.

As this particular activity is fairly mechanical, the teacher can adopt various tactics to sustain interest:
— Students form groups, set missing prepositions (using sentences from the chapter) for other groups to complete.
— Sentences for completion are then used for a quiz – can groups identify what each sentence is referring to, and who is speaking?

Structural practice linked to student response, prediction, etc.

Students can consolidate their control of grammatical forms by completing sentences, while at the same time making explicit their response to characters and situations in the novel. The sentences which follow are more open-ended than the ones in the preceding exercise, and, although the structure is being controlled, the learner's use of language is more personal and creative.

Complete what these characters might say.
Piggy: We won't be rescued unless ....
        Things won't work on the island unless ....
Ralph: We won't be rescued unless ....
        Things won't work on the island unless ....
Jack: I don't want to be rescued unless ....
        We won't have a good time unless ....

Letter in a bottle

Although we have chosen this activity as a follow-up to chapter II, it could be inserted almost anywhere, and could be repeated later in the novel.

The teacher writes one of the names: Piggy, Ralph, Simon or Jack on slips of paper so that there is one for each member of the class, and roughly equal numbers of slips for each character. Students draw one each, at random. Each learner then has to imagine that they are the character whose name they have drawn: they have rescued an empty corked bottle from the plane and have gone alone down to the beach to write a letter home. Inventive groups will need brief instructions only. More dependent groups can be given more guidance, for example:

Tell your parents: where you are.
           how you feel.
           what you want them to do.
           what you miss most.
           what you like most on the island.
           etc.

Teachers can pre-teach letter format and useful language if this is necessary.

If students do not reveal the identity of 'their' character, an amusing listening activity can follow: each learner reads their letter out loud, and the class tries to guess the character who could have written it. This leads to good discussion on various facets of personality.

Figure 11 shows a few examples of 'letters in a bottle' written by students in a lower-advanced class (first year after Cambridge First Certificate). They are uncorrected.

Dear Daddy,

I hope this letter will reach you, but I'm quite sure you will find it.

- we had an accident, I don't know exactly what had happened, but we were dropped out of the plane. All boys are now on an island where it is very warm and it seems to be a good island.

- Daddy, the boys elected me to be their chief! And I'm sure I'll be able to lead them, there's another boy who is a head-boy of a choir, but they don't like him and I think he doesn't really know how to behave in such a situation without any grown-ups. He wants only fun and adventure, but he didn't even kill a pig when he could - Daddy, I know, what you taught me how to survive, don't I? We have to build shelters and to provide for enough water and food. And - Daddy- we were lightening a big signal fire so you can see where we are when you're looking for me in this area to rescue me and the others.

Daddy, I promise you I'll be able to cope with the facts until you come and fetch us.

Love, Ralph

PS: You always wished to have a tough, strong son, didn't you?

Figure 11A

Dear Auntie Phillis,

I hope you will receive this message I am sending in a bottle and you will be able to do something about the situation I am living. I am on a lost island and thank God I am not alone – all the other boys that where on the plane with me are still alive, only the pilot is missing.

We have got food and water but I really miss your wonderful cakes. We are trying to do our best to survive but we lack of organisation: especially the youngest boys are difficult to keep under control. I am really scared because this island seems bewitched. Sometimes all the other boys behave wildly. They want to do just what they like and they don't reason.

I talked to them but they don't want to listen to me: sometimes I think I am the only one that can still use his brain. Please do something! Send somebody to rescue us as soon as possible. At the airport they must know roughly the position where the plane landed.

Tell them to locate where this island is and then send a plane or a ship to rescue us. I wish I was with you instead of being on this island where I haven't got a friend.

All my love

Piggy –

Figure 11B

41, Turneville, Rd
London, W. 14

Note: If someone finds this letter
Would you please send it to
the adress above. Thanks.

Dear Mum and Dad:
                     I am alright
so far but very frightened and I
miss you all.

Nights in the yungle are very
~~scaring~~ scarey as you can hear
the noises of all the wild
animal and insects.

We have lit a permanent fire
on the mountain so that the
people who are going to rescue
us find us easily. Unfortunately
we don't know where we are
but we are all optimistic that
sooner or later we will be rescued

No one was injured during the crash
and they are all very ~~happy~~ nice
boys!
Please don't forget me as I am
trying to be tough but deep
in my heart I am struggling
~~and~~ with despair and
insecurities

                     Love

                     Simon.

Figure 11C

You have the conch

Each student is told to imagine that they are on the island, with the boys. The conch is passed to them, and they are allowed to say whatever they like about the present situation on the island, and the best course of action to adopt.

This can be done as an impromptu oral activity, or as a speech delivered after some preparation time.

Oral review

We have emphasised how important it is, in reading a long text, to keep the whole narrative in the mind of the reader so that he or she can go backwards and forwards easily over the part read while maintaining an overall view. There are various ways of doing this, but here is one which is well suited to this part of the book, that is, once chapters I and II have been read.

Students are given a list of words from the two chapters:

meeting	hunting	specs	plane
choir	rules	names	pilot
chief	beastie	smoke	count
pig	fire	rescue	conch

Students sit in small groups of four or five. In turn, each selects one word from the list and talks about the part of the story to which his or her chosen word relates. The next person takes another word, and so on. The listening students can add comments or other relevant details.

This can be useful preparation for written work. If repeated from time to time, it also ensures that each student has a sense of responsibility to the group for home reading.

A variation can be an oral review of characters. Learners talk about particular characters, using, in turn, the words from a given list as above. The list is written on the board or a copy is given to each student.

Chapter III Huts on the beach (pages 52–62)

In chapter III, Jack continues his hunt for meat, as yet unsuccessfully, while Ralph despairs of ever getting the other boys organised enough to build shelters. Simon is helpful but in an enigmatic way. He wanders off into the forest to be by himself in a quiet clearing. This is a short chapter, well suited to home reading.

Complete the sentences

This is a simple activity which combines comprehension work and structure practice (see Worksheet 25). It can accompany home reading.

Read chapter III of *Lord of the Flies*, then complete the following sentences.

Jack is a little frightened. This is shown when he ....

Simon is the sort of boy who ....

Ralph grumbles because ....

Jack is determined to ....

In the clearing in the jungle, Simon seems ....

The littluns are unreliable and this is indicated by their

....

Worksheet 25

Spot the speech

This quiz can be used as a class follow-up to home reading. It can be written or oral. Students identify the speaker and what each quotation is about, without referring back to the book.

1. 'He's queer. He's funny.'
2. 'I thought I might kill.'
3. 'You and your fire.'
4. 'Never get it done.'
5. You're chief. You tell 'em off.'
6. 'As if it wasn't a good island.'

Missing poster

This is a writing activity of the kind outlined on p. 65, where an appropriate format is illustrated. At this point in their reading of *Lord of the Flies*, students are asked to write a 'missing' poster for Simon.

Film trailer

Students are told that the director of the film version of *Lord of the Flies* is compiling some extracts of dialogue from the book as part of a trailer to advertise the film. He or she has allotted 30 seconds of the trailer to this chapter. In groups, students as film directors and screenwriters have to select what they consider to be crucial 'snippets' of dialogue which can be put together in short sequences to total 30 seconds of shooting time. Each group of students selects, times, rehearses, and performs. Differences between group choices are discussed. If a trailer for the entire book is produced at the end, the choices for chapter III can then be reviewed and modified. This re-examination is an important aspect of the dynamics of overall response.

For a group that needs a lot of support, the teacher might offer a range of dialogue extracts from chapter III and ask them to choose the most important and dramatic, to make up the 30 seconds. They might also assess which of the quotations are most representative of the mood, setting, movement and events of the chapter.

Here are some examples of dialogue extracts from chapter III:

'If I could only get a pig.' (page 60)
'But you can feel as if you're not hunting – but being hunted.' (page 57)
'They talk and scream. The littluns. Even some of the others. As if . . . As if it wasn't a good island . . . ' (page 56)
'I thought I might kill.' 'But you didn't.' 'I thought I might.' (page 55)
'The best thing we can do is get ourselves rescued.' 'Rescue? Yes of course! All the same, I'd like to catch a pig first.' (page 58)
'Don't you want to be rescued? All you can talk about is pig, pig, pig!' 'But we want meat!' 'And I work all day with nothing but Simon, and you come back and don't even notice the huts!' (page 59)
'He's buzzed off.' 'Got fed up . . . and gone for a bathe.' 'He's queer. He's funny.' (page 59)

Here are two lists of words from chapter III of *Lord of the Flies*, which have some features in common. Can you think of a word which would describe what all the words in each list have in common? Write this word in the blank at the head of the list.

....

trotted   surveyed
stole forward   peered
steal up on   gazed
picked his way   glanced

Now, here are some words which describe a family of words. For each word, write words or expressions that belong to this family.

Sounds   *Emotions*   *Plant life*

Worksheet 26

Families of words

Worksheet 26 is a homework exercise for vocabulary enrichment, to follow reading of chapter III.

Chapter IV   Painted faces and long hair (pages 63–82)

Within the natural tempo of island life, the boys' fortunes continue to fluctuate. The small boys are largely absorbed in play, but with underlying fear of their plight. Jack paints his face for more effective hunting. Ralph sees smoke on the horizon but Jack and his hunters have let their own smoke signal die out. Ralph is incensed and, as Jack returns triumphantly with his first pig, a row breaks out in which Jack picks on Piggy and breaks his glasses. A new bond is forged between Piggy and Ralph.

This is a long chapter but has plenty of action and excitement. Pages 71–2 would make good class reading; students can read silently or listen to the teacher or a recording. The following activities offer a range of ideas for exploiting this material in class and for homework.

Jungle poem

In this activity, students first reread pages 61–2 from the end of chapter III, and any other parts of the book read to date that focus on describing the island itself. They are then asked to produce a 'tanka' – a Japanese form of poem comprising five lines with 31 syllables, in the following sequence: five, seven, five, seven and seven. They can use any words they wish including those in the text. (Using a format which stresses syllables rather than the traditional English forms, where internal stress and rhythms have to be taken into account, is usually easier for the foreign speaker.) The aim of the poem produced should be to bring out one theme, such as movement, colour, mood, or sound.

For weaker groups, first build up a resource bank of words. Learners skim through the chapter and extract all words which refer to the theme chosen. These words are put up on the board, then the class is asked to extend the bank by adding all the words and phrases they can think of or find in their dictionary.

Here is an example produced by an upper-advanced multilingual group:

Island movement	
Surging sea below	(five syllables)
Pigs crashing through dry bushes	(seven syllables)
Palms, wind shimmering	(five syllables)
Shoot light in myriad shafts	(seven syllables)
The beast's ear is flickering.	(seven syllables)

Another enjoyable form is the *acrostic*. Here, learners are asked to produce poems about the main characters in the book, so that the first letter of each line, read vertically, spells his name. Here are two examples:

> Strange, quiet boy
> In tune with the island
> Makes his way to the jungle heart
> Opens his being to the beast's voice
> Never to escape its force.

> Poor, fat, wise man
> In physical awkwardness
> Gets ridicule from his peers
> Gains none of the friendship he craves
> Yet deserves the ear of all.

Do-it-yourself grid

This activity helps reading comprehension and vocabulary enrichment. Students often benefit from exercises which they have devised themselves. Here are instructions to help students produce a simple grid of the kind they have already used in preceding chapters:

Make up a grid like the ones we have used in chapter I (or invent a new kind) for someone else in the class to complete. The aim is to bring out some of the differences we see in chapter IV between Biguns and Littluns.

Punishment

In this chapter the fire is allowed to go out, and the boys are not rescued. This raises the issue of the sorts of punishment that would be needed to follow violation of rules. This activity is a natural follow-up to 'Rules' in chapter II (Worksheet 24).

Learners are asked to complete a questionnaire (Worksheet 27), imagining themselves to be stranded on the island, in their own identity.

Group 'Just a minute'

This activity can be used as revision work in class. Those teachers who have played 'Just a minute' with their language classes will have discovered that it is really a daunting task to talk without hesitation, deviation, or repetition for even 15 seconds in a foreign language. This variation merely makes it a team game which incorporates revision of the story so far.

The class is divided into teams of four or five. Each student talks about the story so far for a maximum of 15 seconds, at which point the teacher

Imagine that you are stranded with the group of boys on the island of *Lord of the Flies*. For each broken rule in the left-hand column, choose one of the punishments listed in the right-hand column or suggest your own.

Broken rule | *Suggested punishment (tick one)*

1. Not attending meetings.
   a) No punishment. ☐
   b) Extra work. ☐
   c) Less food. ☐
   d) Other (name your preferred ☐
      punishment: ....

2. Letting fire go out.
   a) No punishment. ☐
   b) Extra work. ☐
   c) Looking after fire for a month. ☐
   d) Other: .... ☐

3. Attacking another boy with intention to harm.
   a) No punishment ☐
   b) Extra work. ☐
   c) Imprisonment. ☐
   d) Other: .... ☐

4. Hiding food.
   a) No punishment. ☐
   b) Less food. ☐
   c) Extra work. ☐
   d) Other: .... ☐

5. Not using proper lavatory spot.
   a) No punishment. ☐
   b) Extra cleaning duty. ☐
   c) Spanking. ☐
   d) Other: .... ☐

6. Interrupting at meetings or speaking when you haven't got the conch.
   a) No punishment. ☐
   b) Public apology. ☐
   c) Extra work. ☐
   d) Other: .... ☐

7. Not doing proper share of work – building shelters, etc.
   a) No punishment. ☐
   b) Extra duties. ☐
   c) Public reprimand. ☐
   d) Other: .... ☐

Worksheet 27

claps his or her hands and counts to three. The next person in that team must take over at this point, and so on, until a minute has elapsed. The team then gains four points. If one member of the team stops before 15 seconds then the other team takes over. Repetition is not counted as a reason for losing the subject, nor is hesitation up to a maximum of three seconds. Deviation from the subject, however, is, and if another team spots it, they can claim the subject, with the referee's approval.

The teacher can change the subject whenever necessary from say 'story' to 'character', 'the island', 'the fire', 'the beastie', 'littluns', etc.

The activity makes an excellent revision session for 10–15 minutes and works best when the rules and rhythm of this game are well established.

Snowball wall chart

As the number of named boys increases, it is worthwhile making a wall chart of a line of boys from smaller to bigger, each outline having a name above it and a brief description inside it. This simple representation helps to make more concrete the growing number of details which become difficult for memories to hold.

Alternatively, the wall chart could be a sociogram: each boy is represented by a circle and circles are put in groups according to friendship patterns. The quality of relationships could be signalled by linking circles with different types of line, for example:

———————————— good friend

—·——·——·——·—— gets on well with

— — — — — — — — — — neutral towards

→ → → → → → → → does not like

—» —» —» —» hates

Diary

A diary is a creative writing activity that can be used systematically as reading progresses, thus serving as a sort of revision summary. Different students are asked to write diaries for different characters, or allowed to choose their favourite. From time to time, learners read current sections of their diary out loud: this brings out different assumptions about what each character would wish to write and different views of their personalities.

Moviemaker

In this chapter, there is a heated confrontation between Ralph, Jack and Piggy. The class is divided into three groups. Each one is to be a mini-production unit, with instructions from an overall director about how he or she wants the confrontation scene to be shot. This is most easily explained by the use of role cards, as illustrated below. The groups begin by reading or rereading pages 75–80.

Role card Group A

The director insists that this scene is rewritten a little so that the argument is *more* heated than in the book.

Stage 1: As a group, decide on possible changes.

Stage 2: Rewrite the dialogue.

Stage 3: Appoint actors and rehearse the rewritten scene.
Remember it is a scene highly charged with emotion!

Role card Group B

The director insists that this scene is rewritten a little so that the argument is *less* heated than in the book.

Stage 1: As a group, decide on possible changes.

Stage 2: Rewrite the dialogue.

Stage 3: Appoint actors and rehearse the rewritten scene.
Remember to reduce the level of emotion in this scene!

Role card Group C

The director insists that this scene is changed a little so that Piggy and Ralph are more aggressive towards Jack and so that Jack is more apologetic than in the book.

Stage 1: Decide on possible additions/deletions.

Stage 2: As a group, modify the dialogue to accommodate the required changes.

Stage 3: Appoint actors and rehearse the rewritten scene.
Remember to make Jack less threatening and Piggy and Ralph more aggressive.

After discussion and rehearsal time, each group performs its scene for the director (the teacher). The other groups watch and try to guess what sort of changes the director wanted from the original text. After all the groups have performed, there is a discussion on how this scene might be depicted in a film. Would it be played as it is in the book? Shortened? Which of the changed scenes did the class prefer? What modifications could they suggest?

Chapter V   Beast from water (pages 93–103)

Almost the whole of this chapter is taken up with the assembly called by Ralph after the killing and eating of the pig. His purpose is two-fold: first, he wants to reassert the rules of the island and their importance; then, he wants the boys to talk about their fears and thus bring them out into the open and defuse them. But the assembly ends chaotically and Ralph, Simon and Piggy are left lamenting the orderly adult-dominated lives they had before coming to the island.

Although fairly long, the chapter contains a lot of speech and is not unduly difficult to read. Learners could be asked to read it at home without worrying too much about any words or phrases that are not fully understood.

The language of persuasion

This class activity can follow home reading. Its aim is to study ways in which the spoken language can be used for persuasion.

Ralph has carefully thought out what he wants to say in the assembly he calls, and how he intends to say it: 'the speech was planned, point by point'. After drawing students' attention to this aspect, the teacher asks them to think about the means which the novelist shows Ralph using in order to persuade his audience. On three different sections of the board, he or she writes three techniques used by Ralph. Students, in groups, find as many examples as they can in Ralph's speech and write them up beside each heading, for example:

Using short, simple sentences:
'Then there's huts. Shelters.'
'We need an assembly. Not for fun.'
'We decide things. But they don't get done.'

Repeating key words:
'That's dirty. I said that's dirty.'
'We need an assembly. An assembly to put things straight.'
'We were going to have water . . . Now there's no water.'

Rhetorical questions: (questions used for effect, rather than to get an answer)
'Who built the shelters?'
'Who built all three?'
'Is a fire too much for us to make?'

The class is asked to add other headings if they can, and then to examine Jack's and Piggy's speeches in a similar way. Discussion of the effectiveness of each speaker's persuasive methods can be followed by a class vote: Which of the three is most persuasive? Which one gets the greatest audience response? The teacher can also ask students to vote on whether they consider these rhetorical devices to be within the characters' age group, or whether they are imported from a more adult perspective.

Minutes of the meeting

This writing activity practises writing in an 'official', impersonal register and transforming direct into reported speech.

In meetings, one person is usually responsible for keeping minutes: an official record of what has been said. Students imagine that they have been appointed to write up the minutes of this chapter's assembly. If necessary, the teacher supplies a format and examples of the kind of reporting that is required.

The class is divided into three groups, the activity discussed and prepared, then the writing is done either as a group activity or as individual homework. Group A's task is to write minutes of Ralph's part of the meeting, from the start of the assembly up to 'And be happy' (page 90). Group B's task is to write minutes of Jack's part, from 'So this is a meeting to find out what's what' (page 90) to ' . . . but there is no beast in the forest' (page 91). Group C's task is to write minutes of Piggy's talk and the littluns' up to the end of the assembly.

As follow-up after the writing has been done, or in the next lesson if it has been set as homework, teams are formed consisting of three students, one from each of the groups. Each team produces a complete set of minutes by collating the three separate accounts. The resulting minutes are displayed for the class to see and compare.

Conflict scale / continuum

The conflict between Jack and Ralph which begins to intensify in these chapters will eventually trigger off a series of tragic events. The following class activity helps students to have a greater awareness of what the attitude of each boy implies, and to explore their own reaction to these attitudes.

The class is divided into two. Working in pairs or groups of three, they fill in Worksheet 28: half of the class fills it in from Ralph's point of view,

---

Think about Ralph and Jack's attitudes to the island. Make notes about how each boy would answer questions on the following.

Good things about the island...
Bad things about the island.......................................
The most important thing to do on the island...
The most important quality in a leader...
The most important quality in a friend..
The way to survive...
The way to be happy..
A proverb that sums up a good attitude to life.................................
A motto...............................
An emblem (plant, flower)...
An emblem (animal)..

Worksheet 28

half from Jack's. Some of the information they need comes from the book, and some from the way they imagine the characters.

When groups have finished, a group that has filled in Ralph's attitudes meets with one that has done Jack's. They compare and discuss choices. Each group in turn then asks the rest of the class to indicate their own feelings about these attitudes, as follows.

A representative from the 'Ralph' team goes to a corner of the room and says: 'Ralph says the way to be happy on the island is to obey rules'. A representative from the 'Jack' team goes to the opposite corner and says: 'Jack says the way to be happy on the island is to hunt and have fun'. Everyone in the class takes up a position against the wall between these two corners, to show how close or how far they feel themselves to be from the two conflicting attitudes.

Chessboard

In this chapter there are growing indications that the idyllic island has its darker aspects as well as its glamorous side. Some of the boys' experiences seem to contain both good and bad elements. The following classroom activity is designed to sharpen students' awareness of those ambiguities.

The teacher prepares a large wall chart in the form of a chessboard, with light and dark squares. He or she tells students that the light squares represent positive aspects of life on the island, and the dark squares represent negative aspects. To set the scene, the class is asked as a whole to think about where they would place the topic 'hunting' on the chess-board, and why. Is hunting a positive aspect of life on the island? (It is exciting, creates a bond between the hunters, and provides the boys with meat.) Or is it negative? (It diverts attention from more important duties, like building shelters or tending the fire, it means that the chance of rescue is missed, it seems to turn the hunters into violent people.)

The class is divided into four groups, each to work with one quarter of the chessboard. The groups are given a set of eight topics relating to this chapter, for example:

Obeying rules.
Sharing work.
Being scrupulous about cleanliness.
Planning things carefully.
Having assemblies.
Expressing fears openly.
Looking after the younger boys.
Tending the fire.

The group's task is to decide whether each of these is a good or a bad thing and to find a quote from the chapter which supports their opinion. They then write the topic on a slip of paper, together with the supporting quote and page number, and pin it on to a light or a dark square in their sector of the chessboard. If they consider any topic to have both positive and negative aspects, they are allowed to pin it on both squares, with different supporting quotes.

When all four parts of the chart have been filled in, lively discussion often results from the fact that topics have been placed on opposite squares by different groups.

Figure 12 shows a quarter of a chessboard, with some of the squares filled in. A grid of this kind, with light and dark squares, can also be given for students to fill in as they read a section at home, with comparison and discussion in the next class lesson.

Figure 12

Chapter VI   Beast from air (pages 104–19)

At the beginning of chapter VI, Ralph's longing for a sign from the adult world receives an ironic reply. During the night, there is an aerial battle above the island and a parachute floats down to the mountain top. When the twins awaken, they are horrified by the sight of the billowing material, which they take to be the long-dreaded 'beast'. They run down the mountain to tell the others. After some deliberation, Ralph leads a party of the bigger boys in search of the beast. Having explored Castle Rock in vain, with Jack, Ralph decides they must continue their search on the mountain.

This chapter divides naturally into three sections:
– The aerial battle and the twins' discovery (pages 104–7).
– The assembly (pages 108–12).
– The search party at Castle Rock (pages 113–19).

The first of these is especially well suited to home reading, and we begin with a choice of worksheets to help students cope on their own.

Worksheet 29 involves a rather elementary kind of right or wrong choice, designed to help weaker students with basic comprehension of the passage. Worksheet 30, for use with the same passage, could accompany home reading, or be the basis of a group activity in class following silent reading of the first three pages.

Read pages 104–7 of *Lord of the Flies*. There are three summaries of these pages. Choose the one you think most appropriate.

1. While the boys were asleep that night, there was a battle between aeroplanes high above the island. A parachute carrying a dead airman came down and became caught in the trees on the mountain top. The twins, when they woke up, saw the moving parachute in the forest and, terrified, ran down to tell the others.

2. The boys were restless and frightened but they looked at the stars twinkling above them and this made them calm again so that they could fall asleep. While they were sleeping there was a great storm above the island with flashing lightning and loud thunder. This was a sign that things would not go well for the boys on the island.

3. The boys were sleeping, so that they did not see a man on a parachute who was coming to rescue them. The parachute was blown over the lagoon and out to sea. Sam and Eric were asleep too, although they should have been on watch. When they woke up, they tried to make a fire but couldn't. They thought Ralph would be angry with them so they ran and told the others they had seen a 'beast'.

Worksheet 29

Within this paragraph, there is an accurate summary of pages 104–7 of *Lord of the Flies*. However, most sentences contain information that is not correct: that is, it does not correspond to what the reader is told in these pages. *First*, strike out the incorrect information. *Then*, use the remaining correct parts to build an accurate summary. You will have to make changes to the punctuation and capital letters. The first sentences have been done for you.

The boys were restless and frightened because they had found snakes in their shelters. They had talked a lot about beasts and this reassured them so that finally they fell asleep. Then they looked at the stars twinkling above them but while they were sleeping they did not see the storm with an aerial battle high above the island. The lightning and thunder were so loud they could not hear a parachute coming down carrying a message in a bottle from the pilot who wanted to rescue them in the middle of the night. Beneath the parachute there was a basket with food and drink for a limp figure which blew far out to sea where it became a mere speck on the horizon. While the twins were playing a game on the shore, the parachute became tangled in the trees that the boys had planted to give shade on the mountain top. There was a terrific popping noise which was a sign from the world of grown-ups. Sam and Eric were determined to find a pig that had fallen asleep, though they should have told Jack about it because he had been on watch. When they woke up later on, they climbed the mountain and hastily looked for wood because there was the fire blazing merrily and they wanted to see if Piggy had gone out of the shelter during the night to search for the beast. They feared Ralph would be angry with them. Suddenly they saw Jack creeping through the bushes with something white and horrible moving behind him and following him in the jungle. They were so terrified they didn't notice that fire was spreading amongst the trees but they managed to run down the mountain and into the sea where they felt safe. Ralph saw them but didn't tell the others because he knew they had seen a terrible monster, as well as planes fighting in the sky.

Worksheet 30

Answer to Worksheet 30
The boys were restless and frightened because they had talked a lot about beasts. Finally they fell asleep. While they were sleeping they did not see a parachute coming down. Beneath the parachute there was a limp figure. The parachute became tangled in the trees on the mountain top. Sam and Eric had fallen asleep though they should have been on watch. When they woke up they hastily looked

for wood because the fire had gone out during the night. They feared Ralph would be angry with them. Suddenly they saw something white and horrible moving in the jungle. They were terrified but they managed to run down the mountain and tell the others they had seen a terrible monster.

A word puzzle

Worksheet 31A shows an easily constructed word puzzle, of the kind younger students usually enjoy, to accompany home reading of chapter VI. The aim is to help learners build vocabulary and move from passive to active mastery of slightly unusual words.

Can you find ten words from chapter VI of *Lord of the Flies*? (The letters of some words may read from right to left or diagonally.)

R	C	R	U	M	P	L	E	D	M
W	E	G	N	I	P	P	O	P	O
J	F	S	L	I	V	E	R	L	H
L	N	W	T	U	H	E	U	C	J
I	Y	I	P	L	E	G	T	T	O
M	R	N	A	H	E	A	G	K	D
B	F	K	C	E	P	S	V	Z	S
W	I	E	I	V	L	P	S	M	B
K	C	D	J	Y	T	N	A	L	S
D	A	N	G	L	I	N	G	O	Y

Worksheet 31A

When you have found the ten words, look up the sentences in which they occur in this chapter. From the context, or using a dictionary if necessary, make sure you understand the meaning of each word. Now choose one of these words to fill the blanks in these ten sentences.

1. The young lad sat on the wall, his legs .... over the edge.
2. 'Be careful as you climb down that cliff,' said the team leader. 'We don't want any of you breaking a .... '
3. When I received another useless advertisement through the post, I just .... it up and flung it into the wastepaper bin.
4. The golden eagle was flying so high above their heads that it was only a .... in the sky.
5. The assistant at the cheese counter cut a thin .... of Cheddar so that I could taste it.
6. The young man paced up and down .... in the hospital corridor as he waited for his child to be born.
7. The table was on such a .... that the pencils kept rolling off.
8. 'Oh dear,' said my father, 'I don't think I can hang the washing out after all. It looks like rain. There's only a tiny .... of blue sky in between those big dark clouds.'
9. As he came in the door, there was a .... of corks and everyone shouted 'Surprise! Happy Birthday!'
10. The lights on the aircraft wings .... as the great jet came gently down to the airfield.

Worksheet 31B

Answers to Worksheets 31A and 31B

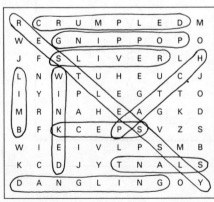

1. dangling	6. restlessly
2. limb	7. slant
3. crumpled	8. patch
4. speck	9. popping
5. sliver	10. winked

It is hoped that working with the ten words within the context of the novel, then in individualised sentences, will reinforce students' ability to use them in different contexts. As follow-up, they can be asked to use each word in a sentence of their own. An amusing variation on this well-known language activity consists of asking students, in pairs, to use all ten words, or as many as they can, in one single sentence. Efforts are read out, and the class awards marks for the following:
− Accurate use of the words.
− Amusing use of the words.
− Imaginative or inventive use of the words.
For variety, learners can be given definitions with which they must match the ten words they have found in the puzzle. It is usually more interesting to give out more than ten definitions, especially if the activity is being done in groups during class time.

The meaning of signs

Students fill out Worksheet 32, then compare their answer with their neighbour's. Each pair then tries, through discussion, to find a common interpretation. They then compare their results with another pair's, and so on.

》》→

At the end of chapter V of *Lord of the Flies*, Piggy and Ralph long for the world they have known, where adults make decisions and ensure a well-ordered life. 'If only they (the grown-ups) could get a message to us,' cried Ralph desperately. 'If only they could send us something grown-up . . . a sign or something.'

The beginning of chapter VI brings a certain answer to Ralph's wish. Which of the following four interpretations best expresses that answer, do you think? If none quite does so, in your opinion, then write your own interpretation against number 5. Then compare your answer with your neighbour's.

1. The boys wanted some sign from the world of adults. They got that sign but did not see it because they were asleep. This means that you must be extremely watchful all the time to seize opportunities as they happen.
2. The sign from the world of adults was a battle in the sky. The sign means that the orderly adult world that the boys remember exists only in their imagination. Reality is different. Reality is quarrels among the boys and war among the adults.
3. The sign that the boys wanted appeared in the form of a dead soldier. The significance of this sign is that people must fend for themselves. It is not any good expecting others to rescue you from the mess you have got yourself into.
4. The boys wanted a sign from the world of adults to reassure them that they were not alone in the world. The fact that there was a battle above the island does show that other people were quite near and that they could hope to be rescued after all.
5. ....

Worksheet 32

Chapter VII   Shadows and tall trees (pages 120–36)

The boys' search for the beast is first delayed while they try unsuccessfully to hunt, then by a hunting dance with one of them acting the part of the pig. Finally, as darkness sets in, Jack taunts and dares Ralph to go up the mountain, and the two of them climb up with Roger. There, they catch a dim glimpse of the tangled, flapping parachute and when the wind stirs it, they flee in panic, convinced that the beast is in pursuit.

A short chapter, with clearly marked events leading up to a suspenseful climax, this is suitable for home reading. Students can be encouraged to read it for the story, without worrying too much if they do not completely understand everything in the two or three descriptive passages which contain a greater density of unfamiliar words. The narrative thread should carry them along.

Choosing and ordering

Worksheet 33 can accompany home reading of the entire chapter.

Here is a list of *twelve* events. *Ten* of these happen in chapter VII. Choose the right ten and put them in the right order so that they tell the story as it happens.

a) Jack goes on by himself to look for the beast but comes back terrified.

b) The parachute comes down to the island and is caught in the foliage on the mountain.

c) The three boys see the beast and run away in terror.

d) Simon goes off by himself through the forest to tell Piggy that the boys are climbing the mountain.

e) A boar comes crashing through the forest. The boys try to kill it, and Ralph hits it with his spear.

f) The boys have a mock hunt, pretending that Robert is the pig: they dance around him and jab him with their spears.

g) The boys set off to look for the beast on the mountain.

h) The boys roll an immense boulder off Castle Rock into the sea.

i) Ralph daydreams of his home as he walks along.

j) Ralph leads the other two to have a look at the beast.

k) Roger is the only one who volunteers to climb the mountain in the dark with Ralph and Jack.

l) The boys follow a pig-run to the base of the mountain.

Worksheet 33

Sculpting

This activity is described and illustrated in Chapter 6 (see p. 81) as an 'ending' activity, but it can also be used in the middle of the novel. In this chapter, there is a subtle but definite shift in the relationships between several of the characters. Rivalry and tension increase between Jack and Ralph, there is new understanding and a growing bond between Ralph and Simon, and Roger emerges as a character in his own right. This makes it a particularly appropriate point for sculpting.

Plausible chains

Learners are paired or put into small groups. Then they are told to think about what *would have happened* if the crucial decision to go up the mountain *had not been made*. They are to write as many sentences as they can, having been given a few examples, such as:
- If the boys *had waited* until daylight, they *would have seen* that the beast was really a dead man hanging from a parachute.
- If Jack *had not taunted* Ralph about his cowardice, Ralph *would have suggested* postponing the climb.
- If Simon *had gone* up with the others, he *would have had* the courage to examine the beast more closely.

When the groups have written as many as they can, all the 'if' sentences are pooled (written on the board or overhead projector; or typed and duplicated for later distribution). The groups are then asked to choose among the sentences the *one* which best expresses:
- The most important factor which determined the decision to go up the mountain in the dark.
- The most important consequence of that decision.

One sentence may be chosen for both, or two different ones for each part. New sentences are often added to the list at this point!

This is quite a simple activity, but the ensuing general feedback and comparison of sentences chosen often generate fairly wide-ranging discussion of a number of issues. On one level, learners are made to think about the complex causes motivating any decision, and to assess whether it was a good decision or not. On a more literary level, in some advanced classes it has led (with some prompting from the teacher!) to talk about the plausibility of a particular chain of events, and about whether the steps which eventually bring about a tragic climax are accidental or unavoidable.

I know what you said, but what do you mean?

The aim of this activity is to sensitise students to the underlying meanings of spoken phrases – often a thorny area for foreign learners, and even for native speakers! Students are asked to consider utterances made by the boys in this chapter and decide on each speaker's intended meaning. We have worked out three variations of this activity, to suit different levels of students or different teaching situations.

A *novel:* 'Lord of the Flies'

VARIATION 1

This is probably more suited to advanced classes. Students are divided into two groups, and each given the task of finding in the chapter phrases that are spoken by one of the boys, where the students feel that the underlying meaning or intention differs from the surface words. When this is done, each group takes turns reading out one utterance to the other group (having previously checked pronunciation and intonation with the teacher, if necessary), asking them to provide an interpretation. There may be cases where one 'right' interpretation seems evident, and others where different interpretations can be defended. One interesting way of carrying out this activity is for the teacher to keep a record, perhaps on the board, of the number of times the whole class could agree on one single meaning, as opposed to the number of times there was disagreement. This can provide a graphic demonstration of the essential ambiguity of speech, and, of course, of the subtlety of the novelist's depiction of it.

VARIATION 2

This is easier. Learners are given quotations, and choose the best interpretation from three possible ones listed. This can be done individually or in pairs. Worksheet 34 illustrates this.

VARIATION 3

This is a listening task. Whenever possible, the activity should include an aural component, because it attempts to heighten learners' awareness of the spoken language. The teacher could use a recording of the novel: either a commercial recording or one he or she has created by reading the appropriate passage on to a cassette. The students listen to the extract, then work with a multiple-choice series of questions, like the ones in

---

Here are ten phrases spoken by the boys in chapter VII of *Lord of the Flies*. Find the place in the novel where each is spoken (the first one is on page 127, the others follow) then decide which of the three possible meanings is closest to what the boy wanted to say or to imply in each case.

1. Ralph: 'Well. We shan't find what we're looking for at this rate.'
    ☐ Let's go on and find the beast.
    ☐ We'd better give up this foolish search.
    ☐ I've given up hope of finding the beast.

≫→

2. 'Shouldn't we go back to Piggy,' said Maurice, 'before dark?'
   ☐ I really care a lot about Piggy.
   ☐ I think we shouldn't be out after dark.
   ☐ I'm afraid to look for the beast in the dark.

3. The twins: 'Yes, that's right. Let's go up there in the morning.'
   ☐ We feel morning is the proper time for a search.
   ☐ We especially like climbing the mountain in the morning.
   ☐ We want to delay the possibility of meeting the beast for as
   long as possible.

4. Ralph: 'We've got to start the fire again.'
   ☐ We must climb the mountain now.
   ☐ I'm reasserting my leadership and insisting on the most
   important thing.
   ☐ A ship might pass by any moment now.

5. Jack: 'You haven't got Piggy's specs, so you can't.'
   ☐ I'm opposing your claim to leadership.
   ☐ You never get things right.
   ☐ The fire isn't important anyway.

6. Ralph: 'If we went back we should take hours.'
   ☐ It's a long way to the shelters.
   ☐ Everyone walks so slowly. You should all hurry up.
   ☐ I don't want to go back. I intend to continue the search.

7. Jack: 'We mustn't let anything happen to Piggy, must we?'
   ☐ We desperately need Piggy's brains.
   ☐ I hate Piggy and I hate you for protecting him.
   ☐ Piggy is so important to our survival that we must look after
   him carefully.

8. Bill: 'Through the forest by himself? Now?'
   ☐ I'm sorry, I didn't quite hear what you said?
   ☐ I don't intend to walk through the forest in the dark by myself!
   ☐ I want to go back to the shelters.

9. Jack: 'Would you rather go back to the shelters and tell Piggy?'
   ☐ Please go back and tell Piggy.
   ☐ You're a coward and you'll run away rather than face danger.
   ☐ I'd like you to do whatever you think is best.

10. Jack: 'If you're frightened, of course.'
   ☐ I dare you to come.
   ☐ Would you come with me, please?
   ☐ Tell me whether you're frightened or not.

Worksheet 34

Worksheet 34. It is better for the whole passage to be listened to, rather than just the isolated quotations reproduced on the worksheet. The 'meaning' or intentional aspect can then be understood not only through intonation and tone, but through the whole situation.

School reports

In their ordinary school life before they came to the island, the boys would receive reports every term, in which their schoolteachers assessed their

NAME: PATRICK MARTIN

Attendance and punctuality:
(Comment only if unusual)

Year Group 4   No. in class 38.   11 yrs 3 mths.

Reading and comprehension	Very good.
Written work	He expresses himself with great originality and draws his words from a wide vocabulary. His writing also suggests depth and clarity of
Spelling	thought but he tends to be untidy and his stories are a little short. Spelling is very good.
Mathematics (Computation and concepts)	He is quick to pick up a new idea in Arithmetic but slow to set work down and this slowness has held him back.

General comment on other subjects

Patrick is a lively, and at times possibly mischievous, member of the class. He is always keen to add to class discussion and is able to draw from an extensive general knowledge. All his written work tends to be untidy.

Class Teacher   *W. a. ...*

Headmaster   Date 13 July 1978

Figure 13*

* Our thanks to Patrick Martin for allowing us to use his report.

academic progress as well as their character and their ability to function in the school's social setting.

Students are asked to imagine that they are a teacher who has to write a progress report on the boys' behaviour on the island so far. They are given an example of an English schoolboy's report (see Figure 13). First, they should suggest appropriate headings for the island situation, then write brief notes under each of the headings for one of the main characters (see Worksheet 35). They are to give some idea of how each boy is managing on the island so far.

This can be done individually, but it is probably more enjoyable when

---

Look at Figure 13 which is an example of an English schoolboy's report.

If you had to write a report on one of the boys on the island, what categories would you use to replace the 'subject' categories of 'reading and comprehension', etc.? Put your categories into the blank form below, then write a progress report on: .... (Simon / Jack / Ralph, etc.).

PROGRESS REPORT

NAME: ....

Attendance and punctuality:
(Comment only if unusual)   ....

No. in group: .... Age: ....

General comments

Class teacher   ....

Headmaster   .... Date ....

Worksheet 35

done as group work, with each group being allocated one character to write about. The reports for each boy are then displayed for the whole class to read. Figure 14 shows some examples of general comments written by a student on Jack and Ralph.

In classes which enjoy improvisations, the reports can lead to the follow-up activity on p. 146.

Jack

Jack is a very good singer. He is ambitious and leads the choir very well. He tries to get used to life on a tropical island and trains himself to become a really good hunter. He has a lot of ideas how to hunt in a proper way. He tries to dominate all the other boys and he can be very rude to weak boys. He hasn't much understanding for little boys and doesn't treat them very kindly. It seems to me that he really enjoys life without his family because he likes being responsible for himself.

Ralph

Ralph is a boy, who knows how to help himself even in difficult situations. He is deliberate and has the capacity of leadership without oppressing the group he leads. He behaves towards his fellows all the same age very kindly and full of understanding. He is social and helps weaker boys. Although he tries not to show it I have the feeling he misses his usual environment and his family.

Figure 14

Interview with the school counsellor

On the basis of the teacher's report, one of the boys (Jack, Piggy, Simon, or Ralph) is asked to go and see the school counsellor. Role-play cards are made up for the counsellor, according to the reports written in the previous activity. Working in pairs, students create the interview, one taking the role of the counsellor, with help from his card, the other taking the role of the boy, and drawing on his knowledge of the character, gained from his reading of the novel so far.

The example shows a role-play card for the counsellor who has been asked to see Simon.

Role card: Instructions for school counsellor

You have been asked to see ....SIMON............ . On his last school report, his teacher has written:

> A dreamy boy who appears to be very reflective but has difficulty communicating with the others. Definitely a "loner". He sometimes seems quite disturbed.

Try to find out more about Simon. Try to find out:
- How he feels about the leaders of his group, Jack and Ralph.
- How he feels about being on the island.
- What he does when he goes off into the forest on his own.
- What he would like to tell the others.
- What he likes best on the island.
- What he dislikes on the island.
- Any other thing you feel would help you understand this boy.

Chapter VIII   Gift for the darkness (pages 137–59)

The rivalry between Jack and Ralph comes to a head as Jack tries to replace Ralph as leader. When the boys do not vote for him, he stalks off by himself, but is soon joined once again by his choir. Together they hunt and kill a pig and leave its head stuck on a stick as a sacrifice to the 'beast'. Unknown to them, the scene has been watched by Simon, who has a 'vision' in which the 'Lord of the Flies' speaks to him. The hunters later raid the other camp to get fire, and they invite everyone to their feast.

A long and in many ways complex chapter, but very important to the unfolding of the novel. It may be a good idea to plan one or two listening passages, and ensure sufficient time for appreciation of the symbolic power of the 'Lord of the Flies'.

Reaction words

Worksheet 36 accompanies home or silent class reading of the beginning of the chapter. Its aim is to improve students' vocabulary and especially their awareness of the emotional dimension of words describing human reactions.

Read pages 137–46 of *Lord of the Flies*. At the beginning of this chapter, we see the boys trying to cope with the terrible fact that there *is* a beast on the mountain. Which of the words listed below could be used to describe the reaction of each boy to the news?

frightened	determined to survive	incredulous
apathetic	apathetic	curious
aggressive	panic-stricken	defeated
depressed	determined to ignore it	wondering
despairing	determined to make	matter-of-fact
belligerent	the best of it	sensible
heartsick	rational	excited

Match each boy's name to as many appropriate words as possible.

Jack ....

Ralph ....

Piggy ....

Simon ....

Sam 'n Eric ....

Worksheet 36

Solutions

Worksheet 37 can also accompany home reading and then gives rise to discussion in class.

At the beginning of chapter VIII of *Lord of the Flies*, the boys each propose a solution to the dilemma they find themselves in. In the right-hand column are many possible solutions. Match each boy's name to the solution he proposes.

	Build rafts and sail away.
Jack	Fortify the shelters.
	Build the fire on the shore.
Ralph	Climb the mountain and have another look.
	Go and live at Castle Rock.
Piggy	Change leadership.
	Give up.
Simon	Pretend nothing happened.
	Group together and attack the beast.

What would you have done in the boys' position?

Worksheet 37

A peace offering

In the central part of this chapter, Jack and his hunters offer a kind of sacrifice to placate the beast. This activity attempts to make learners explore the concept of a 'peace offering' with which people try to ward off evil.

In groups, learners try to list as many situations as they can in which peace offerings of some kind are resorted to. A few examples can be given to start them off. They could be everyday ones like:

You come home later than you promised. How do you placate your wife/ mother/father/boyfriend . . . ?
You forget an important occasion. What do you do to redeem yourself?
Your teacher is cross because you have not handed in your work on time. What do you do or say to remedy the situation?

Or they could be more unusual examples like:

As you're crossing a field marked 'private', you see an angry farmer waving a pitchfork. What can you do?
You find a burglar in your home at night, with a knife . . . ?
You find a Martian sitting on your windowsill, with a ray-gun . . . ?

After comparison of the situations imagined by various groups, and personal recollections if these come up, discussion can be turned to the particular peace offering devised by Jack and his hunters – is it simply a more extreme form of the kind of offering learners have found in their own lives, or is it a darker, more ominous thing? Is it appropriate? disgusting? etc.

Humans? Animals? Or savages?

In a previous chapter, Piggy asked the boys: 'What are we? Humans? Animals? Or savages?'

The break-up of the island community gives renewed force to the question. This writing and discussion activity attempts to get learners to consider whether or not these are quite separate categories, and what each really means.

The class is divided into groups, each of which has responsibility for one or two pages in this chapter. Their task is to write out, on slips of paper, in clear, correct, simple English, the things that happen in their pages. For example:

The boys refuse to vote for Jack as leader.
Jack is humiliated and cries.
Piggy and the twins bring Ralph fruit to cheer him up.
The hunters paint their faces.
The hunters leave the pig's head for the beast.
Piggy and the twins build a fire on the beach.
The hunters invite the others to their feast.
The hunters enjoy killing the pig.

Meanwhile, the teacher prepares a chart with three large headings:

HUMANS   *ANIMALS*   *SAVAGES*

When writing is completed, each group in turn reads out one of its sentences, then puts it up on the wall chart in the appropriate column. The class as a whole has to agree that the event described by the sentence is characteristic of human, animal, or savage behaviour. In cases of disagreement, or where the class agrees that the behaviour could fit two or even three of the categories, the sentence is quickly written out again on a new slip and the two sentences are put up in their respective categories. There is often lively discussion, as students are made to reassess their ideas about what these three words, which are so crucial to the novel, really imply.

Grammar exercise

This is a team game to practise the past perfect. The class is divided into teams. Each team is given a paragraph to study. Two useful paragraphs

149

are: page 143 ('The greatest ideas are the simplest ... ') and page 146 ('Far off along the beach ... ').

Each team now extracts simple sentences from the text, starting each one with the word 'Now'. For example: 'Now there was something to be done', 'Now they worked with passion', 'Now Piggy was full of delight in Jack's departure', etc.

Each team then fires a 'Now' sentence at another team, which has to respond by one perfectly formed sentence beginning 'Before', without using more than two of the same main words. For example:

Now there was something to be done.	Before, they had not known what to do.
Now they worked with passion.	Before, they had been apathetic.
Now Piggy was full of delight in Jack's departure.	Before, he had feared Jack.

Vocabulary enrichment

Students are given some expressions which are used to describe movement at the beginning of the chapter. Some of these expressions also indicate the mood or emotion accompanying the movement.

jerked away	walked a few paces along	shuddered violently
turned towards	panic flight down the mountain	marches away
came stealing out	squats by the fire	twisting his hands
stayed back	crept to the platform	went on
running away	rose obediently	

They are then asked to list as many of these as they can under the following headings:

Fear   Secrecy   Menace   Determination   Defiance

Finally, they find movement words from the rest of the chapter and fit them into these columns or add new columns if necessary.

The Lord of the Flies speaks

In the final section of chapter XIII, Simon 'hears' the Lord of the Flies speaking to him in the voice of a schoolmaster. What Simon hears is partly a recollection of his past, partly a formulation of his thoughts about their present predicament, and partly a prediction of things to come.

If the activity is done in class, it starts with silent reading of the passage, followed by general discussion about the kind of things Simon hears. Then the class is divided into pairs. Each pair is given one character from the novel. They imagine that their character is sitting alone with the Lord of the Flies, and write what the pig's head says to him.

As individual homework, learners can be given some help in the form of a few prompts, for example:

Imagine that you are the Lord of the Flies. .... comes alone to sit with you in the clearing. Remembering the kind of things you said to Simon, speak to this boy. Give him the advice you think he needs. Tell him the truth about his situation on the island, without sparing him. Make sure you tell him:
– What his particular weaknesses are.
– How he relates to the rest of the group and what they think of him.
– What is going to happen to him on the island.

Chapter IX   A view to a death (pages 160–70)

This brief chapter is full of suspense and action, and well suited to class-room treatment. An extract from it makes excellent listening material.

The chapter is a dark one. It marks the break-up of the fragile community into two distinct camps led by Ralph and Piggy on the one hand and Jack and Roger on the other. The constitution, such as it was, shatters. At the same time, a storm signals the return of fear and the power of ritual to keep fear at bay and cement the group temporarily. The ritual, however, summons the darker recesses of the boys' personalities, and they collectively harness their individual aggression in a semi-conscious orgy of death. The unwitting Simon, returning to dispel fears about the beast, becomes the victim. Civilisation snaps, violence stamps its authority on the island.

Doodle and listen

This activity combines relaxed listening with free-running creativity. The class listens to a recording of (or to the teacher reading) pages 164–9, from the point at which Ralph and Piggy join Jack and the others. They are given a piece of paper, preferably with an inset empty rectangle, and are told to draw or write whatever comes into their minds in response to the events they hear about. At the end of the reading, the class is put into small groups and their efforts discussed, if they wish to do so. Some students prefer to keep their doodles private and simply to incorporate them into their own notebooks as records of their response to this particular part of the book.

Students may at first be puzzled by the lack of a formal structure for this listening task. Its advantage lies in the fact that learners remain relaxed yet active while they listen. The teacher must emphasise that it does not matter if they produce nothing, and that individual artistic talents are not relevant.

The power of the group

It is quite common for individuals to be persuaded to do something uncharacteristic in order to remain accepted by a group of friends.

Students are given a questionnaire (Worksheet 38), which they answer individually. They are then put into small groups to discuss and compare their answers, and to tell others about the things they did. Then the class is brought back together. Each group is asked to talk about one event they heard about in their first discussion.

The teacher then asks the class to give their suggestions as to why the boys killed Simon. Were they really vicious under the veneer of their civilisation? Could they be described as temporarily insane? Were they rendered helpless by the dancing and chanting?

If learners are embarrassed by the personal nature of the questionnaire, they may not benefit from the activity. Teachers must judge according to their particular groups of learners. In some cases it may be better to use other ideas to present the theme.

Have you ever done anything (either individually or with others) that was daring or wrong to prove yourself part of a group of friends?
.................Yes   .... No

If 'yes', what was it? Tick the following list if appropriate:

- ☐ Stolen something from a shop, house, school, garden, car.
- ☐ Gone up to someone and asked a question or told them something.
- ☐ Eaten or drunk something unusual or daring.
- ☐ Hurt someone or something.
- ☐ Played a practical joke or trick on someone.
- ☐ Thrown something.
- ☐ Ridden or driven something in a daring way.
- ☐ Something else, name it: ....

How did you feel afterwards?
How do you feel about it now?
If you have never done anything of this kind, can you explain why not?

Worksheet 38

Ritual activities

The impromptu ritualised dancing and singing in chapter IX leads to a grisly death. Any society, however, incorporates a certain ritualistic element. After a warm-up about the nature of rites, students in groups brainstorm a list of ritual activities which they as individuals take part in, and mark them national, local or personal. Then they are asked to nominate the activities on the list which they feel most involved in at the time they happen.

Afterwards, groups compare results and discuss differences, and reasons for them. Students are asked for their reactions to the ritual chanting and dancing in this chapter. In what ways is it different from their own experience? Does it fulfil any social function? Why does it get out of hand? Why didn't a single boy stop and shout: 'It's Simon, stop!'

What if?

This is a suitable spot in the book for the kind of speculation described in Chapter 6 (see p. 83). What if the parachutist had survived intact? What would have happened to the boys? How would their life have been altered? The class can be divided into groups, half imagining that the surviving airman is an English-speaking friend, the other half imagining him as an alien foe.

Language exercise: figurative language

This is a chapter rich in striking similes.

' . . . The Lord of the Flies hung on his stick like *a black ball* . . . '
' . . . made the split guts look like *a heap of glistening coal* . . . '
'(Simon) . . . walked . . . like *an old man* . . . '
' . . . Jack painted and garlanded sat there like *an idol* . . . '
' . . . The movement . . . began to beat like *a steady pulse* . . . '
'The shrill scream was like *a pain* . . . '
' . . . let down the rain like *a waterfall* . . . '

The teacher discusses with the class the images created by these similes, asking them to suggest why these particular correspondences were chosen, and what the effect is on them when they read the passage. All suggestions are allowed, as this is an exploratory activity. Then students are asked to provide comparisons for the following descriptive sentences, adapted from this chapter. This can be done for homework.

page 160 The flies gathered round the pig's head like . . .
page 161 Simon staggered like . . .
page 162 The clouds loomed like . . .

page 165   The boys ate the meat like . . .
page 168   The sticks fell on to the beast like . . .
page 170   Simon's dead body moved out towards the open sea like . . .

In the feedback session, the learners are asked to compare their similes in groups to see if they have used similar ones. Some may be read out and the vividness of the imagery discussed.

Simon's epitaph

Using the outline of a tombstone, students write a short epitaph for Simon, beginning 'Here lies Simon . . .' (Worksheet 39).

Look at the epitaphs in Figure 5 on p. 64. Then write a suitable memorial for Simon on the stone below.

Here Lies
SIMON

Worksheet 39

Newspaper reports

The class is divided into three groups. Each group is composed of reporters writing for a particular newspaper with a different style from the other two. Tasksheets are given to each, as follows:

Newspaper A

The *Daily Mercury* is a newspaper which sensationalises its news reports and tends to exaggerate. It emphasises violence and likes to use lots of adjectives. It is generally anti-youth and welcomes opportunities to attack young people's crimes.

Tasks: 1. As a group, decide on a headline for an article about Simon's death.
2. Brainstorm for adjectives and phrases to use to describe the events surrounding the death, remembering the 'house style'.
3. Individually, write an article of 120 words about what happened on the island that evening.

Newspaper B

The *Western News* is a newspaper which concentrates on the personal angle and gives a lot of detail about any individuals involved in an event. It plays down a sensational approach and seldom examines issues surrounding issues.

Tasks: 1. As a group, decide on a headline for an article about Simon's death.
2. Brainstorm for adjectives and phrases to use to describe the events surrounding the death, remembering the 'house style'.
3. Individually, write an article of 120 words about what happened on the island that evening.

Newspaper C
The *Morning Globe* is essentially a serious newspaper; it detests
sensationalism and too much interest in personalities and tries to
examine the underlying issues.

Tasks: 1. As a group, decide on a headline for an article about
           Simon's death.
        2. Brainstorm for adjectives and phrases to use to describe
           the events surrounding the death, remembering the
           'house style'.
        3. Individually, write an article of 120 words about what
           happened on the island that evening.

Chapter X   The shell and the glasses (pages 171–86)

After Simon's death, Piggy and Ralph have difficulty coping with the
implications of what they have done. Most of the other boys have joined
Jack's group of hunters. After a violent raid, Jack and some of his group
make off with Piggy's glasses. This chapter is suited to a mixture of class
treatment and home reading.

Pledges

The break-up of the boys into two very different groups raises the question of what each stands for. The teacher explains the idea of a 'pledge'
and gives examples. Then students, in groups, write the pledge of
allegiance for each community of boys on the island, according to the
students' assessment of what each community values. A formula is given
for starting:

The Hunters
   I, ..., solemnly swear that I will ....

The Conchies
   (same formula)

When each group has prepared its pledges, these are read out and
similarities and differences discussed. This provides an opportunity for
the teacher to bring out the implications of the polarisation that has taken
place amongst the boys. Was it inevitable? Why has it happened? Was
there any way in which it could have been prevented?

A good leader

One of the principal issues in the novel concerns the ability of a leader both to command respect and co-operation, and to embody acceptable social values. Singly or in groups, students arrange the following leadership qualities in order of importance:

1. Sensitivity to the views of the group.
2. Charismatic personality.
3. Ability to see situations in terms of broad goals.
4. Adaptability.
5. Sticking to a decision once it has been made.
6. Involving as many people as possible in decision-making.
7. Delegating tasks but taking final responsibility.
8. Strong personality.
9. High intelligence.
10. Willingness to put the well-being of the whole group before personal considerations.
11. Refusal to tolerate dissent.

As Ralph and Jack have very different styles of leadership, students are asked which of the two boys most closely represents the ideal leader suggested by their list.

Accuse and deny

The class is divided into two: accusers and deniers. Accusers have to think of as many different statements or questions as they can, which accuse the deniers of murdering Simon. Deniers have to think of as many statements as possible to avoid admitting personal responsibility.

After a set time for preparation, say ten minutes, the class is put into pairs in two circles facing each other. Accusations and denials begin. When the teacher claps once, accusers rotate clockwise and interaction recommences. When the teacher claps twice, deniers rotate anticlockwise one space.

Examples of possible accusations...	*and denials...*
Admit your guilt, murderer!	I was on the outside all the time.
You are responsible for Simon's death.	I was in a dream.
But you did murder him, even if you were in a dream.	I wasn't in my right mind.
You are a murderer, aren't you?	It wasn't me, honestly.
You are guilty, you can't deny it.	I had nothing to do with it.
You are a cold-blooded murderer.	It was dark.
Why did you do it?	I was frightened.
We know you were one of the murderers.	I couldn't see what I was doing, could I?

Part C   *Working with a complete text*

Character fantasy

Worksheet 40 could be done as homework and followed by class discussion.

Assume that the boys are now grown up. For each category in the grid below insert an appropriate entry based on what you imagine might be the choice of each character.

	Job	Type of car	Favourite holiday	Favourite colour	Favourite drink	Favourite food
Ralph						
Jack						
Piggy						

Worksheet 40

Chapter XI   Castle Rock (pages 187–201)

This intensely dramatic chapter reaches a climax in the story. Ralph and Piggy try to retrieve Piggy's glasses but Jack and his group are in no mood for compromise. Piggy is killed by a large falling boulder, the conch is shattered, the twins are captured and Ralph runs off in terror.

If students have been drawn into the fiction, there may be a case for not breaking the spell by too many activities, but simply allowing the class to read or listen to the uninterrupted text. A good place to start class listening of the chapter would be page 193, when the two groups of boys confront each other. Here, more than ever, it is difficult to prescribe set pages for home reading as many students will want to read on and find out what happens. The listening time in class would then aim to provide a revisiting of the text, enrichment, not just repetition.

The following activities work well when the chapter has been read.

Diplomacy

This is a fantasy activity which involves rewriting part of the chapter or adapting it for role play.

In this chapter, Ralph's appeal to Jack's humanitarian instincts fails; disaster ensues. Perhaps Ralph needed to use a little more diplomacy and guile? What could Ralph have done and said which might have produced compromise or a peaceful end to his mission?

In groups, students try to think of as many diplomatic solutions as possible. They are then asked to script the dialogue (together, or as homework) to be acted out later. In classes where it would be appropriate, students can improvise a role play to be presented in front of other groups. In each case, the class tries to imagine Jack's response.

This is often a useful exercise because classes sense that any attempt at diplomacy would be rejected by Jack at this point in the story, and this can lead to insights into the nature of the inevitable quality that is part of tragedy. Alternatively, some groups are eager to accept any diplomatic overtures, to avert the terrible happenings at the end of the chapter. Again, drawing this response into the open has the effect of sharpening learners' awareness of the implications of events in this part of the novel.

Which is better?

At the moment of greatest crisis between Jack's and Ralph's groups, Piggy three times shouts out a question to the 'savage' band inside their fortress of Castle Rock:

'Which is better – to be a pack of painted niggers like you are, or to be sensible like Ralph is?'
'Which is better – to have rules and agree, or to hunt and kill?'
'Which is better, law and rescue, or hunting and breaking things up?'

At the end of chapter XI, with classes which enjoy quite structured oral activities, a debate can be planned on the issue of social order which underpins these questions. The motion is: 'This class agrees that law and order must be the first priority in any civilised society.'

In the first step, every member of the class tries to think of as many arguments as possible for or against. These are noted down by a secretary for each side, on the board or in individual notebooks.

Step two is preparation of the speaking team. This can be done during the lesson or as an out of class activity, as appropriate. Each side is represented by a team of three people – two to argue their side of the debate, the third to cope with rebuttal of their opponent's arguments.

Step three is the debate itself, with a student presiding if at all possible. The two representatives from each team speak in turn, for one or two minutes, then the third member rebuts. The floor is then open to questions.

The final stage is a general vote to carry the motion or defeat it.

Echoes

This simple activity attempts to make readers aware of patterning in the novel (see Worksheet 41). It is best done as group work in class, so that students can help each other with the task of tracking down echoes. The teacher circulates and gives clues if necessary.

In chapter XI of *Lord of the Flies*, there are some words, some expressions and some events which echo others that were in previous parts of the novel. Look at this list. Can you remember or find where these occurred before? Is there any difference now in what each of them means or implies?

Roger throwing stones
heaving a large rock down
painted faces
'the storm of sound'
'waxy'
'playing the game'
'you're acting like a crowd of kids'
'a sense of delirious abandonment'
'a sense of *power* began to *pulse* in (his) body'

Worksheet 41

Chapter XII Cry of the hunters (pages 202–23)

The violence of the band of 'savages' reaches its climax as they hunt the wounded and terrified Ralph through the island, setting fire to the forest in which he is hiding to force him out into the open. Finally, Ralph bursts out on to the beach, where he and his pursuers are confronted by a rescue party that has just landed – attracted, ironically enough, by the smoke from the fire.

This is a fairly long but suspenseful chapter, whose dramatic quality easily carries the reader along. Simple class listening (accompanied, perhaps, by noting down of impressions, or doodles as described for chapter IX) is very suitable for the extremely vivid description of the chase (pages 215–20). The following activities are for use after the chapter has been read.

Point of no return

This activity, very appropriate as a follow-up to *Lord of the Flies*, is described in Chapter 6 (see p. 82).

What if?

Students are asked to note down quickly their response to the following question: Imagine that the plane had deposited a group of girls on the island. Would the outcome have been different? Quickly jot down whatever possible differences come into your mind.

Feedback and comparison of answers is revealing of students' ideas about the causes of the tragedy on the island, and their opinions on male/female stereotypes.

Highlights

This is a variation on the activity described in Chapter 6. Here, learners are asked to choose the book's most powerful pictures, in this way: they describe the six mental snapshots they would choose for a large poster to advertise the film of the book. This can be done as a group activity. In teams of six, learners decide upon the six most powerful 'pictures' in the book. Each then has the task of writing the description of one of these images (a paragraph, plus title).

Results are displayed so that the pictures described can be compared.

Inquest on board ship

This activity is in three parts.

First part: a general brainstorming session with the whole class. Imagine that on the way home, the Chief Officer decides to investigate what really happened on the island. What questions would he need to ask? What answers would be given by Ralph? Jack? Roger? Sam 'n Eric? One of the little boys? It is useful to jot down the questions and answers, either on the board or in a notebook.

Second part: role play/improvisation. Roles are distributed: the presiding officer, his panel of inquiry, five boys. With the help of the recorded questions and answers, they enact the inquest scene.

Third part: the verdict. This is a simulation. The class is divided into groups or four or five: these are now the presiding officer and his panel of inquiry. They have just witnessed the questioning of the five boys, and their task is now to arrive at a verdict, and to write a report on the incident which includes recommendations for the treatment of the boys when they return to England. (The report can be discussed in the group and written then, or done later as an individual task.)

The book on a postcard

Students distil their impressions of the novel in exactly 50 words (see Figure 15).

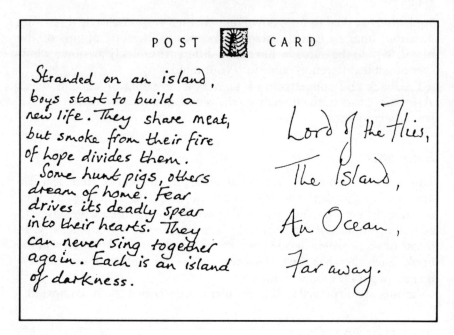

POST   CARD

Stranded on an island, boys start to build a new life. They share meat, but smoke from their fire of hope divides them. Some hunt pigs, others dream of home. Fear drives its deadly spear into their hearts. They can never sing together again. Each is an island of darkness.

Lord of the Flies,
The Island,
An Ocean,
Far away.

Figure 15

8 Plays

Most of the activities discussed in previous chapters can be adapted to plays as well as other genres. An added element in presenting a play, however, is its particular dramatic quality, which it is important to bring out as much as possible in the classroom. Being able to take students to a performance is obviously a great help, as are films or videos. Many plays are available on records or cassettes nowadays, especially suitable for listening exercises; in the absence of curriculum or exam constraints, this would certainly be a factor in choosing a play to read with a class.

With groups that respond well to drama activities, putting on one scene, or a short play, can be both enjoyable and rewarding. Many students love planning costumes, sets, props, lights, and so on. When full-scale staging is not feasible, a prepared reading of a previously studied scene, at the front of the class and with a few props, can also be fruitful. What is not so successful, in our opinion, is asking a student to read aloud an unseen or minimally prepared role. Working in a foreign language, the learner usually has difficulty combining the simultaneous demands of comprehension and language production. In fact, good play reading is not really all that easy, even in one's own language. That is why we prefer other kinds of activities to help students deepen their understanding of the text and the dramatic situation, followed by listening periods in class, or, if cassettes are available, in the language laboratory or at home.

In this chapter we look more closely at ways of working through a whole play, or rather, two very different plays. Until now, on the whole, we have chosen to illustrate our ideas through modern texts, for the opportunities they offer both of useful language transfer and of insights into contemporary social, political or cultural aspects. But modern works, of course, rest upon and interact with a whole line of predecessors. And many students, especially if they are intending to go on to literary studies, are keen to master some of the classics they have heard about. We have therefore chosen as our example for ways of working with a complete long play, Shakespeare's *Romeo and Juliet*. We have found it accessible and interesting for pre-university classes. Its theme of love in a setting torn by civil strife is universal and still very poignant today. It is a play that is often produced, so that we have been able to take students to performances, or to show them the very beautiful Zeffirelli film.

Although to avoid repetition we do not go through the play in the same detail as we have done for *Lord of the Flies*, we hope that these ideas will stimulate interest and help learners overcome the barriers posed by language. With secondary school pupils or non-specialist adult classes in mind, we have aimed at comprehension and enjoyment first and foremost. The various activities should also help students to a better understanding of dramatic structure, development of character, the mechanisms of tragedy, and so on. But we have not gone into questions of background: Shakespeare's life, the Elizabethan period and its theatre; nor into more scholarly issues regarding the establishing of the text. We have concentrated above all on getting classes to feel the immediacy and the pathos of the central theme, as well as the power of the poetry.

These two aims have also underpinned our work with the language of the play. Certainly, students have to be helped with sixteenth-century idioms and structures, and with the extraordinarily rich, compact expression of complex concepts. Here as elsewhere, though, we have encouraged learners to read for gist and comprehension, to feel they can appreciate a scene even if they do not understand every single thing about it.

For contrast, we then look at a very brief modern American play, Edward Albee's *The Sandbox*, where the language presents very few problems but where students may have to be helped to see and appreciate the play's full dramatic import.

Romeo and Juliet by William Shakespeare*

Feud for thought

The underpinning to the well-known tragedy of the two young lovers is the bitter family feud between the Montagues and Capulets which permeates the atmosphere in the city of Verona, and creates an ominous tension in the play. There is no indication in Shakespeare's text of the origin of the feud – it is just a fact.

The following warm-up activity aims to draw a class into the play's setting by asking them to speculate about the origins of the inter-family strife. These are the stages in the activity:

1. Before the students arrive for their lesson, the teacher arranges the desks/chairs into two separate clusters in two different corners of the classroom.
2. When the students enter the room, the teacher asks them to sit down without disturbing the desks/chairs. He or she then asks them to

---

* References are to the Cambridge University Press edition of *Romeo and Juliet*, edited by G. Blakemore Evans, published in paperback 1984.

speculate about what is going on. What might the two 'camps' signify? Speculation is fed by informing the students that the classroom is a city, and that they are some of its inhabitants.

3. Once it has been established that the two groups are families separated by an ancient feud, the teacher announces (if this has not already been guessed) that one family has the name Montague, while the other group are Capulets. The city is Verona in Italy.

4. Next, the teacher asks each family to brainstorm and discuss possible causes of the feud. What event(s) started it all off? A sheet of ideas can be supplied to classes in greater need of support.

Possible causes of the feud between Montagues and Capulets
An unsolved murder.
A theft of valuable jewellery.
One of the families discredited the other by exposing corruption.
An extra-marital affair between a Montague and a Capulet which ended in the suicide of one of the lovers.
Competition for political and economic power in Verona.
One of the families spread a rumour that the other family was cheating the Catholic church of money.

5. After each family group has discussed the origin of the feud and agreed upon their story (or stories), the two families are asked to put their desks/chairs into two lines facing each other.

    The teacher asks the families to begin to accuse each other of starting the feud and to explain the original situation. Accusations should be met by angry denials and the teacher should try to fuel the animosity between the two groups without taking sides.

6. After accusations and denials have been traded, the teacher says that he or she wants the two families to retain their identities while the play is being studied. Thus, for any play reading or enactment of scenes, Capulets will be drawn from the Capulet family and Montagues from the Montague family. Similarly, if an activity like sculpting (see p. 81) is undertaken, characters will be drawn from the appropriate camps.

Wordplay/Swordplay

The very first scene of *Romeo and Juliet* fairly bristles with puns and plays on words, and this can sometimes be rather discouraging for foreign students about to tackle the play. If warm-up activities have sensitised the class to the mood of a city deeply torn by internal strife, however, it will be easier for students to see how the language actually articulates the feud itself. Like the swordplay that follows them, these initial exchanges are full of parry and thrust. The two servants enter with their swords drawn and their wits fully sharpened. Bawdy and aggressive, their language

165

builds up a highly charged atmosphere. One word sparks off another: a verbal equivalent to their barely restrained eagerness for the fray.

The following activity is a way of helping students to see how much is compressed into these apparently frivolous exchanges, designed at one level to secure the attention of the audience. It also helps clarify the dynamics of this first scene. In the first stage, the activity is done by the class as a whole. Students are given the following statements, which represent the gist, in modern English, of the first six exchanges:

1. We'll not carry coals.
2. We're not colliers.
3. If we're 'in choler' (angry) we'll draw our swords.
4. We'll draw our necks out of the collar.
5. I strike quickly when I'm moved.
6. But you're not easily moved to strike.

Students are also given the following set of definitions (worksheet, or board):

coals = a form of fuel
carry coals = a low, menial task

colliers = coal-miners
colliers = a term of abuse (for the Elizabethan audience)

choler = anger (a word no longer used in modern English)

collar = a yoke (symbol of having to work hard under a master)
collar = a hangman's noose

moved = made to feel a strong emotion, in this case anger
moved = motivated, given a reason to do something

The task is now to construct a diagram which shows how each statement relates to the others, and what its effect is (that is, whether it is intended as an aggressive statement but with no particular target, or as a particular threat against the Capulets, or used to tease each other or, in later lines, to make bawdy jokes).

In Figure 16, worked out on a white board, the statements were placed within boxes that were colour-coded for effect (black for generally aggressive, red for teasing). Links between the statements were indicated by lines:

⟶ an arrow = a connection in the meaning of the words
∿∿∿ a wavy line = a connection in sound (two words sound alike)
═══ a double line = explanation of a term or expression

In the second stage of the activity, the class is divided into four groups. Two of these are given the next six exchanges in Scene 1, the other two are given the following six. Appropriate definitions are also given, or more advanced classes might be asked to find these themselves, in their dic-

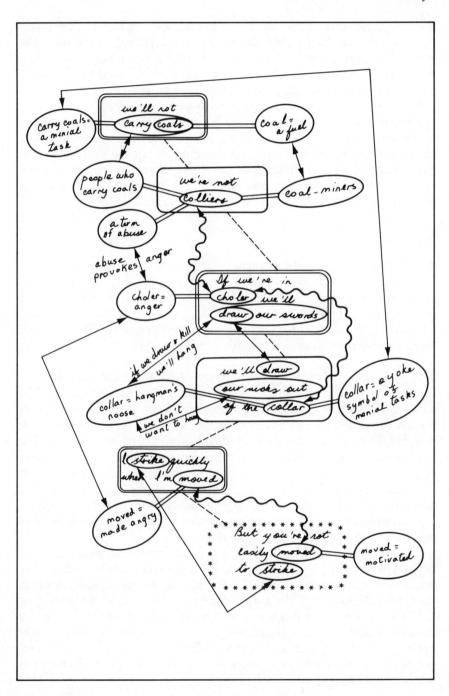

Figure 16

tionary or glossary. Each group designs a diagram for its exchanges, either following the pattern already set, or devising a new one. The finished diagrams are compared and discussed, or posted up for class members to compare at their leisure. A further task could be to join the three series in a master diagram, perhaps on a large wall chart.

It will be seen that this is a means of externalising a quite conventional analysis of the text. The fact that students are given the gist, and a set of meanings, does however reduce problems of simple comprehension, allowing learners to concentrate on the dynamics of the exchanges. The visual element usually makes it easier for students to grasp the textual analysis, while they on the whole enjoy the challenge of finding a way of representing quite complex relationships in a graphic manner.

A visual snowball

With a play that carries the linguistic richness and complexity that *Romeo and Juliet* does, it becomes vital to keep the spirit of the story alive by visual means. Clearly the excellent video versions of the play could be used alongside the reading of the text, but many language learning situations do not include video facilities, and in any case it is difficult to hire video-cassettes for extended periods of time, and they are expensive to buy.

In pairs, within their family groups, the Montagues and Capulets have the task of producing a simple visual presentation for each scene. The basic visual elements should suggest the main events or the atmosphere in a particular scene. Short quotations can be woven into each design. If possible, learners should be supplied with poster card and felt pens; but the teacher should stress that simple designs are often the most striking, and that artistic expertise is not the main requirement. The fact of working with someone else also helps reduce the anxiety some students feel about their ability to draw. Each pair in turn is responsible for adding a representation to depict one scene, and pairs are likely to have more than one go, as there are 24 scenes in the play.

As each scene design is completed, it can either be displayed on a Montague wall or a Capulet wall, as appropriate; or scenes as they accumulate are put into a family folder until the end of the play, at which point they are exchanged as a sign of the end of the classroom feud.

When the entire play has been read, the visual snowball can be used for revision purposes. Each scene design cues the students' memories of events, atmosphere, and language. In addition, the quotes on each visual can be used as the basis for a quotes team quiz. Figure 17 shows how this activity could be started.

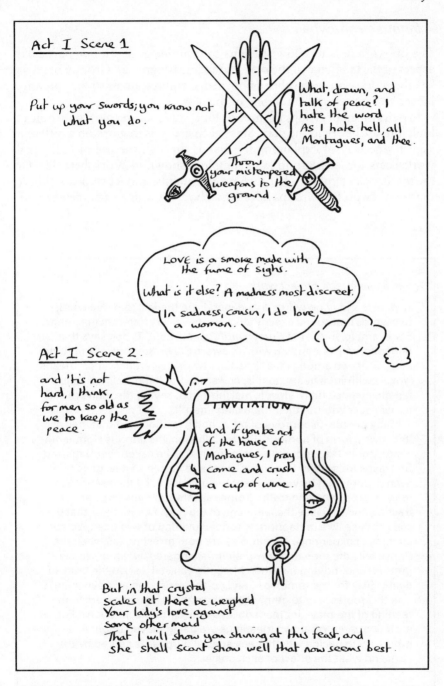

Figure 17

A language snowball

The object here is to allow students to examine in depth one particular aspect of the language of the play, as reading progresses. Groupwork also lets them draw on each other's knowledge and resources so that they are helped to a better understanding of the play.

In pairs or small groups of three or four, students are given one topic to look into as they read the play. Since each group is to work on a different aspect, one way of explaining the task is through the use of individual worksheets for each group (an example is shown in Worksheet 42). Or the teacher can explain what each project entails, and let students choose the one they prefer. Groups have a notebook in which each member can

---

Puns – language project work

A 'pun' is a play on words that depends on the fact that one word, or two words that sound exactly alike, can have very different meanings. For example, in Act I of *Romeo and Juliet* (I.1.65), Tybalt says that Benvolio, who is standing with his sword drawn amongst the fighting men, is 'drawn among these heartless hinds'. 'Heartless hinds' means 'yokels without a heart', that is, cowardly. But 'hinds' also means a female deer, so that Tybalt is making a pun, saying the men are like female deer without their male deer ('hart').

Many people disapprove of puns, and it is often said that they are 'the lowest form of humour'. Doctor Johnson, the famous eighteenth-century critic, thought puns (or 'quibbles' as he called them) marred Shakespeare's style: 'A quibble, poor and barren as it is, gave him such delight, that he was content to purchase it, by the sacrifice of reason, propriety, and truth'. Some readers still think puns are distracting and trivialise the language of the play. Others think that they can produce, like metaphors, a sudden overlap of two unexpected spheres of experience so that they are both arresting (as when the Prince tells the men to throw their 'mistempered' weapons to the ground) and moving (as when Mercutio can still jest on the brink of death: 'Ask for me tomorrow, and you shall find me a 'grave' man'.).

In this project, try to gather as many puns as you can from your reading of the play. Jot them down in your group's notebook. For each one, state what two meanings are being played upon. As a group, try to decide whether any special purpose is served by the pun, and what the effect of each one is.

Worksheet 42

jot examples noticed as they read, as well as their thoughts and comments upon them.

Topics could include: puns; paradoxes; various kinds of imagery – of light and darkness, of flowers, of birds and animals, of celestial bodies and the spheres, imagery used to foreshadow the tragic outcome; rhetorical questions; use of ribald language; the language of violence; language that has a performative aspect: that is, of politeness, command, mockery, etc.; epithets and images used to delineate old/young or love/hate.

One effective way of ensuring that each group's work produces feedback for the whole class is to ask the groups to prepare a poster or wall chart to display the results of its project. When the entire play has been read, a date is set for completion, followed by a poster exhibition in the classroom, hallway or common room. The requirement for a visual presentation can tap quite considerable creative resources in many students, and it makes the whole endeavour more memorable.

For classes preparing exams, the material gathered during the project can be used to support the writing of an essay on any of the particular points studied, or on the language of the play as a whole.

The Prince's speech

Worksheet 43 is a home reading worksheet for Act I Scene 1.

≫→

The Prince of Verona arrives while the Capulets and the Montagues are fighting. He stops them and says he will no longer tolerate such behaviour in his city. Read the following statements. Some of them have a meaning that is the *same* as, or is *similar* to, the Prince's. Mark these S. Others have a *different* meaning. Mark these D, and then rewrite the sentences so that they reproduce accurately what the Prince says.

S	D	
		1. You are citizens who do not obey laws; you shatter our peace and shed your neighbours' blood.
		2. I am glad you are willing to listen to me at last.
		3. You fighting men are like beasts.
		4. The only way you have of calming your anger is through bloodshed.
		5. Put down your weapons and listen to me, or you will suffer torture.
		6. I am so angry with your fighting that I intend to move away from this city.
		7. This is the second time that Capulets and Montagues have fought in the streets of our city.
		8. These brawls have great and serious causes.
		9. You have forced ordinary citizens to take up arms to stop your fights.
		10. If any of you ever fight again, you will be banished.
		11. I order everyone to leave. If anyone remains, he will be put to death.
		12. Old Capulet and Old Montague must both come with me now to the place of judgment where I shall pass sentence upon them.

Worksheet 43

Complete the summary

The summary in Worksheet 44 refers to the last part of Act I Scene 1 and could be done as homework.

Read from the end of the Prince's speech (I.1.104) to the end of Scene 1. Then complete the following sentences so that they form a summary of this part of the play.

After the Prince has left, Old Montague asks his nephew Benvolio to tell him .... Benvolio explains. Lady Capulet is glad that her son was not in the fight but she wonders where Romeo is. Benvolio says that he met Romeo that morning, when both he and his cousin .... Benvolio did not speak to Romeo then because .... Old Montague explains that Romeo has developed the habit of going out, before dawn each day, to weep and sigh. When the sun rises Romeo .... His father cannot understand why Romeo is behaving in this way. He would like to find out, so that .... Benvolio promises to try .... The Montagues leave, and Romeo appears. His cousin asks him why he is so sad. Romeo answers that although he is in love, ... Benvolio wants to know who the loved one is. But Romeo will only say that it is someone who has sworn to .... Benvolio advises Romeo to forget her and to look at .... Romeo protests that .... The two young men leave.

Worksheet 44

The language of love

These are activities designed to sensitise students to one area of language within the play: the language of love, and the concepts and conventions that underlie it.

In order to allow students better to appreciate particular characteristics of the Shakespearean universe, it is useful to look first at what 'love' means and how it is expressed in our modern world, both in contemporary English and, for monolingual groups, in their own culture. A popular way of doing this with adolescents or young adults is through an analysis of pop songs.

The class is divided into small groups. Each chooses a different song to examine (an English-language one if possible – many are familiar to students; or a song in their own language, to be analysed in English). Worksheet 45 can be used.

Groups then compare notes and try to establish an overall 'profile' of the attitudes to love and to lovers implicit in the songs, and of the kind of language used to convey them. The profile is retained for later comparison with the play.

An alternative way of trying to assess contemporary views of love and its language is through the use of a questionnaire such as the one illustrated in Worksheet 46. Students are each provided with several copies of it, one to answer themselves. Then, for homework, they ask other people for their answers, preferably people of different age groups from their own. If this can be done in English (for example, by questioning language assistants or other English speakers in the school or town), valuable language practice can be gained, and students will often learn many new terms and expressions.

In situations where this is impossible, students can ask questions in their L1, then translate the answers on to the form.

Once again, pooling of results and discussion are both very important.

Write notes on the lyrics of the song you have chosen, answering the following questions.

1. What is 'love' like, according to this song? Choose a spot on the continuum. Is it . . .

    | supremely important | relatively unimportant |

    | marvellous, full of joy | terrible, painful |

    | lasting | ephemeral |

    what else?..

2. Words that describe love (does the song have any images or comparisons?):.....................................
3. Words that describe the loved one (images? comparisons?):

    ....
4. If you're in love, according to the song:.............................
    How do you behave?.............................
    How do you feel?.............................
    How does the person who is loved behave/feel?.............................

Worksheet 45

Answer the following questions about the nature of love.

1. Which of the following statements comes closest to your idea of what love is? (Tick one, or more.)
   ☐ Love is a paradise.
   ☐ Love is hell.
   ☐ Love is a disease.
   ☐ Love is a state of madness.
   ☐ Love is a religion.
   ☐ Love is an all-consuming fire.
   ☐ Love is a kind of warfare.
   ☐ Love is an ephemeral nonsense.
   ☐ Love is ....

2. How important, how valuable is it for you? Which of the following sentences comes closest to your opinion?
   ☐ The most important thing, the only valuable thing in the world.
   ☐ A good thing, but not the only good thing in the world.
   ☐ A mixed blessing.
   ☐ A disaster: it always ends in tragedy.
   ☐ A pleasant illusion, cloaking the reality of sex.
   ☐ An unpleasant illusion, distorting our idea of relations between the sexes.

3. If you love someone, what would you be most likely to compare him or her to?
   ☐ a flower: ....
   ☐ a bird: ....
   ☐ an animal: ....
   ☐ a celestial body: ....
   ☐ a part of nature: ....
   ☐ something else: ....

4. If a man loves a woman, this is how he behaves:
   ☐ Writes poems to her.
   ☐ Sends her flowers and gifts.
   ☐ Weeps and sighs if she doesn't respond.
   ☐ Acts in a manly, masterful way.
   ☐ Conceals his love.
   ☐ ....

5. If a woman loves a man, this is how she behaves:
   ☐ Gives him gifts.
   ☐ Pretends to love someone else.
   ☐ Conceals her love.
   ☐ Tells him about it.
   ☐ Sighs and weeps if he doesn't pay attention to her.
   ☐ ....

This is best done in groups in the next class lesson: each group compiles a list of its results and outlines the kind of attitudes and the kind of language which emerge from their survey.

The next step is to turn to the play. When we first meet Romeo (I.1.159) he is convinced that he is deeply in love with Rosaline. He is a conventional lover, behaving and talking in the way then expected of lovers. It is important for students to understand these conventions, so that any later change in language or behaviour can be appreciated. This kind of comprehension is the aim of the following activity.

The class together examines two short scenes in which Romeo appears before he meets Juliet. This can be done by listening to a recording, or to the teacher's reading, with brief elucidation of any major difficulties in the text. They are then, in groups, given Worksheet 47, which gathers, under six categories, the pronouncements on love made by Romeo and Benvolio. Each group decides what view of love is being proposed in each case. After feedback and discussion of their conclusions, students are asked to compare the attitudes and language of the two young men in the play with the kind of language and concepts that emerged from their previous inquiry into modern-day stances. Each group is given the task of drawing out from the comparison any specific aspects that seem to be particular to the play and its time span, whether these relate to ideas, words, images or opinions.

The Petrarchan Lover's code

This is a good point in the play for the activity 'Codes', described in Chapter 5 (see p. 73). Romeo, at the beginning of the play, conforms to the stereotype of an ideal courtly lover. In fact, Mercutio teases him about it, saying that Romeo is trying to outdo the famous love poet Petrarch himself, by using his kind of poetic language and imagery (his 'numbers'): 'Now is he for the numbers that Petrarch flowed in. Laura to his lady was a kitchen wench . . . ' (II.4.38).

From the material gathered on their worksheet, and from their discussions, students should now be in a position to write 'Rules of feeling and behaviour' for such a lover.

This acts as a consolidation for the extended investigation into the language of love that students have been engaged upon. A further follow-up activity, designed to compare Romeo's language before and after he meets Juliet, is described after the classroom activity of role play and discussion which is outlined next.

Love at first sight

In Act I Scene 5, Romeo and Juliet meet for the first time and express their

Read the two scenes in which Romeo and Benvolio talk about Romeo's love (I.1.160–237 and I.2.45–102). Here are some of the things that the two young men say about love and the experience of being in love. The phrases have been grouped together in six categories. Your task is to decide together whether a certain definition of love emerges from each set of phrases, and write an appropriate heading. The first one has been done for you.

Love is . . .
a state full of paradoxes

(*Love is:*)
heavy lightness
serious vanity
bright smoke
cold fire
sick health
still-waking sleep

Love is . . .
....

sad hours seem
   long
Griefs of mine own
   lie heavy in my
   breast
(*love is:*) a sea
   nourished with
   lovers' tears
Shall I groan and
   tell thee?
In sadness, cousin,
   I do love a woman

Love is . . .
....

Alas that love, so
   gentle in his view
Should be so tyran-
   nous and rough in
   proof!
She will not stay the
   siege of loving
   terms
Nor bide
   th'encounter of
   assailing eyes
She'll not be hit with
   Cupid's arrow

Love is . . .
....

a madness most
   discreet
Not mad but bound
   more than a mad-
   man is
Shut up in prison,
   kept without my
   food
Whipped and
   tormented

Love is . . .
....

Bid a sick man in sad-
   ness make his will
One pain is
   lessened by
   another's anguish
One desperate grief
   cures with
   another's languish
Take thou some
   new infection to
   thy eye
a choking gall

Love is . . .
....

When the devout
   religion of mine
   eye
Maintains such
   falsehood, then
   turn tears to fires
Transparent
   heretics, be burnt
   for liars

Worksheet 47

immediate love for each other in the form of a sonnet which culminates in a kiss. The following discussion and role-play activity precedes the reading of this scene and sets the mood for it.

Students are paired off (one boy and one girl, if possible) and are asked to plan a short scene in which a boy and a girl meet for the first time and are strongly attracted to each other. The teacher offers a choice of situations in which the encounter can take place – a train journey, a dance, a party, a bus stop, a park, on holiday, for example. A maximum length of fourteen lines of dialogue is set but students are free to decide which of the lovers does what proportion of the talking.

The scene is then written, with the teacher assisting as necessary. When any two pairs are ready, each pair in turn performs its scene for the other. The teacher circulates and selects pairs to perform their scenes for the whole class. The language used in the scenes is discussed. Is it romantic? Does it contain any metaphor? What differences are there between the man's and the woman's language? Does the scene involve any physical contact, like a kiss? Do actions speak louder than words?

Before and after

After the classroom warm-up just described, students, having now invested something of themselves in the theme of love at first sight, read or listen to Act I Scene 5, in which Romeo and Juliet first meet at the Capulets' ball. With the help of a worksheet (Worksheet 48) they make notes on the language Romeo uses both before and after he meets Juliet.

When the completed worksheets are compared and discussed after this activity, or in the next class lesson, the feelings expressed by Romeo, as well as the language he uses, are compared to those noted in the earlier exercise done in class (Worksheet 47).

Romeo and Old Capulet

On discovering that Romeo, a Montague, is present at his masquerade, Old Capulet does not have him thrown out. He seems to have heard good reports of Romeo and stops the angry Tybalt from attacking Romeo and breaking up the party. Tragic events move so quickly thereafter that Romeo never has the opportunity of trying to persuade Old Capulet that a marriage between himself and Juliet would be an admirable way of healing their family quarrels. However, this situation which never occurs provides the basis for a fantasy writing activity.

Students are asked to imagine a meeting between Romeo and Old Capulet. Would Capulet receive Romeo politely or angrily? Would Romeo, with all his youthful charm, be able to persuade the old man? Would the ancient family feud sour their encounter and cause it to end bitterly?

The teacher can also try to elicit the sort of language that might emerge (nowadays) in the course of such a conversation. For example 'I'd like to

Listen to Act I Scene 5 in which Romeo and Juliet first meet. Make notes about the way Romeo expresses his new love, using the following headings.

	Words/expressions	*Metaphors/images*
The way Romeo refers to his new love.		
The way he talks of himself as a lover.		
What he says of love itself.		

Are any of the expressions or metaphors noted above the *same* as ones already expressed by Romeo or Benvolio in the previous scenes? Mark them S.
What is the effect of these 'echoes'?
☐ ironical
☐ emphasises continuity in Romeo's character
☐ emphasises the short space of time between his loves
☐ (other?) ....

Compare the language and imagery noted above with Worksheet 47.
Is one set:
☐ more concrete than the other?
☐ more 'flowery' than the other?
☐ more convincing?
☐ focussed more on the experience of love?
☐ focussed more on the loved one?
What other differences can you see between them? ....

Worksheet 48

ask your permission to marry Juliet / to ask for Juliet's hand in marriage'; 'It's out of the question. No Montague will ever marry a daughter of mine', etc.

When the preparatory phase has been completed, the conversation can be written, either as homework, or more enjoyably, using the technique in which the class sits in a circle and the dialogues rotate, first left and then right, thus enabling each student to write, alternately, as Romeo and as

Capulet, and to produce a different conversation with the students on either side of him or her. (This is described on p. 59.)

The balcony scene

Worksheet 49, which is a jumbled summary, accompanies home or class reading of the balcony scene (II.2).

Read the balcony scene (Act II Scene 2). Then try to rewrite the following summary sentences, in paragraph form, in the correct sequence.

a) Romeo at last speaks and they share the distress of the feud between their families.
b) Juliet warns him of the dangers should he be discovered in the garden.
c) After another brief absence, Juliet comes back and they arrange a time for Juliet's messenger to be sent to him the following day.
d) From a hidden position, he listens to Juliet.
e) With the approach of dawn, they reluctantly part.
f) Romeo steals into Juliet's garden without being seen.
g) He hears her declaring her love for him and her sadness that family rivalries should come between them.
h) These worries are interrupted by the nurse's call, at which point Juliet says she will be back in a few minutes.
i) On her return, Juliet asks Romeo to send word the next day, if he intends to marry her.
j) When she asks Romeo if he loves her, he openly declares his great love, but Juliet is worried by the suddenness of their strong feelings for each other.

Are there any *important* events or declarations which are in the scene but not in this summary? Write them down if you think there are, and add them to your summary.

Worksheet 49

Answers: f, d, g, a, b, j, h, i, c, e

The balcony scene: a follow-up listening activity

This is a classroom activity to deepen students' understanding and appreciation of the balcony scene. Having mastered gist through home reading and the accompanying worksheet, students now listen to a recording of Act II Scene 2. (A video, if available, can be used in the same way.) The teacher plays the recording through without stopping. At the end, he or she asks students to jot down quickly, in one or two sentences, a description of the part they liked best, or found most memorable or most moving. Students then get together in pairs to compare notes and explain why they made their particular choice.

Each pair is then given its own specific task to carry out as they listen a second time to the scene. One is responsible for making notes about Juliet, the other about Romeo. Here are some examples of task slips that different pairs might be given (14 task slips, one for each pair in a class of 28):

1. Jot down any references to the sun made by Romeo.
   Jot down any references to the sun made by Juliet.
2. Jot down any references to the moon made by Romeo.
   Jot down any references to the moon made by Juliet.
3. Jot down things said which show Romeo being bold.
   Jot down things said which show Juliet being bold.
4. Jot down things said which show Romeo being reticent.
   Jot down things said which show Juliet being reticent.
5. Jot down religious imagery used by Romeo.
   Jot down religious imagery used by Juliet.
6. Jot down expressions of fear or apprehension spoken by Romeo.
   Jot down expressions of fear or apprehension spoken by Juliet.
7. Jot down any very simple, straightforward statement made by Romeo.
   Jot down any very simple, straightforward statement made by Juliet.
8. Jot down questions asked by Romeo.
   Jot down questions asked by Juliet.
   Mark rhetorical questions R (questions where the speaker doesn't really
   want or expect an answer).
9. Jot down any metaphors or comparisons from nature, that is, flowers,
   birds, etc. in Romeo's speeches.
   Jot down any metaphors or comparisons from nature in Juliet's speeches.
10. Jot down references to family made by Romeo.
    Jot down references to family made by Juliet.
11. Jot down references to marriage made by Romeo.
    Jot down references to marriage made by Juliet.
12. Jot down any concrete plans for the immediate future expressed by
    Romeo.
    Jot down any concrete plans for the immediate future expressed by Juliet.
13. Jot down any expression of concern about safety expressed by Romeo.
    Jot down any expression of concern about safety expressed by Juliet.
14. Jot down wishes expressed by Romeo.
    Jot down wishes expressed by Juliet.

The recording is played with a few pauses to allow students to take notes. When this has been done, students are given a series of questions on a

Answer the following questions, supporting your answer in each
case with a quotation from the 'balcony scene' (II.2). If you haven't got
an appropriate quotation, ask a classmate.

Which of the two lovers:
is more practical?   Romeo/Juliet
Quotation: ....

is more imaginative?   Romeo/Juliet
Quotation: ....

is more attached to his/her family?   Romeo/Juliet
Quotation: ....

is more extravagant in speech?   Romeo/Juliet
Quotation: ....

is more fearful of the consequences of their love?   Romeo/Juliet
Quotation: ....

is more confident?   Romeo/Juliet
Quotation: ....

is more forceful?   Romeo/Juliet
Quotation: ....

is more realistic?   Romeo/Juliet
Quotation: ....

is more clear-sighted?   Romeo/Juliet
Quotation: ....

Worksheet 50

worksheet (see Worksheet 50). They must provide answers supported by
quotations from the play. Each pair will already have gathered material
appropriate for one or other of the questions. The pairs must now consult
one another and, by pooling their resources, find a quotation to support
their opinion on each question.

Angel's advocates

In Act III Scene 1, trouble is brewing once more between Montagues and
Capulets. A fight is imminent between Tybalt and Mercutio.

As a first step, students read the scene silently, to get a basic understanding of it. The class is then divided into two groups. One group, of

four to 12 students, consists of the characters in this scene. They choose roles and rehearse their reading of the scene.

The remaining students in the class are asked to imagine that they can travel through time and be transported into the play. They choose a point somewhere between lines 34 and 131, where they are to appear and try to keep the peace. Each student can deliver one speech to achieve this aim.

Before the time travel takes place, students, in pairs, brainstorm to build a range of arguments they can use in their speeches. They then individually write the speeches, with the teacher helping as necessary.

The next stage involves a dramatic performance of Act III Scene 1. Before the scene commences, the teacher nominates the 'time-travelling angels' who will stand up during the scene, at their chosen point, and deliver their speeches. As each interruption occurs, the students with the official roles in the scene are instructed to 'freeze' while each angel's speech is being delivered, then to continue the scene.

To end the session, the teacher and students discuss the impact of the interruptions and consider whether anything could have prevented the two deaths in that scene.

Then and now

Worksheet 51 is a matching activity to help students understand Act III Scene 3, as they read it on their own.

≫→

Match each of the speeches from *Romeo and Juliet* (III.3) on the left with the modern colloquial expression which is nearest to its meaning.

[3.3] *Enter* FRIAR [LAWRENCE].

FRIAR LAWRENCE

Romeo, come forth, come forth, thou fearful man:
Affliction is enamoured of thy parts,
And thou art wedded to calamity.

> You're banished from Verona, but there are lots of other places to live.

[*Enter*] ROMEO.

ROMEO Father, what news? What is the Prince's doom?
What sorrow craves acquaintance at my hand,
That I yet know not?

FRIAR LAWRENCE   Too familiar
Is my dear son with such sour company!
I bring thee tidings of the Prince's doom.

> Don't tell me I'm banished. I'd rather die.

ROMEO What less than doomsday is the Prince's doom?

FRIAR LAWRENCE A gentler judgement vanished from his lips:
Not body's death, but body's banishment.

ROMEO Ha, banishment? be merciful, say 'death':
For exile hath more terror in his look,
Much more than death. Do not say 'banishment'!

FRIAR LAWRENCE Here from Verona art thou banishèd.
Be patient, for the world is broad and wide.

> What bad news are you going to give me now?

ROMEO There is no world without Verona walls,
But purgatory, torture, hell itself:
Hence 'banishèd' is banished from the world,
And world's exile is death; then 'banishèd'
Is death mistermed. Calling death 'banishèd',
Thou cut'st my head off with a golden axe,
And smilest upon the stroke that murders me.

> Being banished is the same as death. It's just death under a more pleasant name.

> Can my sentence be anything other than death?

> You've had more than your share of bad luck. But here is the Prince's decision.

> Come here. What rotten luck you've been having!

> You're in luck: not condemned to death, just banished.

Worksheet 51

Plotting movement

This activity helps classes imagine a production of the play, even if they do not actually put it on; it can be done individually or in groups.

Students are asked to plot on paper, preferably graph paper, the movements of actors in one particular scene. The graph paper represents the stage area, and each character's movements are indicated by a different type of line, with numbers corresponding to the speeches uttered. It is preferable for students to use different colours instead of the conventions shown here. The task can be quite complex, as with the swordplay scenes, or the scene at the Capulets' feast; or simpler, as in the scenes in Juliet's bedroom. The example shown in Figure 18 is from Act III. Juliet, alone after Romeo's exit, has to face first her mother, then her extremely irate father, then the Nurse's heartless advice to reject Romeo.

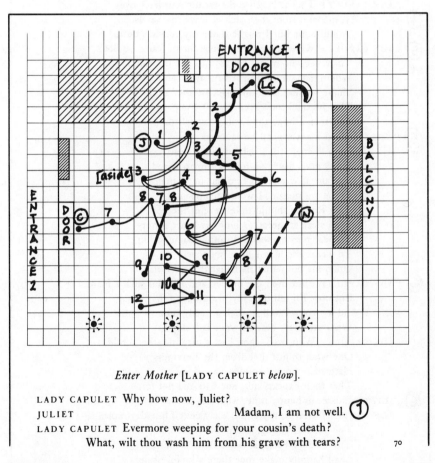

Enter Mother [LADY CAPULET *below*].

LADY CAPULET Why how now, Juliet?
JULIET   Madam, I am not well. (1)
LADY CAPULET Evermore weeping for your cousin's death?
          What, wilt thou wash him from his grave with tears?   70

(Figure 18)

And if thou couldst, thou couldst not make him live;
Therefore have done. Some grief shows much of love,
But much of grief shows still some want of wit.
JULIET Yet let me weep for such a feeling loss.
② LADY CAPULET So shall you feel the loss, but not the friend 75
Which you weep for.
JULIET   Feeling so the loss,
I cannot choose but ever weep the friend.
LADY CAPULET Well, girl, thou weep'st not so much for his death
As that the villain lives which slaughtered him.
JULIET What villain, madam?
LADY CAPULET   That same villain Romeo. 80
③ JULIET [*Aside*] Villain and he be many miles asunder. –
God pardon him, I do with all my heart:
And yet no man like he doth grieve my heart.
LADY CAPULET That is because the traitor murderer lives.
④ JULIET Ay, madam, from the reach of these my hands. 85
Would none but I might venge my cousin's death!
⑤ LADY CAPULET We will have vengeance for it, fear thou not:
LC Then weep no more. I'll send to one in Mantua,
Where that same banished runagate doth live,
Shall give him such an unaccustomed dram 90
That he shall soon keep Tybalt company;
And then I hope thou wilt be satisfied.
⑤ JULIET Indeed I never shall be satisfied
J With Romeo, till I behold him – dead –
Is my poor heart, so for a kinsman vexed. 95
Madam, if you could find out but a man
To bear a poison, I would temper it,
That Romeo should upon receipt thereof
Soon sleep in quiet. O how my heart abhors
To hear him named and cannot come to him, 100
To wreak the love I bore my cousin
Upon his body that hath slaughtered him!
⑥ LADY CAPULET Find thou the means, and I'll find such a man.
But now I'll tell thee joyful tidings, girl.
JULIET And joy comes well in such a needy time. 105
What are they, beseech your ladyship?
LADY CAPULET Well, well, thou hast a careful father, child,
One who, to put thee from thy heaviness,
Hath sorted out a sudden day of joy,
That thou expects not, nor I looked not for. 110
⑥ JULIET Madam, in happy time, what day is that?
LADY CAPULET Marry, my child, early next Thursday morn,
The gallant, young, and noble gentleman,
The County Paris, at Saint Peter's Church,
Shall happily make thee there a joyful bride. 115
⑦ JULIET Now by Saint Peter's Church and Peter too,

He shall not make me there a joyful bride.
I wonder at this haste, that I must wed
Ere he that should be husband comes to woo.
I pray you tell my lord and father, madam,   120
I will not marry yet, and when I do, I swear
It shall be Romeo, whom you know I hate,
Rather than Paris. These are news indeed!
LADY CAPULET Here comes your father, tell him so yourself;
And see how he will take it at your hands.   125

Enter CAPULET *and Nurse.*

CAPULET When the sun sets, the earth doth drizzle dew,
But for the sunset of my brother's son
It rains downright.
How now, a conduit, girl? What, still in tears?
Evermore show'ring? In one little body   130
Thou counterfeits a bark, a sea, a wind:
For still thy eyes, which I may call the sea,
Do ebb and flow with tears; the bark thy body is,
Sailing in this salt flood; the winds, thy sighs,
Who, raging with thy tears and they with them,   135
Without a sudden calm, will overset
Thy tempest-tossèd body. How now, wife,
Have you delivered to her our decree?
LADY CAPULET Ay, sir, but she will none, she gives you thanks.
I would the fool were married to her grave.   140
CAPULET Soft, take me with you, take me with you, wife.
How, will she none? doth she not give us thanks?
Is she not proud? doth she not count her blest,
Unworthy as she is, that we have wrought
So worthy a gentleman to be her bride?   145
JULIET Not proud you have, but thankful that you have:
Proud can I never be of what I hate,
But thankful even for hate that is meant love.
CAPULET How how, how how, chopt-logic? What is this?
'Proud', and 'I thank you', and 'I thank you not',   150
And yet 'not proud', mistress minion you?
Thank me no thankings, nor proud me no prouds,
But fettle your fine joints 'gainst Thursday next,
To go with Paris to Saint Peter's Church,
Or I will drag thee on a hurdle thither.   155
Out, you green-sickness carrion! out, you baggage!
You tallow-face!
LADY CAPULET   Fie, fie, what, are you mad?
JULIET Good father, I beseech you on my knees,
Hear me with patience but to speak a word.
[*She kneels down.*]

187

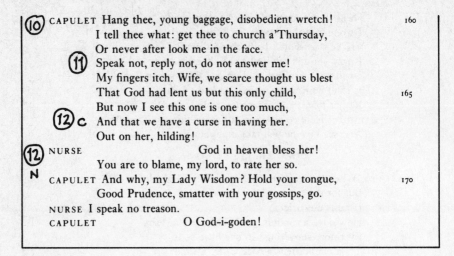

CAPULET Hang thee, young baggage, disobedient wretch!   160
I tell thee what: get thee to church a'Thursday,
Or never after look me in the face.
Speak not, reply not, do not answer me!
My fingers itch. Wife, we scarce thought us blest
That God had lent us but this only child,   165
But now I see this one is one too much,
And that we have a curse in having her.
Out on her, hilding!
NURSE   God in heaven bless her!
You are to blame, my lord, to rate her so.
CAPULET And why, my Lady Wisdom? Hold your tongue,   170
Good Prudence, smatter with your gossips, go.
NURSE I speak no treason.
CAPULET   O God-i-goden!

Figure 18

Friar Lawrence's letter

In Act IV Scene 1, Friar Lawrence tells Juliet that he intends to send a letter to Romeo to tell him that Juliet is to feign death, and to ask Romeo to come back so that he and Friar Lawrence can be with Juliet when she awakes:

In the meantime, against thou shalt awake,
Shall Romeo by my letters know our drift.
And hither shall he come;   (IV.1.113)

Students, in groups, discuss what Friar Lawrence would say in his letter, and how best to phrase it in order not to alarm Romeo but to reassure him. Then, individually, perhaps as homework, each learner writes Friar Lawrence's letter in modern idiom.

I'd do anything for you, dear, anything . . .

By the time the students are approaching the end of the play, they are bound to have identified with the situation of the two lovers and to have thought about what lovers are prepared to do rather than live without each other. This activity aims to draw out the students' own potential response to a similar situation in their own lives.

If it is available, a song from Lionel Bart's *Oliver*, a musical version of Dickens' *Oliver Twist*, can be used as a first step. The students are asked to write down some of the things that the singer says he would do for his

---

For a man/woman I loved, I feel sure that I would:

1. Move to another city or town rather than live without him/her. ☐
2. Change my religion rather than live without him/her. ☐
3. Deceive or disobey my parents, rather than live without
   him/her. ☐
4. Wait any number of years for him/her to return if we were
   separated, rather than live without him/her permanently. ☐
5. Give up my job to look after him/her if he/she had an incurable
   illness, rather than live without him/her. ☐
6. Give up my life, if he/she died rather than live without him/her. ☐

Worksheet 52

loved one, while they listen. The teacher quickly goes through the lyrics after the class has told him or her what they heard.

Next, the learners are given Worksheet 52, and they tick the things that they feel sure they would do for someone they loved, rather than live without that person.

In groups, students compare answers and explore differences between their views. After a short plenary discussion to widen the discussion, students are asked to reconsider the decision made by Romeo and Juliet. Would they say that this decision indicates that the lovers were mad? emotionally unbalanced? immature? deluded? . . .

Discussion based on prioritising

This is an activity designed to stimulate oral expression and to help students think about the 'inevitability' of the tragic outcome.

Students in small groups or pairs study the following list of possibilities:

The tragedy would not have happened if:
a) The stars had been in a different configuration when Romeo and Juliet
   were born.
b) Lady Capulet had been a better mother, so that Juliet had felt able to
   confide in her.
c) The apothecary had been less poverty-stricken, and refused to sell Romeo
   the poison.
d) Friar John had been able to deliver Friar Lawrence's letter to Romeo,
   instead of being prevented by chance from doing so.
e) Romeo had been less impetuous and waited instead of taking poison so
   quickly. ⟫→

f) Juliet had refused to take the potion.
g) Friar Lawrence had arrived at the tomb a few minutes earlier.
h) Romeo's page Balthasar had disobeyed his master and quickly raised the alarm.
i) The two families had sought to be reconciled instead of keeping to their old quarrel.

Students are asked to choose three and place them in order of importance: first, second and third. They must then decide which of the following statements fit each of their three choices:

Tragedy results from a chance coincidence of events.
Tragedy results from pre-ordained fate.
Tragedy is caused by human error.
Tragedy results from a flaw in the human character.
Tragedy does not happen in real life: it is a distortion of probable events imposed by the writer.

After discussion in groups and then comparison of choices made, students could be asked to prepare a short oral presentation (one or two minutes) in which they justify their choice of one (or more) of the above statements by referring specifically to the play.

The Sandbox by Edward Albee*

There are good reasons for using this play with foreign learners: it is very brief, and its simple, everyday language presents few problems. Although on one level it can be read as a rather biting comment on the American way of life – and death – there is a sense in which it also mediates issues that are universal: how to cope with the elderly; how to face approaching death; how to retain human feeling within the dehumanising rituals of social intercourse. These are themes which may not appeal to the younger reader: the play is probably more effectively used with mature students or with learners in their final secondary school years.

One difficulty in presenting the play stems from its modern style, which

* in *The Zoo Story and Other Plays*

may break with the reader's expectations. The long warm-up session described below was devised to allow students to become thoroughly immersed in some of the themes before they come to the play itself. This often has the effect of relaxing learners so that they enter into the spirit of the play and enjoy it rather than worrying unduly about 'what it is saying'. The meaning of this kind of play is intimately linked with what it *is*, and it therefore suffers from being paraphrased. This is one reason for our recommendation that teachers try to have their students put the play on, in a more or less elaborate form. Its small cast, almost bare set, and simple language make it ideal for a full-scale performance, where this is possible and desirable. Even a minimally staged reading performance in class, however, will convey something of its dramatic quality and allow students to appreciate the force of its imagery, as well as its humour and irony (see 'Reading and performing the play' on p. 193).

The play is a sort of modern fable about death. A couple, Mommy and Daddy, carry the woman's mother, 'Grandma', on to the stage and put her into a sandbox. They then sit down to await the event which has brought them here: Grandma's death. Mommy and Daddy are very anxious to preserve all the conventions and do everything in a tasteful way. They have even hired musicians for the occasion. But these social graces cover a callous lack of feeling. Grandma, who seems at first in her second infancy, is gradually revealed to be a plucky old lady with a lot of life left in her. But to no avail. The pleasant young man who has been doing exercises in the background, and who is the Angel of Death, eventually comes forward to perform his appointed role. Grandma is at first surprised, then resigned, while Mommy and Daddy, having shed conventional tears, go briskly back to their own lives.

Warm-up

This is an activity which involves discussion and writing and is done in class prior to reading the play. The aim is to get learners thinking about relationships between the generations, and elicit their own feelings about them.

The class is divided into groups of three or four. Half the groups receive Worksheet 53A, the others Worksheet 53B. If it is necessary, the teacher explains the idea of an 'agony aunt' column in a newspaper or magazine, and asks the class to imagine that they must supply useful advice for people with real problems. (They are not told at this stage that the material comes from a play.)

Groups discuss an appropriate response, write it, then each member of group A meets with one member of group B to compare problems and answers. A general feedback session follows, with discussion of the questions raised.

'Aggie Neeont' is the pseudonym used by a group of reporters who, together, write the advice column for their newspaper. Imagine that you are that group of reporters, and that you have received the following letter from a reader. Compose a suitable reply to be published in the column.

Dear Aggie Neeont,

Please tell me what we can do about my mother who is ruining my life and my marriage.

My husband has worked very hard to build up enough money to let us live in comfort in a nice suburb of the city. Two years ago, I decided that my mother ought to leave her farm and come and live with us. It seemed the right thing to do. She really couldn't cope any longer on her own. My husband went to a lot of trouble to sell her farm and to fix up our spare room for her. He put in a little stove so that she can make herself a cup of tea, and he bought her a set of dishes for her own use.

She doesn't appreciate any of this and never stops complaining about everything. She claims we've taken her money. She's even told the neighbours that we make her sleep under the stove and eat from a single dish like a dog. I'm sure having her here is affecting our standing in the neighbourhood because she will not give up her farm ways.

What can we do? She gets hysterical when I mention a home and I'm sure we would have to carry her physically to get her to go. My husband is no help. He just says: "She's your mother ... whatever you say." I want to do everything nicely but I'm getting tired of waiting for her to go.

Yours,
DESPERATE

Worksheet 53A

'Aggie Neeont' is the pseudonym used by a group of reporters who, together, write the advice column for their newspaper. Imagine that you are that group of reporters, and that you have received the following letter from a reader. Compose a suitable reply to be published in the column.

> Dear Aggie Neeont,
>   I don't know why I'm writing to you as I'm sure you can't help. My problem is that I think my daughter and son-in-law are trying to get rid of me.
>   I was married when I was 17 to a farmer but my husband died and I had to raise my daughter all by myself. Now she's married this rich fellow. They dragged me off the farm where I had lived all my life. I guess I ought not to complain as they've given me a nice bed under the stove and a blanket and my own dish. But they say I have got to go. Well, I don't intend to move. They'll have to carry me out bodily if they want me to go away. There's no respect these days for old age.
>   I guess the only way out is for me to die. That would solve the problem for everybody.
>
>   Yours,
>   Lived Too Long.

Worksheet 53B

Reading and performing the play

At the end of the warm-up activity, which will usually take up a whole class lesson, learners are given the play to read at home. If this is not appropriate, reading can be deferred to the next class lesson.

Home reading can be accompanied by a worksheet to highlight one

---

In *The Sandbox* we meet a young man, a middle-aged couple, and an old lady. The way each one behaves is a mixture of what we expect from the old and the very young. List as many aspects as you can for each character, under the headings given.

	Behaviour appro- priate to children	Behaviour appro- priate to grown-ups
Mommy and Daddy		
Grandma		
Young man		

Which character seems to you most 'childish'? Why?

Worksheet 54

particular feature of the play. For example, Worksheet 54 focusses the student's attention on ideas of childhood and old age.

A performance is planned for the next lesson. Roles are given out, with non-actors assuming responsibility for arranging a set (at the front of the classroom) and providing the props (these are minimal: chairs, a sandbox or something to represent one, a bucket and spade). In many classes, there will be one person at least who can play a musical instrument but if not, the 'musician' can mime in time to a recording. The cast need not memorise their lines but are asked to practise reading them so that they can carry off their performance fairly fluently. Providing that a relaxed atmosphere is maintained, we have found that students enjoy this kind of staged reading a great deal.

Follow-up activity

This activity is suggested for advanced students studying literature as a main part of their course, or preparing to do so at the higher education level.

An interesting aspect of *The Sandbox*, which links it to one of the mainstreams in contemporary drama, is its play on the idea of theatricality, of appearance and reality, of 'roles' in life and 'roles' in dramatic productions. Realist plays attempt to portray life as it is led outside the theatre. *The Sandbox* portrays this 'outside' life as though it were itself a staged play.

A teacher wishing the students to reflect on this aspect could first ask them to skim through the short play once again and extract all the references where characters speak of their lives as though they were in fact engaged in a play. This can be done singly or in groups, and the resulting list put up on the board. It should include items such as:

Grandma: You're . . . you're an actor, hunh?
Young man: Yes, I am.
Grandma (to the musician): Honey, do you play all through this part?
Daddy (starting): What was that?
Mommy: It was an off-stage rumble . . . and you know what *that* means . . .
Young man: Uh . . . ma'am; I . . . I have a line here.
Young man (prepared; delivers the line like a real amateur): I am the Angel of
    Death. I am . . . uh . . . I am come for you.
Grandma: What I meant was . . . you did that very well, dear.

The teacher asks students to give their impressions about this aspect of the play. Do they find it startling? off-putting? Does it stop them from believing in the characters? What could be its purpose? How true to their own experiences is it? Have they ever felt as though they were involved in a performance in their lives, instead of behaving spontaneously?

This general discussion is followed by a task in groups (or discussed in groups then written individually as homework): to write a very short sketch in which some situation in their real life is depicted as though it were a stage play. Situations with a strong element of ritual immediately spring to mind, since participants in them often feel as though they were playing a stage role: getting married, going through a graduation/christening/confirmation ceremony, appearing in court (swearing the oath exactly like in a film), going for a job interview, attending a funeral, etc. Some of these can be suggested if learners are at a loss for ideas.

This exercise often stimulates the interest of students in the theme and how it is handled by other modern dramatists. It can be explored further by reading other plays that embody it, for example Tom Stoppard's *The Real Inspector Hound* or David Hare's *A Map of the World*.

9 Short stories

Short stories are often an ideal way of introducing students to literature in the foreign-language classroom. For the teacher, they offer many immediate and striking advantages:
— Their practical length means they can usually be read entirely within one or two class lessons. Slightly longer works can be sectioned in the same way as novels or plays, but still be completed in a few lessons.
— They are less daunting for a foreign reader to tackle or to reread on his or her own, and are more suitable when set as home tasks. Students get that feeling of achievement at having come to the end of a whole work, much sooner.
— They offer greater variety than longer texts. A teacher can choose very different short stories, so that there is a greater chance of finding something to appeal to each individual's tastes and interests.
— Short stories are especially valuable for sessional courses, summer courses or the like; or for teachers with shifting classes: evening courses, for example, or continuous-intake adult classes.

We hope that the ideas on the following pages will encourage a creative use to be made of this rewarding genre. We have always found that being creative in presenting and exploiting the text is, if anything, even more important with short stories than with longer works. They are so brief that if we are not careful, they may be less involving for the foreign reader: there is not enough time to be drawn into the fiction and feel really at home within its created universe. They are also extremely compressed. This is of course what makes them such a delight: when a short story writer is successful, he or she encapsulates experience with a masterly economy of language and imagery. We are invited to see the universe in a grain of sand. But this compression can make it difficult for foreign readers to appreciate the quality of the work, even when they understand its surface meaning. When they look at the grain of sand, they must be helped to see the universe within it, and to respond to it on an emotional level.

For this reason, care and preparation are needed for successful presentation of short stories. The grids and activities suggested in previous chapters are just as valuable here, partly because they diversify classroom procedure and make it more enjoyable, partly because they encourage students to go back over the pages read, look more closely at the detail, mull over what is happening. Rereading is a key element in the full appreciation of short stories: because of its concision, a short story's full richness is hardly ever revealed in a first reading.

We have assumed that class time need not always be devoted to the actual process of reading the short story, either silently or out loud. Some activities depend upon students having been given the story previously to read on their own, usually with the suggestion that they read for gist without stopping to look up every unknown word. Other activities give learners a taste of the plot or theme of a particular story, which they are then left to read on their own. If classwork is to have any repercussion on the reading habits of students, they must be encouraged to become more independent in the foreign language, just as they are, presumably, when they choose a bedside book in their own language.

'The hitchhiker' by Roald Dahl*

This simple but effective story holds the reader's interest throughout. It concerns a writer who is enjoying a drive in his new car. He stops to pick up a hitchhiker and becomes intrigued when he is unable to guess the man's occupation. The hitchhiker tempts the writer into testing the maximum speed of the car but the experiment is brought to a halt by an equally speedy policeman on a motor cycle. He takes down details of the two men and warns the writer that a heavy fine and loss of licence are inevitable. The journey continues and the hitchhiker's 'skill' is revealed – he is a 'fingersmith'. He shows the writer some of the belongings he has picked from his pockets during the ride. The writer is astonished but overjoyed to discover that his passenger also has something belonging to the policeman . . .

For classroom purposes the story divides neatly into four sections which can be presented for listening or reading or a combination of both. The following activities aim to integrate different language activities and to maximise student involvement and response.

Warm-up

Students are asked to study some photographs of various hitchhikers (see Figure 19) and to decide whether or not they would give each of them a lift. Each decision must be accompanied by an explanation. Students are grouped to compare decisions briefly. For a more structured warm-up, the teacher can use a simple worksheet (see Worksheet 55). If necessary, the whole activity can be preceded by some practice of appropriate

* in *More Tales of the Unexpected*

Figure 19

language using one of the photos (for example, 'He looks . . . ', 'He looks a bit . . . ', 'He looks as though . . . ').

Study the four photographs of hitchhikers in Figure 19 and complete the boxes below.
You can assume the following:
– You are alone in your car.
– You are not in a hurry.
– It is safe to stop your car if you want to.
– Hitchhiking is permitted along this road.
– It is daytime.

Photo no.	Sex M/F	Approx. age	Possible occupation	Appearance (face, clothing, personality, etc.)

Are you going to stop for the person in photo 1?   YES/NO
Are you going to stop for the person in photo 2?   YES/NO
Are you going to stop for the person in photo 3?   YES/NO
Are you going to stop for the people in photo 4?   YES/NO

Now discuss the reasons for your decisions in groups.

Worksheet 55

Reading or listening in sections

Students read or listen to the *first section* of the story (ending 'The secret of life . . . is to become very very good at somethin' that's very very 'ard to do'). The writer has picked up the hitchhiker but is unable to find out what he does for a living. The class is asked to consider what it knows so far about the hitchhiker and then to choose the occupation he seems most likely to have, using the following list as a prompt: carpenter, ice-cream salesman, knife-sharpener, artist, vet, musician, blacksmith. Choices are compared and students asked to justify the chosen occupation in terms of the story's content.

The *second section* of the story describes the encounter with the police-man (ending 'Then he kicked the starter and roared off up the road out of sight'). The language is straightforward so a response activity is appropriate: students are asked to imagine that the same event has happened in their country or countries. What would be the differences in the police-man's behaviour, attitude, questions, and the eventual punishment? If necessary, the teacher puts these questions on a simple questionnaire. Students discuss in groups and possibly improvise a sketch of the parallel situation in the target language to illustrate the differences they perceive.

The *third section* of the story (ending 'Because you've got fantastic fingers') satisfies the readers' or listeners' curiosity as they find out that the hitchhiker is a pickpocket. His 'fantastic fingers' are his special skill. As a light-hearted response activity, the teacher asks the students to think about their own special skills. Then he or she tells them to write their prime skill on a piece of paper. The skill doesn't have to be very special, just something that each of them is good at. The teacher collects the slips of paper and puts them into a hat together with his or her own! Students then take out one piece of paper each (not their own) and try to guess who is the possessor of the special talent written on it.

The *final section* of the story reveals the surprise. The hitchhiker has pickpocketed the policeman's notebook with all the details of the two men and of the offence in it. He has saved the day. An attractive way of commencing this final part of the narrative is to ask the class to try to predict the end of the story.

As follow-up, after reading or listening, several activities work well:
- Students have to determine the exact point in the story at which the hitchhiker took the policeman's notebook. They write down words from the story that mark the chosen point. Results are then compared.
- Students are asked to write a newspaper article about the incident with the headline 'POLICEMAN TAKEN FOR A RIDE'.
- Students are put into pairs for an improvised role play. The teacher gives each pair a story-related situation to think about and then act out. Situations include the following:

- Policeman and writer meet in a pub shortly after the incident; police-man is off-duty.
- Policeman's wife is talking to next-door neighbour over the garden fence; neighbour has read a newspaper account of the incident.
- Hitchhiker meets policeman in motorway café the same day; police-man asks for his notebook.

Students prepare their respective sketches and each situation is per-formed for the rest of the class by volunteering pairs. The teacher monitors for later language repair work, as necessary.

'The star' and 'The spread of Ian Nichol' by Alasdair Gray*

These are two extremely compact stories incorporating a strongly surreal element.

In 'The star', a young boy sees a 'star' drop from the sky into the back yard of his house. He finds it and treasures it, secretly. When he takes it to school, however, he is caught looking at it by his teacher. Rather than relinquish it, he swallows it and becomes a 'star' too.

In 'The spread of Ian Nichol', Ian Nichol, a riveter, finds he has a lump on a bald patch at the back of his head. It spreads and gradually becomes a complete double, another Ian Nichol. A struggle for ownership of identity ensues. When that is finally resolved, each of the two discovers a lump at the back of his head . . .

Group work and mime

In this activity, the stories are presented without the usual warm-up, and mime is used to stimulate interest in these and other contemporary short stories and in extensive reading. The aim is to develop self and group reliance in comprehension; to encourage individual class members to share their own interpretations of the stories without the feeling that there is a single 'right' view.

FIRST STAGE: READING AND UNDERSTANDING

The class is divided into two halves, with the explanation that each is going to read a different short story. 'The star' is distributed to one half, 'The spread of Ian Nichol' to the other half, and interest is built by mentioning that these are unusual stories. Students read, marking any unknown words with pencil.

When the stories have been read once, students are placed into groups of four, and asked to discuss difficult vocabulary and check understand-

* in *Unlikely Stories, Mostly*

ing of the story. The teacher helps out if the combined group cannot guess the meaning of any word or expression.

SECOND STAGE: MIMING THE STORIES

The small groups are told that they have to prepare a mime of the story they have read and then perform it for one of the groups which read the other story; they need mime only the main narrative and can divide it into scenes if they wish. Groups then perform their mimes and the watching group guesses aloud the story-line being performed. (With larger classes, the teacher might need more than one room.)*

THIRD STAGE: READING THE SECOND STORY

When mimes have been completed, the other stories are distributed so that each student can read the story they saw mimed. Students are paired, one from each of the groups formed in the first stage. Each student helps the other with any difficult words in the second story.

FOURTH STAGE: DISCUSSION

The teacher has several choices at this point. He or she can simply ask the class to say which story they liked best, which they thought most unusual,

---

* The miming of stories also works very well for stories read privately at home. Students then start the class by preparing the mime (second stage).

In 'The star' it is possible to build up a good picture of Cameron, the boy. Find quotes from the story which indicate or suggest the following qualities.

secretiveness	lack of confidence
loneliness	lack of love
fear	other?
shyness	

Which of the following ideas or things do *you* most readily associate with the image of the star in the story?

a marble	imagination	eternal life
suicide	a longing for love	flight from reality

Write down any other thoughts you have on the possible meanings associated with the star. Discuss your thoughts with others in your group.

Worksheet 56

'The spread of Ian Nichol' is an unusual story. Perhaps it does not have a moral in the traditional sense, but if you were asked to supply one, what would it be? Here are some possible morals. If none of them seems appropriate, make up your own and say why you think it suitable. Even if you choose one of the morals from the list, justify your selection.

Moral 1: Everyone is afraid of meeting a double.
Moral 2: Narcissus got it all wrong.
Moral 3: Inside everyone there's another personality trying to get out.
Moral 4: No form of birth control is safe.
Moral 5: Creativity isn't always original.
Moral 6: Whatever you do, life goes on relentlessly.
Moral 7: Know 'thyselves'.
Your moral: ....
Your choice and reason: ....

Worksheet 57

etc. and, after a short discussion, give out worksheets for homework, or the teacher can read both stories to the class at the beginning of the next literature lesson, then let students go through the worksheets together in groups (see Worksheets 56 and 57). This usually produces a good range of views and debate, and it builds confidence in expressing personal interpretations, rather than simply relying on received ones.

'The edge' by R. K. Narayan*

This is a fairly long story, with some vocabulary that may be unfamiliar, best suited, therefore, to more advanced levels. At first, the story seems almost plotless, as it gradually builds up a picture of its endearing central character: Ranga, a knife-grinder in India. A wealth of details sketch his background and idiosyncratic personality, his love for his daughter, his repeated conflicts with his wife, his pride in his trade and his relationship with his customers. Eventually, though, Ranga encounters officials from the government's sterilisation programme. They cannot understand what having a child means to this poor illiterate man, while he at first fails to realise why exactly he is being offered the princely sum of 30 rupees. In a final irony, the knife-grinder runs away, unwilling to have the sharp instruments of his trade used on *him*!

* in *Malgudi Days*

Part C   Working with a complete text

Warm-up activities

SPECULATING ABOUT THE TITLE

Students are told that they are going to read a story called 'The edge'. Can they think what 'edge' is being referred to? What expressions do they know containing the word 'edge'? For example: the sharp or blunt edge of a knife, the edge of a cliff, the edge of town, to live on the edge of poverty, the edge of sanity / the edge of madness, a sharp-edged tongue, to be on the edge of a breakthrough, to be on the edge of a breakdown, etc. All suggestions are accepted at this stage. The teacher puts them on the board, while students jot them down in their notebooks. They are to be kept for the follow-up activity (see p. 209).

COMPARING LIFESTYLES

This is designed to elicit students' attitude to the central situation in the short story. Students are asked to think about what life is like for a very poor, illiterate man in a small rural village. What differences would there be between that person's life and the life of someone who has been educated and lives and works in an urban environment (their own lives, if that is the case)? This can be done as a general class discussion, although working in groups, with a grid like the one in Worksheet 58 often ensures a more evenly distributed participation.

When the various groups have filled in their grid, there is a general feedback session to establish an overall class grid.

A listening activity

Students read ten statements about the first section, which they are about to hear. Two of them are false. Their task is to tick the correct statements and mark the two incorrect ones, with an X (see Worksheet 59).

The teacher then reads out the first section (34 lines – approximately two-and-a-half minutes' reading time) once or twice as necessary. The worksheet acts as a mini-summary to guide students into the story, and also introduces and explains some of the terms needed for comprehension – *dhoti*, peripatetic, grinding, etc.

After answers have been checked, the teacher asks students for their impressions of the main character, so far. As many details as possible about his personality are elicited and jotted down, to be kept for later reference.

After this first encounter with the text, students can do the 'intensive' vocabulary exercise which is described next, or the class can go on to a reading of the first three pages, to be followed by a discussion sparked by an 'interpretation' questionnaire (Worksheet 60).

Write comments on the contrasting lifestyles of the two kinds of people below.

Attitudes to:	An illiterate person in a small rural community	An educated person in an urban environment
Time: What does it mean? How important is it?		
Family: What does it mean? How important is it?		
Community: How does an individual relate to his community?		
Communication with others: How can an individual communicate with others?		
The central government: How can an individual relate to it?		
A job or trade: What does it mean? How important is it?		
Age: What does it mean? What are its special rights, privileges or duties?		

Worksheet 58

You are going to hear the first part of a short story by R. K. Narayan called 'The edge'. Before you listen, read the following statements. *Eight* of them describe the facts in the short story accurately. *Two* of them are false. As you listen to the story, tick (√) the statements which are true. Mark the two incorrect statements with an X. *The statements are not in order.*

1. He was dressed in a *dhoti*, a shirt and a turban. (A *dhoti* is a loose-fitting cloth worn around the middle part of the body, by Hindus.)
2. He carried a portable grinding machine operated with a pedal.
3. He had become a millionaire by sharpening swords for a Maharaja.
4. He liked to think that he could sharpen all kinds of instruments, not just knives.
5. He did not work in one single place, but was peripatetic (he moved from place to place).
6. His name was Ranga, and he would never tell anyone his age.
7. He did not have a moustache, but had a very full beard.
8. He was a man who loved to talk on and on.
9. He had a lot of trouble persuading tailors and barbers to have their knives sharpened.
10. He had a loud voice and used to walk in the city streets calling for people to come and have their knives and scissors sharpened.

Worksheet 59

A vocabulary game

For this exercise, learners are given the first page of the short story to read (23 lines). The teacher has prepared as many slips of paper as there are students in the class. Half the slips have one difficult or unusual word from the text; the other half have a definition of one such word. The example shown is worked out for a class of 30 students.

Example: 15 words and their definitions, each one to be put on a slip of paper and used for a vocabulary game based on page 1 of 'The edge' (for a class of 30).

Words	*Definitions*
pressed	Urged strongly; compelled; forced.
tactics	The art or skill of organising your efforts to reach a desired aim.
scythe	An instrument for cutting grass or other crops. It has a long thin curving blade and is held with both hands. It is used with a long sweeping motion.

hatchet	A small or light axe with a short handle, for use with one hand.
loquaciousness	The condition of someone who is talkative, who loves to talk.
patchy	Resembling a patchwork; made up of different bits and pieces; having an uneven appearance.
tuft	A bunch of small things, usually soft and flexible – like hairs, feathers, etc., fastened at the base together.
overlaid	Put or placed over something else.
almanac	A calendar of months and days, with calculations and forecasts based on the stars.
a *dhoti*	A loose-fitting cloth worn around the middle part of the body, by Hindus.
khaki	A dull brownish-yellow colour. Often used for military uniforms.
sonorous	Of sounds: loud, deep, or resonant.
high-pitched	Of sounds: high in tone, squeaky.
grindstone	A disk of stone turning on a central axle and used for grinding, sharpening or polishing.
peeler	A tool used to strip anything of its outer layer, or its skin or rind (for example, oranges, carrots, etc.).

The teacher puts all the slips into a container and lets each student choose one. By reading out their word or definition to each other, students must now try to find their partner.

This activity is usually rather chaotic at first, and the noise level can be rather high, so that it can only be used in situations where there is no danger of disturbing neighbouring classes. But learners enjoy it, and it is an effective way of getting them to use the context to try to guess meanings.

As soon as pairs begin to form, the teacher puts two pairs together. Each pair asks the other two whether they can provide a definition for their word: 'Do you know what "almanac" means?' If the second pair can answer they get a point. They then go on to the next pair and repeat the procedure.

An 'interpretation' questionnaire

Students read the first three pages of the short story (up to the paragraph beginning 'Ranga physically dwelt in the town no doubt . . . ').

They are then given Worksheet 60 to fill in, singly or in groups. These are not questions of fact or comprehension, which can be given a right or a wrong answer. Rather, they try to make learners think about some of the underlying issues within the text – they try to make them interpret it.

This type of questionnaire must be adapted to the level of the class. We have found that it is useful to give students one or two suggestions to get

Try to give as many answers as possible to the following questions.
A few suggestions have been made for you.

1. Ranga never told anyone his age. Why not?

   He didn't know it.

   He had forgotten it.

2. Ranga walked about the streets of Malgudi 'in a blissful state'.
   Why was his state blissful?

   He loved his work.

   He didn't have to watch the clock.

3. Ranga was careful when he had to do business with tailors or
   barbers. Why?

   He could not depend on them.

   They refused to have their knives sharpened.

4. What words could you use to describe Ranga's attitude to his
   work?

   persistent

   cunning

5. Ranga did not care much about food. Why not?

   He didn't want to spend too much money on food.

   He thought eating was necessary but not interesting.

Worksheet 60

Other suggestions
1. He didn't want to be stereotyped.
   He didn't think it important.
   He thought it would give others power over him.
2. He wasn't worried about his appearance.
   He trusted in fate to be good to him.
   He didn't have a boss to nag at him.
3. He never knew what their reaction would be.
   He had to work hard to convince them.
   He couldn't trust them.
4. aggressive, full of pride in his skill, determined, caring, crafty . . .
5. He thought hunger would go away if he took no notice.
   He wasn't interested in any personal comfort.

them started, but not too many, because that tends to cramp their own imagination. Literary specialists and more advanced learners need fewer suggestions, general students and less advanced classes need more. A few suggestions are made after Worksheet 60, from which a teacher preparing such a worksheet might choose.

Comparing the completed worksheets and justifying choices in pairs or groups is followed by general feedback and discussion.

Ordering events

The class is now asked to read the bulk of the short story – up to the part where Ranga meets the sterilisation team – probably as homework. (They read up to the paragraph beginning 'He noticed a coming vehicle . . . ').

Worksheets 61A and 61B, which lead to the construction of a flow-chart, can accompany home reading. The comparison and discussion of the flowcharts can be reserved for the next class lesson, otherwise the whole activity can be done in class after students have read the section on their own.

Students are given a list of 14 events which make up the story of Ranga's life as we know it, up to the point where he meets the government officials. The events are given in a jumbled order. Learners must order them according to Ranga's chronology, then fit them into the diagram of the flowchart they have also been given. (For an advanced class, the teacher asks students to devise their own flowchart to portray the stages of Ranga's life.) The completed flowchart is shown in Figure 20.

Reading to the end

The class is now poised to finish the story, perhaps as home reading. It is useful to pause a moment before doing so, to review what has been learned so far and try to guess how the story might develop from this point. Once the whole story has been read, there are a variety of follow-up activities to choose from.

Reviewing 'edges'

Students are asked to return to the list of 'edges' they wrote down before starting to read. In groups, they must now choose three of those expressions, the three which are more appropriate to the story, and grade them in order of importance. When lists are compared at the end of this activity, there is often fruitful disagreement and an ensuing discussion on the story's many levels of meaning and symbolism. For homework, students are asked to write one sentence justifying each one of their three choices.

Here is a list of 14 events in Ranga's life as we know it so far. Put them in the right order so that they tell his story as it happened.

a) His wife refuses to move to town with him.
b) The village smith demands a share of his profits and often wants a drink at the tavern as well.
c) He walks through the streets of his village but cannot make enough money. His wife is discontented because they are so poor.
d) When his first line of moustache appears, he starts working as a knife-grinder.
e) His wife's temper improves.
f) He consults the schoolmaster to find the right date for his departure to the city.
g) He strikes his wife and she retaliates with the broom, driving him out of their home.
h) He sets up his grinding wheel as an assistant to the village smith, under the big tamarind tree.
i) His daughter is old enough to be sent to the Mission school. His wife wants the child to leave school because it is too expensive, but Ranga insists that she must be educated.
j) Ranga goes on a journey to explore the possibilities of work in Malgudi, a town 25 miles away. He decides it is the place for him.
k) His wife has tantrums and won't serve him food when he has been to the tavern.
l) He decides to try his luck as a peripatetic sharpener.
m) Ranga decides on a compromise: he works in Malgudi but visits his family every other month for a few days.
n) He wants his wife to try a sip of drink. She hates it and spills it all over the floor.

Worksheet 61A

Here is a diagram of a flowchart for the events in Ranga's life. When you have ordered the 14 events, put them into the appropriate box in this chart. The time flow in this chart is from top to bottom: that is, earlier events are higher than later events. Boxes on the same level indicate events happening at the same time. An arrow (↓) indicates that one event has *caused* another.

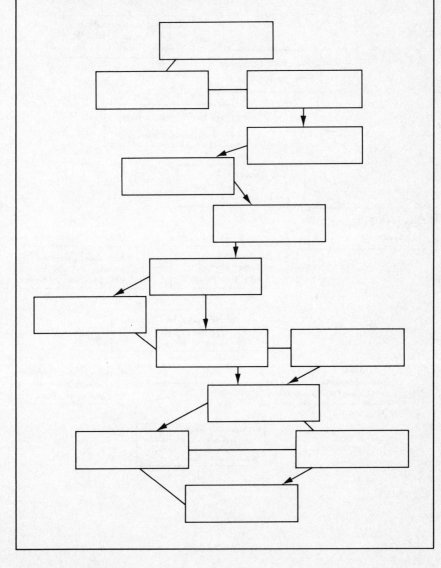

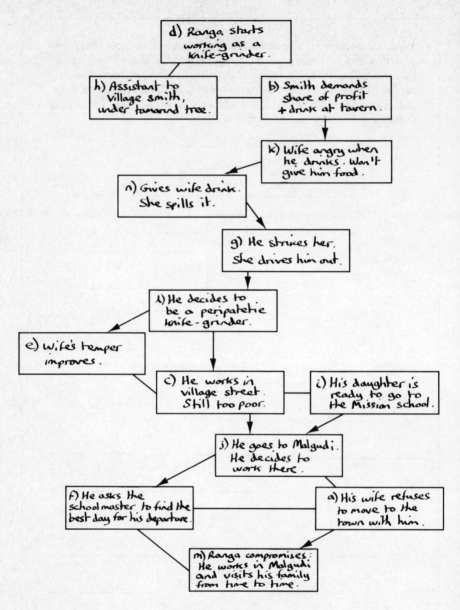

d) Ranga starts working as a knife-grinder.

h) Assistant to village smith, under tamarind tree.

b) Smith demands share of profit + drink at tavern.

k) Wife angry when he drinks. Won't give him food.

n) Gives wife drink. She spills it.

g) He strikes her. She drives him out.

l) He decides to be a peripatetic knife-grinder.

e) Wife's temper improves.

c) He works in village street. Still too poor.

i) His daughter is ready to go to the Mission school.

j) He goes to Malgudi. He decides to work there.

f) He asks the school master to find the best day for his departure.

a) His wife refuses to move to the town with him.

m) Ranga compromises: He works in Malgudi and visits his family from time to time.

Figure 20

A grid leading to essay-writing

Students are given a grid to fill in (Worksheet 62). They are to jot down a brief quotation from the story (with page reference) which would give the reader information about each heading. This is intended as a class activity. Half the class is asked to fill in details about Ranga, the other half

---

Find a brief quote indicating Ranga's/Ranga's wife's attitude to the following. Write it in the appropriate box, with a page reference.

	Attitude
food	
task in life	
daughter's education	
women's role	
drinking	
relationships with the other sex	
fate	
poverty	
modern civilisation	
place in the community	
the younger generation	

Worksheet 62

about his wife. When the task is completed, students are paired to enable them to compare the grids of husband and wife.

As homework, students can write an essay either about one of the characters; or comparing and contrasting their personalities, strengths and weaknesses.

Television reportage

In this classroom group activity, each group must prepare and present a short reportage on the events of the story, as though for a 'special report' to be shown on the evening news programme. Students may be given a framework to start them off, as follows.

The first part of this television programme features Jim/Julia Smith, who is the reader on the 'six o'clock news' every evening, and who starts off by reading the following news item:

'In an attempt to improve living standards in India, the government has been conducting a vigorous campaign aimed at reducing the birth rate. Posters carrying the campaign slogan "Two Will Do" have been put up all over the country. Teams of specialists have been sent to every region so that anyone who already has two or more children can be sterilised. Attractive cash bonuses will, it is hoped, convince people to come forward voluntarily. But in some areas, the programme has been running into stiff opposition. To see how people are reacting to the government's initiative, we go now to our special reporter Christine Carter-Browne, who has been interviewing people in and around the rural town of Malgudi . . . '

Students now prepare this 'special report'. One of them is to be the reporter, the others her subjects: Ranga; the leader of the team of doctors carrying out the sterilisations; Ranga's wife; the village schoolmaster, etc. For a more controversial report, groups can be invited to include interviews with people likely to have strong opinions: for example, the leader of the Anti-Abortion League in Malgudi, the government expert on relief to famine-stricken areas, etc.

The teacher helps students prepare their scripts. They are encouraged to make the interviewees from the story act 'in character' – for example, would Ranga answer the reporter's questions directly? Would he answer briefly or tend to talk on and on? How would Ranga's wife behave? Would she regret the lost 30 rupees? And so on.

When groups are ready, the special reports are presented in front of the class, or put on video if at all possible.

'The open window' by Saki (H. H. Munro)*

This classic short story is very brief and therefore ideally suited to a double lesson of say one-and-a-half hours.

The story is cleverly constructed. Vera, a self-confident 15-year-old, talks a nervous visitor, Mr Nuttel, into believing that her aunt's husband and brother never returned after a hunting trip, but that her aunt still leaves the French window open in the belief that they will turn up. When three figures approach the house, Nuttel flees in panic, while Vera puts her talents for 'romance' to instant use by inventing a far-fetched explanation for her aunt.

Warm-up

A full-scale classroom activity is used as a prelude to the actual reading of the story. It aims to encourage learners' imaginative development, to foster their oral skills, and, above all, to build the desire to read literature. It is particularly successful with students who know each other well.

Each pair is given Worksheet 63 which contains a list of the main characters and a few sentences (extracted from the story, although they do not know this yet). They are then asked to build any story that retains the elements contained in the extracts. Learners new to this kind of creative activity can be given further help by being told to answer the following questions, as they brainstorm for ideas, and by having their attention drawn to key vocabulary items such as the word 'creepy':

1. Who is Mr Nuttel and why is he visiting Mrs Sappleton?
2. What was Mrs Sappleton's tragedy?
3. Who are the figures? Where have they come from and what do they want?
4. Where has the spaniel come from? Whose is it?
5. Why does Mr Nuttel run away in fear?

Once each pair has pieced together its own story, they tell it to other pairs, and listen to other versions, in turn. Then the class is invited to read the original story silently straight through. Immediate reactions are requested, after which the teacher can move into more conventional comprehension work with worksheets, or discussion of character and plot.

Here, as an example, is an imagined story produced by a multilingual lower-advanced class from the stimulus extracts.

Mr Nuttel is a lonely widower, looking for a female companion. He has subscribed to a matrimonial agency and has been matched with a Mrs Sappleton. He visits her house.

Mrs Sappleton is a pathological man-hater. She uses her niece to occupy her

* in *The Penguin Complete Saki*

In pairs, make up a short story (orally). It should contain the elements
listed below. Be ready to tell your story to other pairs.

Principal characters for your story:
Vera, aged 15
Mrs Sappleton, Vera's aunt
Framton Nuttel, a visitor to Mrs Sappleton's house

Elements to include in your story:
'My aunt will be down presently, Mr Nuttel,' said a very self-
  possessed young lady of fifteen; 'in the meantime you must try to
  put up with me.'
'Her* great tragedy happened just three years ago,' said the child.†
'Do you know, sometimes on still, quiet evenings like this, I almost
  get a creepy feeling that they will walk in through that window . . .'
In the deepening twilight three figures were walking across the lawn
  towards the window; they all carried guns under their arms.
Framton grabbed wildly at his stick and hat.
'A most extraordinary man, Mr Nuttel,' said Mrs Sappleton.
'I expect it was the spaniel,' said the niece calmly; 'he told me he had
  a horror of dogs.'

* 'Her' refers to Mrs Sappleton.
† 'the child' refers to Vera.

Worksheet 63

prospective suitors while she spies on them from upstairs to see if she is interested
in nurturing the relationship. In this case, she signals to Vera that she is not. Vera
therefore tells Nuttel that her aunt's three previous husbands disappeared
mysteriously while out on the moors. Nuttel is uneasy. Mrs Sappleton tiptoes
unnoticed down the stairs, carrying a stiletto knife. Suddenly Nuttel sees three
men coming across the lawn carrying guns. He is terrified and rushes out.

The men are policemen investigating the disappearance of a widower called Mr
Johnson. They ask who the man is who rushed from the house. Mrs Sappleton
says it was a man looking for gardening work, and the niece explains that her
aunt's spaniel had reawakened his terror of dogs, which had been formed after he
had been badly bitten by his mother's dog when he was a child.

'Destiny and the bullet' by Gerald Kersh*

This is a very short story with a strong narrative. A man tells of the time
when he was a soldier in China. While on sentry duty, he killed a poor

* in *Read and Relate*, ed. John Ashton and George Bott

man who was looking for food for his family. Years later, the man gets married. He employs a Chinese servant girl. The girl saves the life of his wife and baby son. For the first time he starts to talk to the servant girl. What he discovers about her own life has the painful echo of destiny . . .

Warm-up

The teacher tells the students the title of the story and invites speculation about the possible connection between 'destiny' and 'bullet'. If necessary, students are guided by questions such as: How could a bullet play a part in someone's life? If someone's destiny is to shoot another person can that person change his or her future? Why or why not?

Jigsaw reading

Students read the first part of the story stopping at the point at which the narrator begins to tell his own story of destiny and the bullet. Then the teacher divides the class into three groups. Each group is asked to read a different section of the narrator's story. Students read their respective sections individually and then meet as a group to iron out difficulties of comprehension contained in their portion. After that, new groups are formed in the conventional jigsaw activity progression. Thus each new group has three members, each of whom has read a different section of the story. Every group member retells their part of the story and the overall account is pieced together. Next, the teacher tells the class that the final twist in the story is missing. In groups, they are to discuss a likely ending (that is, they try to work out that the Chinese servant girl is the daughter of the poor man whom the narrator shot). Once an ending has been deduced, students are asked to write it using approximately 120 words. They are advised to study the writer's style and to bear it in mind. Finally, they read the original ending and compare it with their own efforts.

Follow-up activities

Here are some alternatives:
- With advanced groups, the teacher can ask students to make a stylistic analysis of their endings and then to compare them with the original. They report back to the class in terms of the similarities and differences that have been found.
- Students write the conversation that takes place between the narrator and the servant girl *after* he has confessed to her that he killed her father. Then it is acted out in short role plays in pairs.
- A class debate could take place. The motion is: 'This class believes that the narrator was not responsible for the death of the poor man'.

'Sredni Vashtar' by Saki*

This is a concise story that quickly builds up suspense and leads, along classic short story lines, to a dramatic climax. (There is an excellent film version which catches these qualities admirably.) There are some lexical difficulties but they do not obstruct understanding of the main narrative, so that the story can be used to good effect to provide training in gist reading.

A sickly ten-year-old boy lives a miserable life in the house of his spinsterly, domineering cousin cum guardian. He creates a fantasy religious cult in a garden shed, where his idols are a hen and a ferret. When his guardian gets rid of his hen, he prays to the ferret for revenge. She goes down to the shed again . . .

The aim of the activities is to encourage reading for the central features of the story, without undue fear of unknown words; to build up motivation to read the story, so that learners are willing to reread it for more detailed comprehension; to move towards a written composition on the two main characters.

Warm-up

Students are told that they are going to read a very short story. Five key words are written on the board:

BOY   GUARDIAN   FERRET   DEATH   HATE

(Ferret will probably have to be explained.) In groups of three or four, learners try to predict what the story might be about.

After the class has been called together again and has shared predictions, the story is distributed (referenced for line numbers). The class is asked to read it once to find out what the story is. They are told not to use dictionaries and not to worry about unknown vocabulary. This could be set as homework.

Classroom activities

After students have read the story, the original small groups are reconstituted for students to discuss the story and especially the relationship between the boy and his guardian. We have found that discussion is often stimulated by giving each group a grid to fill out (see Worksheet 64). At this point, use of dictionaries is encouraged, to help pinpoint meanings and nuances of words relevant to the quality of the relationship. Com-

---

* in *The Penguin Complete Saki*

'Sredni Vashtar' presents the reader with two strong characters in conflict. Read quickly through the story again, picking out the words or expressions which indicate either positive or negative feelings between Conradin and Mrs de Ropp. Enter as many as you can in the appropriate boxes below, with line references.

+	−
	'disagreeable' (line 7)
	'hated her' (line 17)

Worksheet 64

pleted grids are posted up at the end of this period so that students can compare them.

As a revision/oral activity, students could make a 'trailer'. Groups are told to imagine they are now moviemakers who have finished making a film of 'Sredni Vashtar' but have not yet made a 'trailer', that is, a selection of snippets with a voice-over to whet the appetite of cinemagoers the week before the film is shown. (If the actual film version can be obtained, groups are to imagine they have been commissioned by its director to produce the trailer.)

The moviemakers must devise, act out and do the voice-over for their trailer. This must last no longer than two minutes, and must aim to build up a desire in the audience to come and watch the film next week. Preparation and dress rehearsals follow, within a set time limit. Each group's trailer is then performed for the whole class (this can be done next lesson if time is a problem).

Written follow-up

The teacher can set a homework essay which asks the students to analyse the relationship between Conradin and Mrs de Ropp. A great deal of the material for such an essay will already have been gathered and jotted down in note form on the grid, so that learners are free to concentrate on questions of essay structure, style, and organisation of material.

'The war in the bathroom' by Margaret Atwood*

This unusual short story is set in the form of seven entries in a diary, one for each day of the central character's first week in new lodgings. The themes – the problems of adjusting to new surroundings, and the inevitable clashes that arise when people share a house – are quite wide in their appeal, while the ambiguity of the image projected by the narrator creates enough suspense to carry the reader along. Another advantage from the point of view of the foreign student is the simple, 'everyday' quality of much of the language (there are a few North American terms which may have to be glossed).

This is a fairly long story but its division into definite sections makes it ideal for varied treatment: some used for listening or other classroom activities, others left for individual reading.

Warm-up

The aim is to set the scene, and elicit learners' own feelings about the central situation of moving into new, unfamiliar surroundings. This can be done in a variety of ways, according to the group's needs and the linguistic skills the teacher wishes to emphasise. One way of achieving this is to use visual prompts: for example, pictures of packing cases, removal vans, etc. (see Figures 21A and 21B). Students are asked to think about moving, either the class as a whole or in small groups:

- Have you ever moved? Were you excited? depressed? nervous? etc.
- Would those feelings change if you had to move often?
- Do things get lost when you move?
- Do you enjoy exploring new territory or does it frighten you?
- Do you prefer new things or old, well-used and well-loved things?

Followed by similar questions about sharing a house:

- What kinds of things can cause friction if you are sharing a house?
- Do you think time in the kitchen/bathroom should be rationed?
- What do you feel about noise problems in a shared house?
- What are the advantages/disadvantages of sharing? How do you feel about this?

An alternative warm-up strategy is writing followed by oral feedback. Students are shown pictures without comment, then asked to write down their reactions as spontaneously as possible, in a few sentences, which are later compared and discussed.

Students are asked to make their choices, then compare their answers

---

* in *Dancing Girls and Other Stories*

Figure 21A

with their neighbour's. Further discussion is often sparked by establishing a 'class profile' of favourite objects: the teacher asks how many students chose number 1, number 2, and so on, giving one mark for each choice, so that the overall favourites can be found (see Worksheet 65). Whichever warm-up activity is used, it should take up about 15 minutes to half an hour. The rest of the lesson can then be devoted to a class reading of the first section, 'Monday'.

221

Figure 21B

Listening in class

Students do not yet have the text. The teacher gives them a list of questions to help shape their listening: What is the story about? Who do we meet in it? What is the narrator like? He or she then reads to them, or plays a recording of, 'Monday' (three-and-a-half to four minutes). The language in this first section is simple, and some of the crucial words have

Imagine you are moving into new 'digs' (one room only). You can take with you only three things from this list. Which would you choose?

1. my radio/cassette player
2. my own cutlery (this is called 'silverware' in the story)
3. my own plates
4. glasses (wine glasses)
5. my two favourite books
6. my own sheets and quilt or duvet
7. a teapot (or coffeepot)
8. the teddy-bear (or other toy) I've had since childhood
9. a framed picture of my mother/father/lover/child
10. a good bedside reading lamp
11. my diary/notebook
12. my calendar
13. other item (name it) ....

Worksheet 65

been presented in the warm-up session. For most upper-intermediate or advanced classes no further pre-teaching will be necessary. Students listen, then write comments on the story they have just heard. In particular, they are to indicate what most struck them in it and what they remember most about it.

After students have compared their impressions, first in pairs, then in general feedback and class discussion, they are given 'Monday' to read, and, for home reading, the longer section, 'Tuesday'. The teacher encourages students to speculate about the central character(s), and, if possible, compare notes with others. In particular, learners are asked to note what new facts emerge about the protagonist(s), and his/her/their personality. In 'Tuesday', contradictory clues begin to be picked up by the reader. To accompany home reading, it is useful to give learners a 'focussing' worksheet (see Worksheet 66). The class is asked to start building up a picture of the narrator, which they may want to revise as the story progresses.

In the next class, a similar procedure can be used. Students listen to 'Wednesday' (three to three-and-a-half minutes). The language is very straightforward and most suitable for listening comprehension. Once again, students jot down a description of what they have heard and their reactions to it. In groups, they compare reactions, and their picture of the central character. They are given 'Wednesday' and 'Thursday' for home

One of the intriguing things about 'The war in the bathroom' is that the reader has difficulty building a picture of the narrator. The clues we pick up at the beginning are contradictory and confusing: it is often necessary to go back and look more closely at what we have been told.

Look at the following descriptions and decide which one coincides most closely with *your* picture of the narrator. Add any details *of your own* so that you end up with your view of the narrator's background and character. You may end up with an amalgamation of details from 1, 2, 3 and 4, plus your own thoughts and hunches.

1. The narrator is a disturbed, elderly lady forced to live with her middle-aged daughter who is also rather dependent and shy. The old lady is very protective towards her daughter and not happy to be living in circumstances far below her former standard of living. The old lady is rather religious.

2. The narrator is a youngish woman (in her late thirties perhaps) probably unmarried and a bit of an outsider. She has some mental problems probably caused by an over-rigid upbringing. As a result she is hyper-sensitive and anti-social but reasonably self-disciplined, tidy and clean. She dislikes mess, especially other people's and is petty-minded. She probably grew up in a rural area.

3. The narrator is probably a young graduate student in her twenties who is unemployed and forced to live in a rented room. She is lazy and depressed, and lonely, but very sensitive and observant. She mocks herself by calling herself 'she' from time to time. She is suspicious of men, and enjoys her food. She seems to have middle-class tastes, has regular habits and is careful with money. She needs more privacy.

4. The narrator is probably a writer in her fifties who has a split personality, is obsessed with cleanliness and purity, is paranoid and has probably been in and out of mental hospitals. She is frightened and also aggressive because she needs a lot of personal space in order to remain calm. She is sometimes cruel (perhaps her father was cruel to her) but basically she is a rather sad, compliant woman who is not getting much out of life and is withdrawing into herself.

Worksheet 66

reading. Their task is now to list and describe the people who live in the house, perhaps using a grid with the following headings:

people in the house
age
appearance
character / personality
what the narrator thinks of them

If time is short, or with more advanced learners, the third listening activity may be omitted and students given the rest of the story to read, with the task of up-dating their picture of the narrator. Otherwise, 'Friday', a very short section, can be used for a final listening session (under one minute). 'Saturday' and 'Sunday' are given for silent class reading, followed by group or general discussion of the reader's final impression of the protagonist, and of the story's themes: the intensity of conflict generated in cramped quarters, the cruelty of domestic 'wars', the meaning of 'self' or 'identity'.

Parallel reading

Students who enjoy reading parallel stories could be given Patricia Highsmith's 'The cries of love' (in *Eleven*). This is a story of two elderly ladies who have shared a room for so long that they cannot manage to live apart, but who spend their whole lives plotting increasingly cruel acts of revenge against each other. On a formal level, however, this story provides a striking contrast with 'The war in the bathroom', as it is a fairly straightforward third-person narration. Comparison of the two stories can thus be used in advanced classes to stimulate discussion of the effects of a writer's narrative strategies.

10 Poems

Poems offer a rich, varied repertoire and are a source of much enjoyment for teacher and learner alike. There is the initial advantage of length – many poems are well-suited to a single classroom lesson. Then again, they often explore themes of universal concern and embody life experiences, observations and the feelings evoked by them. Their brilliant concision and strong imagery combine to powerful overall effect. Moreover, poems are sensitively tuned to what, for language learners, are the vital areas of stress, rhythm and similarities of sound. Reading poetry enables the learner to experience the power of language outside the strait-jacket of more standard written sentence structure and lexis. In the classroom, using poetry can lead naturally on to freer, creative written expression. Indeed, poems are capable of producing strong response from the reader, and this memorable intensity motivates further reading of poetry in the foreign language.

When the teacher comes to select poems to share with the students, he or she will need to take into account which poems are suited to their interests, language and maturity levels. Not all poems are serious or complex. There are many poems written in a lighter vein, or with a fairly simple narrative structure. Both these types are well-suited to language learners, especially at the earlier stages. However, the teacher should not be too hesitant about working with more challenging poems, especially ones he or she particularly likes.

Providing that learners can be given help with the personal and linguistic resources they will need, they will be able to attain the fuller enjoyment of a poem that comes from a sense of sharing the poet's created world and becoming, as reader, a new creator of meaning. Once again, we feel that this kind of help can best be provided through a range of group activities. In particular, before a poem is read or listened to for the first time, it is often very important to plan a substantial warm-up activity to arouse the learners' curiosity and involve them in the poem's themes.

As far as is possible, we feel that the activities selected should encourage a sort of productive exploration which feeds the confidence of the learners both to develop their own responses and to read and enjoy poetry in the target language on their own. The aim, ultimately, is to individualise each student's experience of literature.

For our illustrations in this chapter we have chosen just a few of the poems which we have used to good effect in our teaching. The selection demonstrates a variety of approaches which can be used at different levels with students of different ages and interests. In Appendix 2, we have included a list of anthologies that may be useful to language teachers.

'The King of China's daughter' by Edith Sitwell*

This is a set of related activities designed to help students appreciate the lyrical and melodic quality of poetry as well as its metaphorical richness.

Warm-up

The class is asked to recall any songs or nursery rhymes they particularly liked as children. The teacher can often start this off by reciting or singing one that he or she remembers with pleasure, or that his or her children especially enjoy. In monolingual classes, favourite rhymes or songs are compared, and learners are asked to note any points of similarity between them. In multilingual classes, students are encouraged to recite or sing in their own language, so that other students can hear the rhythm or melody of the original, then to explain meanings in English. Once again, the class is asked to look out for any points of similarity between the various rhymes recalled.

The teacher then distributes the text of three or four English nursery rhymes. Suitable ones could be: 'I saw three ships', 'I saw a ship a-sailing', 'Lavender's blue', 'The old woman toss'd up in a basket', 'I had a little nut tree', etc. – the texts of these follow. The teacher reads them out to the class, then asks learners, in pairs, to list as many similarities as they can between the various rhymes, and, if possible, between these and the ones previously remembered. (Recordings of sung versions are ideal, if available.)

> *I saw three ships*
>
> I saw three ships come sailing by,
> Come sailing by, come sailing by;
> I saw three ships come sailing by,
> On New Year's Day in the morning.
>
> And what do you think was in them then,
> Was in them then, was in them then?
> And what do you think was in them then,
> On New Year's Day in the morning.   ⋙→

* in *The Faber Book of Modern Verse*, ed. Michael Roberts

Three pretty girls were in them then,
Were in them then, were in them then;
Three pretty girls were in them then,
On New Year's Day in the morning.

And one could whistle, and one could sing,
And one could play the violin –
Such joy there was at my wedding,
On New Year's Day in the morning.

I saw a ship a-sailing

I saw a ship a-sailing,
A-sailing on the sea;
And oh! it was all laden
With pretty things for thee.

There were comfits in the cabin,
And apples in the hold,
The sails were made of silk,
And the masts of beaten gold.

There were raisins in the cabin,
And almonds in the hold,
The sails were made of satin,
And the mast was made of gold.

Lavender's blue

Lavender's blue, dilly, dilly,
Lavender's green;
When I am king, dilly, dilly,
You shall be queen.
Call up your men, dilly, dilly,
Set them to work,
Some to the plough, dilly, dilly,
Some to the cart.
Some to make hay, dilly, dilly,
Some to cut corn,
While you and I dilly, dilly,
Keep ourselves warm.

The old woman toss'd up in a basket

There was an old woman toss'd up in a basket
Nineteen times as high as the moon;
Where she was going I couldn't but ask it,
For in her hand she carried a broom.

Old woman, old woman, old woman, quoth I,
O wither, O wither, O wither, so high?
To brush the cobwebs off the sky!
Shall I go with thee? Ay, by-and-by.

There is a feedback session when the class pools similarities noted. These usually include features such as repetition of key phrases, strong rhythm, simple rhymes, recurring reference to kings, queens, precious things such as gold and silver, strange happenings or transformations, expressions of love or happiness, vivid but sometimes mysterious images, etc. The teacher elicits comments on whether students remember these features as being appealing to them when they were children, and whether they are so still.

The teacher then asks the class to look more particularly at this short nursery rhyme:

> I had a little nut tree
> Nothing would it bear
> But a silver nutmeg   (*a variant version:* But a silver apple)
> And a golden pear.
>
> The King of Spain's daughter
> Came to visit me,
> And all for the sake
> Of my little nut tree.

The teacher reads the poem once or twice, and asks students to place a little mark, in their copy of the poem, over the words that are stressed. These are then compared, any differences discussed, then learners read the poem softly to each other, in pairs.

The teacher then tells the class that an old professor was said to have been at work for many years on a very thorough and detailed interpretation of this poem. After his death, however, nothing was found in his papers but a few unintelligible scribblings; among these there was a list of words which could only be made out with difficulty. The teacher writes these words in a column at the left-hand side of the board (or on different boards, if the classroom has more than one):

hard/soft
edible
rich, precious
fruitful/barren
exotic/magical
attraction
power
love/sex

The class is then asked, in groups of three or four, to choose any two words, and try to decide how they relate to the poem. When they have agreed amongst themselves, one of the group goes up to the board and writes his or her group's explanation, as briefly as possible, against the appropriate column. The teacher can write a first sentence of his or her own to start off the exercise, if students need an example.

It is best to treat this as a brainstorming exercise, in which odd or unusual explanations are welcomed, and to set a fairly short time limit for it. When time is up, the class considers the various links made. Are any not clear? Students are encouraged to question members of other groups about what they meant. Are there any words or sets not chosen? Why not? Can the class together supply any explanations for these? The teacher then asks students to nominate the word or set that they feel is most important or most illuminating. Finally, the teacher asks students to say whether it is possible to indicate what the concrete images could mean.

Reading the poem

The preceding activities will probably occupy the whole of a first lesson. At the beginning of a second lesson, perhaps after a break, or the next day or week, the teacher tells students that he or she is going to read them a modern poem and that their task is to list as many differences as they can between it and 'The little nut tree'. They may wish to remind themselves of the nursery rhyme by rereading it quickly. The teacher then reads the poem out, perhaps twice, with lots of expression.

The King of China's daughter

The King of China's daughter,
She never would love me
Though I hung my cap and bells upon
Her nutmeg tree.
For oranges and lemons,
The stars in bright blue air,
(I stole them long ago, my dear)
Were dangling there.

The Moon did give me silver pence,
The Sun did give me gold,
And both together softly blew
And made my porridge cold;
But the King of China's daughter
Pretended not to see
When I hung my cap and bells upon
Her nutmeg tree.

Students note down differences and compare them afterwards with their neighbour's. A class list is drawn up on the board by a nominated student. Then the teacher distributes the text or displays it on the overhead projector. Students, in groups of three or four, read the poem, asking each other's help with any difficulties they might encounter. The teacher writes on the board three items: cap and bells, oranges and lemons, porridge cold. He or she circulates, ensuring that students between them have picked up the references underlying these, to traditional lore: the 'cap and bells' is the symbol of the jester or fool who was also often thought of as a 'bard' or storyteller; oranges and lemons feature in many children's songs as exotic and precious fruit, and as the name for a traditional children's game; porridge also occurs in games and rhymes, as well as in the very well-known children's story, 'The three bears'.

Each group is now set a double task:

1. Remembering the exercise they did with the 'professor's list of words' in the preceding lesson, they are able to write a similar list of words, or paired words, that would be important to an interpretation of the Sitwell poem.
2. They are to write one sentence which encapsulates the group's view of what the poem is about (for example, one group wrote: 'I am not important to the person who is most important to me').

Comparison of key words chosen, and of the overall interpretation contained within the sentence written, often increases students' appreciation of the poem as a whole.

If there is time, a reading-aloud exercise can follow. The poem divides quite easily into four-line sections, each of which is given to one group to prepare. Stresses are marked as in the initial activity with 'The little nut tree'. The teacher circulates and helps with places where there is variation on the standard pattern (as in the three stressed final words in 'The stars in bright blue air'). When everyone is ready, choral reading is done by each group in turn.

Follow-up

Learners are asked to look back at all the vivid images in the poems they have been reading: sailing ships, the sun, moon and stars, gold, silver, girls singing and dancing, a nutmeg tree, oranges and lemons, cap and bells, etc., then choose the one they like best. They are to write a short note (or poem, if they wish) to a loved one, telling him or her how they feel, through the image chosen.

'My papa's waltz' by Theodore Roethke*

This poem is written in deceptively simple language and evokes strongly the ambivalence of a child's view of a parent. This is a theme within the experience of most people.

Warm-up

The students are asked to complete the following sentences in any way that they feel is appropriate:

A good father . . .
A bad father . . .

Upon completion, comparisons are made in pairs and then the teacher asks for some samples and these are written up on the board. Next, the teacher tells the class the title of the poem and asks for guesses in terms of its likely theme. Then he or she reads the poem to the students having asked them to choose *one* word which captures their first response to its contents. A bank of likely response words is supplied where necessary: 'fear', 'fun', 'tension', 'insensitivity', 'bully', 'dancing', 'drunken', 'pleasure', 'mystery'. Instead of pre-presenting any difficult lexis, the teacher mimes or indicates words like 'dizzy', 'knuckle', 'buckle', 'countenance' during the first reading.

> *My papa's waltz*
>
> The whiskey on your breath
> Could make a small boy dizzy;
> But I hung on like death;
> Such waltzing was not easy.
>
> We romped until the pans
> Slid from the kitchen shelf;
> My mother's countenance
> Could not unfrown itself.

* in *The Faber Book of Modern Verse*, ed. Michael Roberts

The hand that held my wrist
Was battered on one knuckle;
At every step you missed
My right ear scraped a buckle.

You beat time on my head
With a palm caked hard by dirt,
Then waltzed me off to bed
Still clinging to your shirt.

Once the students have heard the poem, they select their word and choices are compared and explained. Then the text of the poem is distributed. Any remaining vocabulary problems are discussed after a silent reading and the students are asked if they wish to change their choice of word. Once again, any changes are discussed. To help to clarify the students' response, the teacher asks the students to make two columns on a piece of paper with the headings 'positive' and 'negative'. He or she then reads out some of the words from the poem and asks the students to assign each word to one of the columns according to whether they feel it has a 'good' or a 'bad' sense in the poem. The columns are then discussed and should reveal the ambivalence of words like 'beat', 'battered'. The students consider whether the father in the poem is 'good' or 'bad'. Their views are related back to the warm-up activity and the discussion is thereby extended.

Reading the poem chorally

This poem has a subtly irregular rhythm and rhyme which carry additional meaning. The subtlety can be drawn out by encouraging the students to read the poem aloud. The following procedure is an enjoyable way of involving the whole class and marks an elaboration of the activity outlined for 'I had a little nut tree'.

The class is first divided into four groups – one group per stanza. Each group is allotted a stanza and examines it in detail. Main stresses are marked and groups circle any words which can be spoken in a way that reveals meaning (for example, slid, battered, scraped, waltzed, dizzy). Next, groups are told to quietly 'drum' the stress pattern of their stanza with their hands until all drummers are in time. A conductor should be appointed to keep disagreements to a minimum. Then the groups read out their respective stanzas quietly, led by their conductor. When each chorus is in reasonable shape, the groups discuss possible improvements – pauses, or other modifications to their 'tune'. Rehearsals continue for a little longer and then the teacher announces that the 'concert' will commence. After an introduction by the teacher, the poem is read by the choral groups in the correct sequence. The performance is discussed and then individual members of each stanza-group are invited to give solo renderings. Finally, the teacher gives a solo performance and there is discussion of differences in the readings. With confident groups, a recording of the concert helps this discussion greatly.

Follow-up

This poem offers plenty of scope for follow-up. The students can be asked to improvise a conversation between the child in the poem and his mother that same evening, or between the father and mother. This usually reveals assumptions about the relationships which are implicit in the poem. Alternatively, the students can be asked to draw up a list of qualities of the 'good father' and then to arrange them in order of importance.

For students who enjoy creative writing, a simple activity starts when the teacher asks the class to imagine that they are young children again. They must try to remember their world at that time and their perceptions of adults, especially their father or a father-figure such as a favourite uncle or brother. They are asked to complete a stanza beginning thus:

> *Father* (or uncle/brother, etc. as appropriate)
> You make me feel . . .
> You give me . . .
> I give you . . .
> I wish . . .
> I . . .

Finally, there are several fine poems written about family life from the perspective of the child. These can be used as a basis for stylistic contrast or as additional reading for the students to do at their leisure. Examples of such poems include: 'Follower' by Seamus Heaney, 'Sorry' by R. S. Thomas, 'Family Reunion' by Sylvia Plath.*

'Telephone conversation' by Wole Soyinka†

This well-known poem vividly illustrates the distastefulness of racial prejudice. The narrator's anger at being on the receiving end of its patronising attitudes is forcefully conveyed. Some of the vocabulary in the poem is quite challenging, but the situation is clear enough for it to be used successfully with advanced classes.

---

* in *Contemporary British and North American Verse*, ed. Martin Booth; *Poem into Poem* by Alan Maley and Sandra Moulding; *Collected Poems* by Sylvia Plath, ed. Ted Hughes, respectively
† reproduced in *Kaleidoscope*, ed. Michael Swan

Warm-up

Before they hear or see the poem, the students are asked to imagine a situation in which a person is looking for a room and is about to telephone a woman who has advertised a suitable room in the newspaper. Half of the class imagine that they are landladies. What will they want to know about anyone who phones up about the room? The other half are prospective tenants. What will they want to know? Each half is given time to consider its questions. Then the teacher asks for questions from each side. These are written on the board and discussed. With suitable groups, the teacher can encourage an improvisation of the telephone conversation and ask the rest of the class for their reactions to the characters. Is the landlady pleasant? suspicious? cool? Is the prospective tenant polite? timid? desperate?

Reading the poem

The teacher reads Soyinka's poem. Difficult words are given initial meaning through mime or manner of delivery. We do not like to pre-present isolated vocabulary items as this spoils the integrity of the first contact with the whole poem.

Telephone conversation

The price seemed reasonable, location
Indifferent. The landlady swore she lived
Off premises. Nothing remained
But self-confession. 'Madam,' I warned,
'I hate a wasted journey – I am African.'
Silence. Silenced transmission of
Pressurized good-breeding. Voice, when it came,
Lipstick coated, long gold-rolled
Cigarette-holder pipped. Caught I was, foully.
'HOW DARK?' . . . I had not misheard . . . 'ARE YOU LIGHT
OR VERY DARK?' Button B. Button A. Stench
Of rancid breath of public hide-and-speak.
Red booth. Red pillar-box. Red double-tiered
Omnibus squelching tar. It *was* real! Shamed
By ill-mannered silence, surrender
Pushed dumbfoundment to beg simplification.
Considerate she was, varying the emphasis –
'ARE YOU DARK? OR VERY LIGHT?' Revelation came.
'You mean – like plain or milk chocolate?'
Her assent was clinical, crushing in its light
Impersonality. Rapidly, wave-length adjusted,

Read the poem 'Telephone conversation'. In the empty bubbles, write what the character might be thinking. If you like, continue the story in boxes 9 and 10.

I chose. 'West African sepia' – and as afterthought,
'Down in my passport.' Silence for spectroscopic
Flight of fancy, till truthfulness clanged her accent
Hard on the mouthpiece. 'WHAT'S THAT?' conceding
'DON'T KNOW WHAT THAT IS.' 'Like brunette.'
'THAT'S DARK, ISN'T IT?' 'Not altogether.
Facially, I am brunette, but, madam, you should see
The rest of me. Palm of my hand, soles of my feet
Are a peroxide blond. Friction, caused –
Foolishly, madam – by sitting down, has turned
My bottom raven black – One moment, madam!' – sensing
Her receiver rearing on the thunderclap
About my ears – 'Madam,' I pleaded, 'wouldn't you rather
See for yourself?'

After the poem has been read with plenty of feeling and eye contact the teacher asks the students for their reactions. This should lead to the concept of prejudice, and more especially, racial prejudice. The poem is then handed out and the teacher reads it for a second time. Following that, the poem is examined in more detail through a range of questions, for example: Why are the landlady's words written in capital letters? What words indicate the emotions of the two speakers? Students are encouraged to guess the meaning of unknown vocabulary items. The teacher then asks the class what the landlady and the caller are thinking while they are communicating with each other. They are reminded that the actual words of the conversation do not seem to reflect the emotion words that they have already identified. A simple cartoon version of the conversation is displayed on the overhead projector (see Worksheet 67) and the students, in groups, consider the likely contents of the thought bubbles. Then groups are given copies of the cartoons and they write in the thoughts. After that, groups exchange cartoons. Finally, a short scene is enacted with one student playing the landlady, another the prospective tenant and two additional voices being the thoughts of each.

Follow-up

Activities could suitably concentrate on creative writing. The students might imagine themselves to be either the landlady or the caller and write a letter about the telephone conversation to a friend or, in the caller's case, a race relations organisation.

More ambitiously, the students could build up a group poem about the landlady. First the teacher distributes to groups of five students a sheet of paper with the following written on it:

Metaphor poem – The landlady
(Animal)   She's...
(Flower)   She's...
(Drink)   She's...
(Weather)   She's...
(Colour)   She's...

The students are told that the poem they are going to write is to be about the landlady in Soyinka's poem. Each student in the group chooses one of the categories in brackets. That category then becomes the basis for a metaphor about the landlady. Each student writes his or her metaphor sentence and then the group's collective efforts are put together to form a five-line metaphor poem. Here is an example:

> *The landlady*
>
> She's a blind peacock strutting in a small circle,
> She's a faded rose with a rotten scent,
> She's iced tea behind lace curtains,
> She's a frost against the summer sun,
> She's the yellow face of prejudice.

'The couple upstairs' by Hugo Williams*

The brevity of this simply written poem leaves plenty of scope for a detailed examination of the effects it creates and the inferences available to the reader.

Warm-up

Students are asked about their neighbours. Do they have neighbours? How close to their house/flat do they live? They are then asked to form pairs, and, using the grid illustrated in Worksheet 68, to interview each other about one or two of their respective neighbours. Findings are discussed as the teacher asks different students what they discovered. The teacher then asks whether they are affected by what their neighbours do. Do they try to 'keep up with the Joneses'? Do they go out together, visit each other's houses? How would they feel if one of their neighbours left?

Reading the poem

Students are told that they are going to hear a poem about neighbours

* in *Contemporary British Poetry*, ed. Blake Morrison and Andrew Motion

Work in pairs and complete the questionnaire about your partner's neighbours.

Neigh- bour number	What are their jobs?	How long have they lived there?	How many in the family?	Inter- ests, hobbies	Eccen- tricities, strange habits	Qual- ities: friendly? noisy? cheer- ful? etc.
1.						
2.						
3.						

Worksheet 68

called 'The couple upstairs'. They are given a gist question to accompany the first listening: What has happened? The teacher reads with plenty of expression and eye contact.

After this first reading and the follow-up to the gist question, the poem is displayed on the board or overhead projector and the teacher reads it once more.

The teacher now says that he or she has a copy of the poem with some notes and questions written on it by English students who used the class text in previous years (see Worksheet 69). The students are asked, in pairs or threes, to study the notes and, concentrating on the ones they find most interesting, discuss what they mean, and whether they agree with statements made. With many groups, at least 20 minutes must be allowed for this. When the groups are ready, the teacher invites comments about the notes and questions.

This activity is a way of getting the students to examine the poem in some detail on their own. The situation is informal and the discussion is not teacher-centred. The notes, handwritten and 'arrowed' into a copy of the poem, make the process of analysis visual and concrete. The jotted-down, open-ended nature of the comments gives students the feeling that they can be more easily explored or challenged. The unanswered questions leave room for student contribution. In short, this format builds initial confidence in the analysis of poetry in a foreign language, and heightens appreciation.

Read the poem, study the handwritten notes and choose the comments you find most interesting.

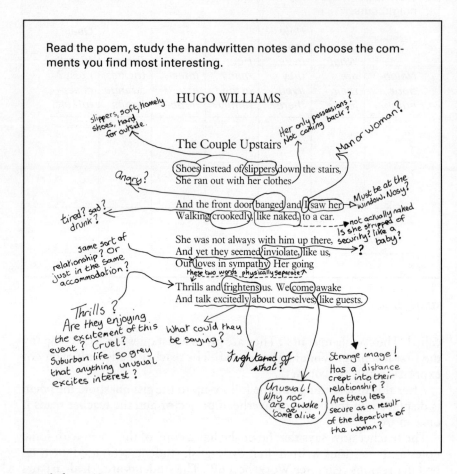

Worksheet 69

Follow-up

Follow-up could include:

Improvisation The teacher returns to the theme and asks the students to improvise the conversation between the couple downstairs and the man (now living alone?) upstairs.

Writing Students are asked to imagine what is going on in the departing woman's mind as she runs down the steps and, turning, just catches a glimpse of the curtain moving in the neighbours' bedroom. This can be written in the form of a 'stream-of-consciousness' – that is, thoughts jotted down as they occur without any deliberate ordering – or as a poem beginning with the line:

Watching, always watching ....
....
....
....

Figure 22 shows examples of poems students have written.

Down the stairs. Turn around, there is still time.
The front door, bang!
Watching, always watching. Yes, dear neighbour, I'm
leaving. Something new to talk about: "Who should
have thought that?"..."They seemed happy." Happy?
I was, once.
The car. Go back, give it a second chance.
No, I'm too tired. Tomorrow, perhaps.
Reverse gear. Still there, watching. Thinking: "What
went wrong?"

Figure 22A

Watching, always watching... As if their whole lives
depended on that... Always watching other people's
unhappiness, so as to forget their own dull and empty lives...
Yes I've just left him! Yes we've just split up!
So what? Leave me cry alone... My pain is pure,
sincere, but your dirty eyes on me... oh I won't
give you the pleasure to see me cry...

Figure 22B

Watching, always watching,
That smug prying female rat

The scorching sting of her spying eyes
Bores my naked back.

Gloating and nodding, but (as) blind as a bat.
Overweening, but outwitted,
She won't even hear her own door bang
When he goes. But the thought of us
Will long keep her awake
Like an unwanted guest.

Figure 22C

'To women, as far as I'm concerned' by D. H. Lawrence*

This poem, like the next one, has proved popular with classes of adult learners or students at the upper secondary school level, because both poems crystallise feelings that lie close to the centre of many lives: feelings about human relationships and the 'games people play' in their dealings with each other. They are an excellent stimulus to discussion!

'To women, as far as I'm concerned' is a short poem, consisting entirely of straightforward statements, with no linguistic problems for advanced students. One way of presenting it is to cut it up into its individual lines, and ask students in small groups to decide on a possible order for them:

The feelings you would like us both to have, we neither of us have.
So if you want either of us to feel anything at all
The feelings I don't have, I won't say I have.
The feelings people ought to have, they never have.
The feelings you say you have, you don't have.
The feelings I don't have I don't have.
you'd better abandon all idea of feelings altogether.
If people say they've got feelings, you may be pretty sure they haven't got
  them.

* in *Selected Poems*

It is important to stress that it is not necessary to guess the 'right' order: the task is rather to arrange the lines in a way that suggests some kind of progression. For example, students have sometimes arranged the lines to show a movement from my feelings, to yours, to ours; or from the general to the particular; or from an idealised view of the world to what it is 'really' like. When this ordering has been done, each group is asked to supply a title for its poem, then compare it with the results achieved in other groups. The task in itself usually sparks off a lively exchange of views about what the poet is saying. These opinions can be further drawn out by a 'continuum' exercise of the kind described in Chapter 5. With one corner of the room representing total agreement and the other total disagreement, learners are asked to take up a position along the wall in between, thereby showing the extent to which they agree with certain statements about the poem, for example:

- The speaker in this poem is quite right in his attitude to feelings.
- People who talk most about feelings don't have any real feelings.
- Perfect honesty between people just isn't possible.
- All social relationships are hypocritical.
- The speaker is quite wrong to presume he knows what another person is 'really' feeling.
- The speaker is self-satisfied, not to say arrogant.
- The speaker is patronising towards the 'you' in the poem.
- The speaker is honest and trying to build up a good relationship with the other person in the poem.
- The poet's title suggests an antagonism towards women.

etc.

The teacher encourages students to justify the position they have taken, and question others at different points about the reasons for their decision.

One question which is often thrown up in the course of these activities concerns the poetic qualities, or otherwise, of this particular work. Is it really a poem? And if so, what exactly makes it one? If the teacher has not told the class that the statements they were ordering in the first phase came from a poem, he or she can ask them what kind of text they feel it is. Very often, learners sense that it is a poem, but they are sometimes worried by the absence of conventional features: imagery, metaphors, rhyme, a stanza pattern. In a general class discussion, the teacher asks students to list as many aspects or qualities as they can which mark this collection of sentences as a poem. Next, students in pairs try to work out a short definition of 'poetry' which fits the poem – or alternatively, which excludes it, if learners think that it is not really a poem at all. Afterwards, definitions are pinned up for learners to compare. The teacher could at this point add a definition of his or her own, and/or one or more famous ones, for example:

What oft was thought / But ne'er so well expressed   (Pope)

Emotion recollected in tranquillity   (Wordsworth)

A poem should be palpable and mute
  As a globed fruit . . .
A poem should not mean
  But be.   (Archibald MacLeish)

Mathematical formulae are satisfying because they express in a very sharp form a very wide law of nature. One expression encapsulates the motion of all the planets and satellites around the earth. I find that very satisfying. I regard poetry as being akin to that.   (D. King-Hele)

The text of 'To women, as far as I'm concerned' follows.

> ### To women, as far as I'm concerned
>
> The feelings I don't have I don't have.
> The feelings I don't have, I won't say I have.
> The feelings you say you have, you don't have.
> The feelings you would like us both to have, we neither of us
>   have.
> The feelings people ought to have, they never have.
> If people say they've got feelings, you may be pretty sure they
>   haven't got them.
> So if you want either of us to feel anything at all
> you'd better abandon all idea of feelings altogether.

'You and I' by Roger McGough*

This poem is on a similar theme, and can follow 'To women as far as I'm concerned', if students have enjoyed the discussion generated by that poem. 'You and I' is slightly more complex linguistically, with some words or expressions that may be unfamiliar to learners – 'try a new tack', 'blinkers', 'placatory', 'crocodile tears' – and some images whose connotations in English may have to be drawn out for students from some other cultures: 'dove and hawk', 'olive branch and thorns'. The discourse pattern built up cumulatively by each succeeding stanza is so strong, however, that the context usually helps learners get the sense of these expressions, with only minimal help from the teacher, so that pre-teaching is not really necessary. The following activity aims at getting learners right into the situation, asking them to imagine what the poet

* in *Waving at Trains*

could have written so that they can assess the strength and vividness of the images in the poem.

The teacher gives the class the title and first stanza only of the poem (written on the board, on a hand-out, or overhead projector). He or she reads it out, explains any difficulties, then asks students to say what the poem is about. Who could the 'you' and the 'I' be? What is their relationship like? Do members of the class recognise this situation? Do they ever feel misinterpreted? Are their own good intentions sometimes seen as aggressive by other people? Do they feel they sometimes distort or misunderstand what others are trying to communicate to them?

The teacher then gives the second stanza, but gapped, in the following way:

> You see both sides. I
> I
> am placatory. You
>
> ....

He or she explains difficulties, and asks for suggestions as to what could complete these sentences. Quite often, the first attempt will produce a too-simple opposition: 'You see both sides. I *see neither*' or 'I *see only one*' 'I am placatory. You *are violent, refuse to give in*', etc. In such cases, the teacher accepts the suggestions, writes them down, then asks students to check whether the second stanza is consistent with the first. 'I see neither' is a *possible* completion, but does it continue the thought: 'I explain quietly but you *hear* me shouting'? Would the thought have been different if the poet had written: 'I explain quietly but you *shout*'? Students usually then revise their first sentence to produce something like: 'You see both sides. I *think you're biassed (unfair/narrow-minded)*' 'I am placatory. You *think I'm insulting you / stirring up trouble / am a trouble-maker*'.

After this first communal writing effort, the teacher gives students in pairs the gapped third and fourth stanzas, and asks them to fill in the missing sections:

I am a dove. You	see an eagle. think I'm warish (war-like). are the wounded lion.
.... You	
offer an olive branch. I	see you throw down the glove (gauntlet). feel you're a bully. think you're antagonistic.
....	
You bleed. I	refuse to be moved. think you're pretending. think you're making a fuss.
.... I	
withdraw. You	think it's just a new tactic. don't believe me. put up new defences.
....	

Some sentences provided by a multilingual class preparing for the Cambridge Proficiency exam are given above, on the right. It is clear from these that students both understood the poem and responded to it with imagination and sensitivity. After comparing their solutions, they were eager to read the poem. There were cries of delight as students realised that they had come very close indeed to the spirit of the poem, but satisfaction too at the vivid metaphorical expression of the original. 'Well', they said, 'after all, he *is* a poet, isn't he!' The text of the poem follows.

You and I

I explain quietly. You
hear me shouting. You
try a new tack. I
feel old wounds reopen.

You see both sides. I
see your blinkers. I
am placatory. You
sense a new selfishness.

I am a dove. You
recognise the hawk. You
offer an olive branch. I
feel the thorns.

You bleed. I
see crocodile tears. I
withdraw. You
reel from the impact.

Appendix 1 With examinations in mind

Some students who are reading works of literature in a foreign language will be working towards a written examination, usually involving essay writing. Sometimes the essays will need to be written in the target language.

Essay writing and examinations are frequently a lonely business. The element of competition and the awarding of marks compound this isolation. In our view, essay writing and marking need to be explored and shared so that the processes at work can be better understood. Every literature essay is a form of communication between writer and reader. Poor marks indicate that the two of them are not in tune: the writer is not meeting the expectations of the reader. Clearly the teacher's written comments or class discussion of an essay question will help students to understand what is expected of them but the teacher has many other helpful options available.

Asking students to set essay questions enables them to appreciate how the working of the question determines what will be relevant in the answer and also gives them a greater sensitivity to the sort of question that particular literary works seem to demand.

Exchanging essays and then marking and reporting on them, or even marking and commenting on their own essays, prior to handing them in to the teacher, can help students to develop greater awareness of their own strengths and weaknesses.

Brainstorming for the relevant content of an essay in groups prior to individual writing is another way of restoring a social dimension to the planning of essays.

With weaker groups, the teacher can supply a checklist of possible points for inclusion in an essay. Students can then be asked to prioritise the points and group them, having first deleted any that are considered irrelevant.

We hope that some of the activities we have described in this book will help students to have a more thorough basic understanding of the literary work and a strong sense of involvement with it. These two factors will help to add substance and life to essay writing in literature.

For teachers seeking an attractive activity that integrates many of the above awareness exercises, the following simulation is offered. It is versatile enough to be adapted to different class sizes and requires a total

247

of about two to two-and-a-half hours in all, although the various parts can also be done separately.

The Examinations Board – a simulation

The idea for this simulation was born out of a desire to make students more aware of what they are doing – and why – when they write literary essays to prepare for examinations. It can be done in part, or in full, according to choice and available time.

Step 1: The sub-committee of the National Examinations Board

Students are divided into small groups, each one representing a sub-committee of the Examinations Board, whose task is to write the questions to be set on an English Literature examination.

We assume a class size of 20 for the purpose of illustrating the simulation, but it can be adapted to other class sizes (see the table at the end of this appendix). Four groups of five students each receive:
– A tasksheet (example follows).
– A sample NEB exam paper, showing the kind of questions set.*
Students read the instructions and the sample papers on other works of literature; then they write two questions for the exam to be set on the work they have been studying.

Discussion and writing take about 20 minutes.

---

* We give two 'sample papers' of different levels, as examples: one is on the short story 'Sredni Vashtar' by Saki, with literary questions set at a pre-university level, for students who have been studying literature as part of a syllabus; the other, on G. B. Shaw's *Pygmalion*, has questions set for advanced students not sitting a specifically literary paper but an exam with a literary essay as part of a language composition paper (for example, Cambridge Proficiency in English). Teachers working for a set exam syllabus might wish to include their own past papers at this stage of the simulation.

The exam questions sub-committee

You are a member of the exam questions sub-committee of the National Examinations Board.

   You are meeting to devise two essay questions for this year's NEB English Literature exam. The two questions will be based on:

Lord of the Flies by William Golding

This book has not been used on the NEB Literature syllabus before. The tradition in the NEB is to offer candidates a choice of *one* from four questions on each work on the syllabus.

The four questions correspond to these four categories:
a) One question on a character or characters in the work.
b) One question on one of the major themes in the work.
c) One 'context' question – that is, using a short quotation from the book as the basis for interpretation and comment.
d) One free or open question with no restrictions.

Your sub-committee is concerned *only* with two questions: of type (a) and (c) above.*

   You can consult your sheet of sample NEB questions on other works of fiction to get some idea of the 'house style'. Please do not imitate any of these questions.

You must submit your two questions after a maximum of **20 minutes' discussion.**

Tasksheet 1

---

* Note to teacher: Vary these categories evenly so that two questions are produced in each category. For example: group 1 – (a) and (c); group 2 – (b) and (d); group 3 – (a) and (d); group 4 – (b) and (c).

NEB/EL/SA (8/03)

NATIONAL EXAMINATIONS BOARD

English Literature Syllabus A

Tuesday 12th June 19XX   9am–12am   3 hours

PAPER 1 SHORT STORIES

Answer **three** *questions* **only** *from this paper:* **one** *question* **only** *may be selected from each one of the sections A, B and C.*

SECTION A: 'Sredni Vashtar' by Saki

1. 'Although Mrs De Ropp is the victim in this short story, our sympathy lies with the young boy, Conradin.'
   Do you agree with this view? Discuss with detailed reference to the story.

2. 'Religion is one of the ways used by human beings to dispose of their enemies.'
   Discuss, with specific reference to 'Sredni Vashtar'.

3.   'I thought you liked toast,' she exclaimed, with an injured air, observing that he did not touch it.
           'Sometimes,' said Conradin.
   Explain how this quotation relates to the story as a whole, and especially to the depiction of the relationship between the two main characters.

4. Discuss the way in which the author brings out the intensity of the emotions simmering in the De Ropp household.

NEB/EL/SB (7/96)

NATIONAL EXAMINATIONS BOARD

English Literature   Syllabus B

Wednesday 14th May 19XX   2pm–4pm   2 hours

PAPER 3   DRAMA

Answer **two** *questions* **only** *from this paper:* **one** *question from* **section A** *and* **one** *question from* **section B.**

SECTION A: *Pygmalion* **by G.B. Shaw**

1. Compare and contrast the characters of Professor Higgins and Alfred Doolittle.

2. What is the importance of Colonel Pickering in this play?

3. Towards the end of the play Higgins says to Liza: 'I presume you don't pretend that *I* have treated you badly?'
   What do you think? *Has* Higgins treated Liza badly?

4. The way you speak is at least as important as what you are.
   Do you agree? Discuss with reference to *Pygmalion*.

Step 2: The executive committee of the National Examinations Board

When time is up and the first task has been finished, students are told to write down the two questions set by their group. Each student now becomes a representative of his or her sub-committee, sent to a meeting of the National Examination Board's executive committee.

The teacher regroups 20 students into five executive committees of four students: each student coming from a different sub-committee, and each bringing his or her sub-committee's two questions.

An easy way of achieving this change-over is as follows: when the teacher gives out tasksheets to the sub-committees in step 1, he or she labels them: A – B – C – D – E, giving one to each member of the group. When the second committee is formed, he or she tells all the A's to go together to one corner of the room, all the B's to go to another corner, etc. In this way, five groups are formed, each consisting of one student from sub-committee 1, bringing with him or her questions (a) and (c); one student from 2, with questions (b) and (d); one student from 3, with questions (a) and (d) and one student from 4, with questions (b) and (c).

Each member of the new executive committee is now given Tasksheet 2. Regrouping, discussion and selection of questions should take about 20 minutes.

The executive committee of the National Examinations Board

You are the executive committee of the NEB, and you have been asked to make the final choice of four questions for this year's English Literature examination. You have eight questions submitted by the sub-committees: two for each of the categories (a), (b), (c) and (d).

Your final choice must be : **four** questions in all, one for each category.

You have **15 minutes** to make your selection.

Tasksheet 2

Step 3: The NEB plenary meeting

All students now meet together with the teacher as vote counter. Each executive committee reports its choices; then, the teacher nominates the final four on the basis of which questions were chosen most often. Any two questions from the same category which have the same number of inclusions are put to an immediate vote.

The marking scheme sub-committee

You are a member of the NEB's marking scheme sub-committee. You are meeting to assign weighting to a number of qualities which the NEB seeks in literature essays.

Your decisions will form the basis of the marking scheme for all NEB examiners.

The NEB supplies a 'list of criteria'. Study the list and add any criteria which you think are missing. Then assign marks to the criteria you consider important, remembering that **each essay answer is marked out of a total of 100 marks**.

For simpler calculations, you may wish to work in multiples of ten.

Tasksheet 3

This meeting should take no longer than 15 minutes. The final four questions are recorded and submitted to the NEB for inclusion on the English Literature examination paper.

The first part of the simulation is now concluded. It usually takes about one hour. The next step can follow immediately, if another hour is available, or it can be done in a later lesson, as appropriate.

Step 4: The marking scheme sub-committee

The class goes back to its original four groups of five students. Each group receives:
– Tasksheet 3.
– A 'list of criteria' from the NEB.

The time allowed for this task is approximately one hour. Each member of the sub-committee should keep a copy of the weighting decided.

》》》→

NEB marking criteria

Criterion	What is meant by this criterion	Marks assigned
1. knowledge of the book	Candidate shows thorough and detailed familiarity with the work.	
2. essay structure	Candidate organises his or her essay in a systematic and logical way.	
3. language	Candidate's use of language is accurate, varied and clear.	
4. illustration	Candidate quotes from the book to support arguments made, amply and relevantly.	
5. relevance	Candidate answers question directly, with no unnecessary material.	
6. coverage	Candidate deals with all main aspects of the topic set.	
7. originality	Candidate expresses his or her own criticism and interpretations, in a personal way.	
Sub-Committee can offer alternative criteria if they wish:		
8.		
9.		

Step 5: Homework

The teacher asks the class to do a test run of the exam paper questions by choosing to answer *one* as their homework.

Step 6: Individual marking of essays

Without prior discussion, the teacher asks each student to mark his or her own essay, using his or her sub-committee's marking scheme and headings. The final mark out of 100 should be recorded. The teacher checks all the essays, marks them in his or her own way, then discusses with the student, either in a written note or in an individual interview, the differences he or she sees between his or her marking scheme and the student's self-marked total.

This can lead on to a very useful discussion between the teacher and the class, in which the teacher establishes his or her own view of what the 'real' examination board's criteria would be for marking students' essays.

Adapting the simulation to different class sizes

Basically, the grouping for step 1 is done through multiples of four, with odd numbers slotted in to the four groups, as shown for class sizes of 13 and 14. For class sizes above 20, use multiples of the basic patterns given: that is, for a class of 24: 2 × 12; for 28: 2 × 14, and so on.

Class size	Step 1 group configurations	Step 2 group configurations
8	AB – AB – AB – AB	AAAA – BBBB
12	ABC – ABC – ABC – ABC	AAAA – BBBB – CCCC
13	ABC – ABC – ABC – ABCC	AAAA – BBBB – CCCCC
14	ABC – ABC – ABBC – ABCC	AAAA – BBBBB – CCCCC
16	ABCD – ABCD – ABCD – ABCD	AAAA – BBBB – CCCC – DDDD
20	ABCDE – ABCDE – ABCDE – ABCDE	AAAA – BBBB – CCCC – DDDD – EEEE

Appendix 2   A resource bank of titles

Language teachers can, in favourable circumstances, help their students
to read more widely by setting up a class library of suitable, unabridged
literary works. A catalogue of titles might indicate approximate difficulty
and include synopses designed to whet the reader's appetite. Occasional
visual displays of particular authors and their works – including perhaps
photographs, theatre programmes, critical reviews, film posters and so on
could serve both to encourage interest and to become the basis of class
projects. Where the possibility exists, film showings, poetry readings,
radio plays and theatre visits will lend further encouragement to students
exploring literature in the target language.

Within existing libraries outside the classroom, a list of suitable titles
for language learners could be made available to students or displayed to
guide their browsing.

When students are using a library independently, teachers might
organise social evenings or classroom sessions during which learners
would talk about books they had read and enjoyed and perhaps read out
favourite extracts. Alternatively, students could write brief reviews of
books read, for display.

The lists of books, plays and anthologies that follow are inevitably only
a small selection of the literary works that we feel will be useful to teachers
working with literature in the ways we have described. The first list in the
resource bank describes in a little more detail some of the works
mentioned in the main body of the book which have accompanying
activities. A complete list of all titles referred to in the activities follow.
The third section has titles of books that we like and judge to be suitable
for language learners, and include some that have been recommended to
us by colleagues. No doubt teachers will find that some of their own
favourites are missing so we hope that our bank will be modified and
supplemented according to the particular interests and constraints
involved.

Books at a glance

The following table gives details of novels and plays for which activities have been
described in the main body of the book. The abbreviations used are as follows:

Level: earliest recommended level, i.e. A = advanced, I = intermediate.

Language difficulty: approximate difficulty of language, i.e. S = simple, M = medium, more challenge.

Length: S = short novel or play, M = medium novel or play, L = long novel or play.

Novels

Author and Title	*Level*	*Language difficulty*	*Length*	*Brief description*	*General comments*
John Fowles, *The Collector*	A	M	M	Solitary young man kidnaps girl and holds her captive.	Suspense and psychological interest.
William Golding, *Lord of the Flies*	A/I	M	L	A group of boys stranded on a desert island struggle to survive, learning bitter lessons about human nature in the process.	A modern classic – universal themes, simple yet powerful plot.
Graham Greene, *Doctor Fischer of Geneva*	I/A	S	S	Man of great wealth plays sinister games with his grovelling entourage.	Economical style – a powerful modern fable.
Patricia Highsmith, *The Talented Mr Ripley*	A	M	M	Young American in Italy murders his friend.	Gripping psychological thriller.
Aldous Huxley, *Brave New World*	A	M	M	Sanitised life in a futuristic society based on genetic engineering.	Intriguing – build-up of suspense – good discussion potential.
Somerset Maugham, *The Moon and Sixpence*	A	M	M	Respectable banker deserts home and wife to pursue the Bohemian life of an artist.	Interesting theme, sustained by a strong central character in a variety of settings.

George Orwell, *Animal Farm*	I	S	S	Animals take over a farm and things gradually go sour.	A well-known and well-loved allegory.
George Orwell, *Nineteen Eighty-Four*	A	M	L	A gloomy futuristic vision of a totalitarian society.	A powerful novel that rewards effort.
F. Scott Fitzgerald, *The Great Gatsby*	A	M	M	Love, sex, corruption and death in a high society setting in 1920s America.	A subtle, evocative masterpiece.

Plays

Author and title	Level	Language difficulty	Length	Brief description	General comments
Edward Albee, *The Sandbox*	A	S	S	Americal couple dispose of an elderly mother.	Biting satire on modern ways.
Raymond Briggs, *When the Wind Blows*	A	M	S	Retired couple struggle to survive nuclear attack on Britain.	Controversial, topical theme – knowledge of English culture helpful.
David Hare, *A Map of the World*	A	M	L	A play written about real events satisfies none of its 'real' protagonists.	A well-crafted variation on the 'play within a play' theme.
Harold Pinter, *Applicant*	A	M	VS	A bizarre job interview.	Good length for class staging, with few props needed – amusing.
William Shakespeare, *Romeo and Juliet*	A	M/D	L	A young couple's love is thwarted by their feuding families.	Universally loved – surprisingly accessible for foreign students.

G. B. Shaw, *Pygmalion*	A	M	L	Professor of speech takes on challenge of transforming poor Cockney girl to pass her off as a duchess.	Period piece that is still witty and entertaining, relevant to modern concerns about gender and social roles.
Tom Stoppard, *The Real Inspector Hound*	I/A	S	S	A spoof on murder mystery plays, which questions notions of 'reality' versus 'appearance'.	Very enjoyable.
Tennessee Williams, *The Glass Menagerie*	A	M	M	Family drama set in the southern USA: a mother's attempts to marry off her crippled daughter.	Moving portrayal of family relationships.

Books referred to in the text

Albee, E. (1962) *The Zoo Story and Other Plays*, Jonathan Cape.

Ashton, J. and G. Bott (1967) *Read and Relate*, Cornelson-Velhagen and Klasing.

Atwood, M. (1984) *Dancing Girls and Other Stories*, Virago.

Ballantyne, R. M. (1982) *The Coral Island*, Penguin Books.

Barrie, Sir J. M. (1967) *The Admirable Crichton*, Hodder and Stoughton.

Booth, M. (ed.) (1981) *Contemporary British and North American Verse*, Oxford University Press.

Briggs, R. (1983) *When the Wind Blows*, Penguin Books.

Brontë, C. (1973) *Villette*, Pan Books.

Dahl, R. (1970) *Someone Like You*, Penguin Books.

Dahl, R. (1986) *More Tales of the Unexpected*, Penguin Books.

Fitzgerald, F. Scott (1950) *The Great Gatsby*, Penguin Books.

Fowles, J. (1968) *The Magus*, Pan Books.

Fowles, J. (1976) *The Collector*, Panther Books.

Gaskell, E. (1977) *North and South*, Oxford University Press.

Golding, W. (1958, reprinted 1983) *Lord of the Flies*, Faber and Faber.

Gray, A. (1984) *Unlikely Stories, Mostly*, Penguin Books.

Greene, G. (1978) *The Human Factor*, Penguin Books.

Greene, G. (1981) *Doctor Fischer of Geneva*, Penguin Books.

Hare, D. (1983) *A Map of the World*, Faber and Faber.

Highsmith, P. (1972) *Eleven*, Penguin Books.

Highsmith, P. (1976) *The Talented Mr Ripley*, Penguin Books.

Huxley, A. (1955) *Brave New World*, Penguin Books.
Irvine, L. (1984) *Castaway*, Penguin Books.
Lawrence, D. H. (ed. W. E. Williams) (1950) *Selected Poems*, Penguin Books.
McGough, R. (1982) *Waving at Trains*, Cape.
Maley, A. and S. Moulding (1985) *Poem into Poem*, Cambridge University Press.
Malamud, B. (1985) *Selected Stories*, Penguin Books.
Maugham, S. (1919) *The Moon and Sixpence*, Heinemann.
Morrison, B. and A. Motion (eds) (1982) *Contemporary British Poetry*, Penguin Books.
Narayan, R. K. (1984) *Malgudi Days*, Penguin Books.
Orwell, G. (1969) *Animal Farm*, Penguin Books.
Orwell, G. (1970) *Nineteen Eighty-Four*, Penguin Books.
Plath, S. (ed. Ted Hughes) (1981) *Collected Poems*, Faber and Faber.
Pritchett, V. (1984) *Collected Stories*, Penguin Books.
Redamond, R. and H. Tennyson (1976) *Contemporary One-Act Plays*, Heinemann.
Roberts, M. (ed.) (1965) *The Faber Book of Modern Verse*, Faber and Faber.
Saki (1982) *The Complete Saki*, Penguin Books.
Shakespeare, W. (ed. G. Blakemore Evans) (1984) *Romeo and Juliet*, Cambridge University Press.
Shaw, G. B. (1969) *Pygmalion*, Penguin Books.
Spark, M. (1963) *The Go-Away Bird and Other Stories*, Penguin Books.
Spark, M. (1967) *The Mandelbaum Gate*, Penguin Books.
Stevenson, R. L. (1971) *Treasure Island*, Penguin Books.
Stoppard, T. (1970) *The Real Inspector Hound*, Faber and Faber.
Stoppard, T. (1983) *The Real Thing*, Faber and Faber.
Swan, M. (ed.) (1979) *Kaleidoscope*, Cambridge University Press.
Thornley, G. C. (ed.) (1958) *Outstanding Short Stories*, Longman Group.
Trollope, A. (1973) *The Eustace Diamonds*, Panther Books.
Waugh, E. (1951) *Scoop*, Penguin Books.
Wells, H. G. (1958) *Selected Short Stories*, Penguin Books.
Williams, T. (1968) *The Glass Menagerie*, Heinemann (and in *Penguin Plays*).

Books for the classroom – further suggestions

Anthologies of poetry

Booth, M. (ed.) (1981) *Contemporary British and North American Verse*, Oxford University Press.
Henri, A., R. McGough and B. Patten (1967) *The Mersey Sound*, Penguin Books.
Hunter, J. (ed.) (1968–81) *Modern Poets 1–5*, Faber and Faber.
Lucie Smith, E. (ed.) (1985) *British Poetry since 1945*, Penguin Books.
Macbeth, G. (ed.) (1979) *Poetry 1900–1975*, Longman English Series, Longman Group.
Summerfield, G. (ed.) (1968–70) *Voices 1–3*, Penguin Books.
Wain, J. (ed.) (1979) *Anthology of Contemporary Poetry Post-War to the Present*, Hutchinson.

Anthologies of short plays

Shackleton, M. (1985) *Double Act, Ten One-Act Plays on Five Themes*, Edward Arnold.

Collections of short stories

ANTHOLOGIES

Adkins and Shackleton (eds) (1980) *Recollections – Ten Stories on Five Themes*, Edward Arnold.
Hadfield, J. (ed.) (1984) *Modern Short Stories 1*, Dent and Sons.
Hunter, J. (ed.) (1964) *Modern Short Stories*, Faber and Faber.
Swan, M. (ed.) *Samphire and Other Modern Stories*, Cambridge University Press.
Swatridge, Dr C. and Dr C. A. Bitter (eds) (1986) *The Man with the Scar and Other Stories*, Macmillan.
Taylor, P. (ed.) (1979) *The Road and Other Modern Stories*, Cambridge University Press.
Updike, J. and Shannon Ravenel (eds) (1985) *The Year's Best American Short Stories* (annual), Severn House.

COLLECTIONS OF SHORT STORIES BY INDIVIDUAL AUTHORS

Bradbury, R. (1959) *The Day It Rained Forever*, Penguin Books.
Dahl, R. (1969) *Kiss, Kiss*, Penguin Books.
Dahl, R. (1979) *Tales of The Unexpected*, Penguin Books.
Greene, G. (1972) *Collected Stories*, Heinemann.
Joyce, J. (1974) *The Dubliners*, Macmillan.
Lawrence, D. H. (1971) *Short Stories*, Penguin Books.
Lessing, D. (1975) *The Story of a Non-marrying Man and Other Stories*, Penguin Books.
Lessing, D. (1980) *The Grass is Singing*, Panther Books.
Mansfield, K. (1973) *Bliss and Other Stories*, Penguin Books.
Thurber, J. (1971) *A Thurber Carnival*, Penguin Books.

Some modern novels

Achebe, C. (1962) *Things Fall Apart*, Heinemann.
Amis, K. (1979) *Lucky Jim*, Penguin Books.
Atwood, M. (1980) *The Edible Woman*, Virago.
Baldwin, J. (1984) *Go Tell it on the Mountain*, Corgi Books.
Baldwin, J. (1984) *Another Country*, Corgi Books.
Banks, L. R. (1971) *The L-Shaped Room*, Penguin Books.
Bellow, S. (1966) *Seize the Day*, Penguin Books.
Bellow, S. (1969) *Herzog*, Penguin Books.
Bradbury, M. (1979) *The History Man*, Arrow Books.
Bradbury, R. (1976) *Fahrenheit 451*, Panther Books.
Brookner, A. (1985) *Hotel du Lac*, Granada Publishing.
Drabble, M. (1969) *The Millstone*, Penguin Books.

Drabble, M. (1977) *The Ice Age*, Weidenfeld and Nicolson.
du Maurier, D. (1976) *Jamaica Inn*, Pan Books.
Ellison, R. (1970) *The Invisible Man*, Penguin Books.
Golding, W. (1955) *The Inheritors*, Faber and Faber.
Graves, R. (1969) *I, Claudius*, Penguin Books.
Greene, G. (1969) *The Quiet American*, Penguin Books.
Greene, G. (1969) *The Power and the Glory*, Penguin Books.
Greene, G. (1979) *The Human Factor*, Penguin Books.
Hemingway, E. (1976) *The Old Man and the Sea*, Panther Books.
Highsmith, P. (1972) *A Suspension of Mercy*, Penguin Books.
Hill, S. (1974) *I'm the King of the Castle*, Penguin Books.
Kesey, K. (1973) *One Flew Over the Cuckoo's Nest*, Pan Books.
Lee, H. (1974) *To Kill a Mockingbird*, Pan Books.
Lodge, D. (1978) *Changing Places*, Penguin Books.
Marshall, J. V. (1980) *Walkabout*, Penguin Books.
Murdoch, I. (1969) *The Bell*, Penguin Books.
Murdoch, I. (1972) *A Fairly Honourable Defeat*, Penguin Books.
Nabokov, V. (1980) *Lolita*, Penguin Books.
Naipaul, V. S. (1969) *A House for Mr Biswas*, Penguin Books.
Naipaul, V. S. (1980) *A Bend in the River*, Penguin Books.
Rushdie, S. (1982) *Midnight's Children*, Pan Books.
Salinger, J. D. (1969) *The Catcher in the Rye*, Penguin Books.
Shute, N. (1968) *A Town Like Alice*, Pan Books.
Shute, N. (1969) *On the Beach*, Pan Books.
Sinclair, U. (1965) *The Jungle*, Penguin Books.
Spark, M. (1969) *The Prime of Miss Jean Brodie*, Penguin Books.
Spark, M. (1970) *The Ballad of Peckham Rye*, Penguin Books.
Steinbeck, J. (1970) *The Pearl*, Pan Books.
Steinbeck, J. (1974) *Of Mice and Men*, Pan Books.
Walker, A. (1983) *The Color Purple*, Women's Press.
Waugh, E. (1970) *The Loved One*, Penguin Books.
Weldon, F. (1980) *Praxis*, Hodder and Stoughton.
Weldon, F. (1982) *Watching Me, Watching You*, Hodder and Stoughton.
Wyndham, J. (1969) *The Midwich Cuckoos*, Penguin Books.
Wyndham, J. (1970) *The Day of the Triffids*, Penguin Books.
Wyndham, J. (1970) *Chocky*, Penguin Books.

Some modern plays

Leigh, M. (1983) *Abigail's Party*, Penguin Books.
Orton, J. (1985) *Loot*, Eyre Methuen.
Orton, J. (1975) *The Good and Faithful Servant*, Eyre Methuen.
Osborne, J. (1957) *Look Back in Anger*, Faber and Faber.
Pinter, H. (1965) *The Birthday Party*, Eyre Methuen.
Pinter, H. (1980) *Betrayal*, Eyre Methuen.
Priestley, J. B. (1965) *An Inspector Calls*, Heinemann.
Shaffer, P. (1977) *Equus*, Penguin Books.

Select bibliography

Alderson, J. C. and A. H. Urquhart (eds) (1984) *Reading in a Foreign Language*, Longman.

Brownjohn, S. (1980) *Does it Have to Rhyme?*, Hodder and Stoughton.

Brownjohn, S. (1982) *What Rhymes with Secret?*, Hodder and Stoughton.

Brumfit, C. J. (ed.) (1983) 'Teaching literature overseas: language-based approaches' *ELT Documents* 115, British Council, Pergamon Press.

Brumfit, C. J. (1985) *Language and Literature Teaching: From Practice to Principle*, Pergamon.

Christison, M. A. (1982) *English through Poetry*, Alemany Press.

Culler, J. (1975) *Structuralist Poetics*, Routledge & Kegan Paul.

Doughty, P. S. (1968) *Linguistics and the Teaching of Literature*, Longman.

Eagleton, T. (1983) *Literary Theory: an Introduction*, Basil Blackwell.

Forum, Vol. XXIII, No. 1, January 1985 (issue devoted to the teaching of literature).

Fowler, R. (1986) *Linguistic Criticism*, Oxford University Press.

Gatbonton, E. C. and G. R. Tucker (1971) 'Cultural orientation and the study of literature', *TESOL Quarterly* 5, 1971, pp. 137–43.

Gower, R. (1986) 'Can stylistic analysis help the EFL learner to read literature?', *ELT Journal*, Vol. 40, No. 2, April 1986, pp. 125–30.

Grellet, F. (1981) *Developing Reading Skills*, Cambridge University Press.

Holden, S. and R. Boardman (eds) (1987) *Teaching Literature*, Proceedings of the 1986 Sorrento Conference, MEP/British Council.

Koch, K. (1983) *Rose, where did you get that red? Teaching great poetry to children*, Vintage Books, Random House.

Leech, G. N. (1969) *A Linguistic Guide to English Poetry*, Longman.

McKay, S. (1982) 'Literature in the ESL classroom', *TESOL Quarterly*, Vol. 16, No. 4, December 1982, pp. 529–36.

Maley, A. and S. Moulding (1985) *Poem into Poem*, Cambridge University Press.

Moody, H. L. B. (1968) *Literary Appreciation*, Longman.

Moody, H. L. B. (1971) *The Teaching of Literature*, Longman.

Nuttall, C. (1982) *Teaching Reading Skills in a Foreign Language*, PLT 9, Heinemann Educational Books.

Traugott, E. C. and M. C. Pratt (1980) *Linguistics for Students of Literature*, Harcourt Brace.

Widdowson, H. G. (1975) *Stylistics and the Teaching of Literature*, Longman.

Widdowson, H. G. (1984) *Explorations in Applied Linguistics 2*, Oxford University Press.

Index

Index